Disability KEY ISSUES AND FUTURE DIRECTIONS

DISABILITY
THROUGH THE LIFE
COURSE

The SAGE Reference Series on Disability: Key Issues and Future Directions

Series Editor: Gary L. Albrecht

Arts and Humanities, by Brenda Jo Brueggemann
Assistive Technology and Science, by Cathy Bodine
Disability Through the Life Course, by Tamar Heller and Sarah Parker Harris
Education, by Cheryl Hanley-Maxwell and Lana Collet-Klingenberg
Employment and Work, by Susanne M. Bruyère and Linda Barrington
Ethics, Law, and Policy, by Jerome E. Bickenbach
Health and Medicine, by Ross M. Mullner
Rehabilitation Interventions, by Margaret A. Turk and Nancy R. Mudrick

Disability KEY ISSUES AND FUTURE DIRECTIONS

DISABILITY
THROUGH THE LIFE
COURSE

Tamar Heller
University of Illinois at Chicago

Sarah Parker Harris
University of Illinois at Chicago

SERIES EDITOR
Gary L. Albrecht
University of Illinois at Chicago

Los Angeles | London | New Delhi
Singapore | Washington DC

HV 1568 .D5699 2012

Disability through the life course

$5.00

Los Angeles | London | New Delhi
Singapore | Washington DC

FOR INFORMATION:

SAGE Publications, Inc.
2455 Teller Road
Thousand Oaks, California 91320
E-mail: order@sagepub.com

SAGE Publications Ltd.
1 Oliver's Yard
55 City Road
London EC1Y 1SP
United Kingdom

SAGE Publications India Pvt. Ltd.
B 1/I 1 Mohan Cooperative Industrial Area
Mathura Road, New Delhi 110 044
India

SAGE Publications Asia-Pacific Pte. Ltd.
33 Pekin Street #02-01
Far East Square
Singapore 048763

Publisher: Rolf A. Janke
Acquisitions Editor: Jim Brace-Thompson
Assistant to the Publisher: Michele Thompson
Project Development, Editing, & Management:
   Kevin Hillstrom, Laurie Collier Hillstrom
Production Editor: Jane Haenel
Reference Systems Manager: Leticia Gutierrez
Reference Systems Coordinator: Laura Notton
Typesetter: C&M Digitals (P) Ltd.
Proofreader: Ellen Howard
Indexer: Terri Corry
Cover Designer: Gail Buschman
Marketing Manager: Kristi Ward

Printed in the United States of America.

Library of Congress Cataloging-in-Publication Data

Disability through the life course / Tamar Heller, Sarah Parker Harris.

p. cm.—(The Sage reference series on disability: key issues and future directions)

Includes bibliographical references and index.

ISBN 978-1-4129-8767-7 (cloth : alk. paper)

1. People with disabilities. 2. Older people with disabilities. 3. Aging. I. Heller, Tamar. II. Harris, Sarah Parker.

HV1568.D5699 2012
362.4—dc23   2011019182

SFI Certified Sourcing
www.sfiprogram.org
SFI-00453

12 13 14 15 10 9 8 7 6 5 4 3

Contents

Series Introduction

The SAGE Reference Series on Disability appears at a time when global attention is being focused on disability at all levels of society. Researchers, service providers, and policymakers are concerned with the prevalence, experience, meanings, and costs of disability because of the growing impact of disability on individuals and their families and subsequent increased demand for services (Banta & de Wit, 2008; Martin et al., 2010; Mont, 2007; Whitaker, 2010). For their part, disabled people and their families are keenly interested in taking a more proactive stance in recognizing and dealing with disability in their lives (Charlton, 1998; Iezzoni & O'Day, 2006). As a result, there is burgeoning literature, heightened Web activity, myriad Internet information and discussion groups, and new policy proposals and programs designed to produce evidence and disseminate information so that people with disabilities may be informed and live more independently (see, for example, the World Institute of Disability Web site at http://www.wid.org, the Center for International Rehabilitation Research Information and Exchange Web site at http://cirrie .buffalo.edu, and the Web portal to caregiver support groups at http:// www.caregiver.com/regionalresources/index.htm).

Disability is recognized as a critical medical and social problem in current society, central to the discussions of health care and social welfare policies taking place around the world. The prominence of these disability issues is highlighted by the attention given to them by the most respected national and international organizations. The *World Report on Disability* (2011), co-sponsored by the World Health Organization (WHO) and the World Bank and based on an analysis of surveys from over 100 countries, estimates that 15% of the world's population (more than 1 billion people) currently experiences disability. This is the best prevalence estimate available today and indicates a marked increase over previous epidemiological calculations. Based on this work, the British medical journal *Lancet* dedicated an entire issue (November 28, 2009) to disability, focusing attention on the salience of the problem for health care systems worldwide. In addition, the WHO has developed community-based rehabilitation principles and strategies which are applicable to communities of diverse cultures and at all levels of development (WHO, 2010). The World Bank is concerned because of the link between disability and poverty (World Bank, 2004). Disability, in their view, could be a major impediment to economic development, particularly in emerging economies.

Efforts to address the problem of disability also have legal and human rights implications. Being disabled has historically led to discrimination, stigma, and dependency, which diminish an individual's full rights to citizenship and equality (European Disability Forum, 2003). In response to these concerns, the United Nations Convention on the Rights of Persons with Disabilities (2008) and the European Union Disability Strategy embodying the Charter of Fundamental Rights (2000) were passed to affirm that disabled people have the right to acquire and change nationalities, cannot be deprived of their ability to exercise liberty, have freedom of movement, are free to leave any country including their own, are not deprived of the right to enter their own country, and have access to the welfare and benefits afforded to any citizen of their country. As of March 31, 2010, 144 nations—including the United States, China, India, and Russia—had signed the U.N. Convention, and the European Union Disability Strategy had been ratified by all members of the European Community. These international agreements supplement and elaborate disability rights legislation such as the Americans with Disabilities Act of 1990 and its amendments, the U.K. Disability Discrimination Act of 1995, and the Disabled Person's Fundamental Law of Japan, revised in 1993.

In the United States, the Institute of Medicine of the National Academy of Sciences has persistently focused attention on the medical, public health, and social policy aspects of disability in a broad-ranging series of reports: *Disability in America* (1991), *Enabling America* (1997), *The Dynamics of Disability: Measuring and Monitoring Disability for Social Security Programs,* (2002), *The Future of Disability in America* (2007), and *Improving the Presumptive Disability Decision-Making Process for Veterans* (2008). The Centers for Disease Control have a long-standing interest in diabetes and obesity because of their effects on morbidity, mortality, and disability. Current data show that the incidence and prevalence of obesity is rising across all age groups in the United States, that obesity is related to diabetes, which is also on the rise, and that both, taken together, increase the likelihood of experiencing disability (Bleich et al., 2008; Gill et al., 2010). People with diabetes also are likely to have comorbid depression, which increases their chances of functional disability (Egede, 2004).

Depression and other types of mental illness—like anxiety disorders, alcohol and drug dependence, and impulse-control disorders—are more prevalent than previously thought and often result in disability (Kessler & Wang, 2008). The prevalence of mental disorders in the United States is high, with about half of the population meeting criteria (as measured by the *Diagnostic and Statistical Manual of Mental Disorders,* or DSM-IV) for one more disorders in their lifetimes, and more than one-quarter of the population meeting criteria for a disorder in any single year. The more severe mental disorders are strongly associated with high comorbidity, resulting in disability.

Major American foundations with significant health portfolios have also turned their attention to disability. The Bill and Melinda Gates Foundation has directed considerable resources to eliminate disability-causing parasitic and communicable diseases such as malaria, elephantiasis, and river blindness. These efforts are designed to prevent and control disability-causing conditions in the developing world that inhibit personal independence and economic development. The Robert Wood Johnson Foundation has a long-standing program on self-determination for people with developmental disabilities in the United States aimed at increasing their ability to participate fully in society, and the Hogg Foundation is dedicated to improving mental health awareness and services. Taken in concert, these activities underscore the recognized importance of disability in the present world.

Disability Concepts, Models, and Theories

There is an immense literature on disability concepts, models, and theories. An in-depth look at these issues and controversies can be found in the *Handbook of Disability Studies* (Albrecht, Seelman, & Bury, 2001), in the *Encyclopedia of Disability* (Albrecht, 2006), and in "The Sociology of Disability: Historical Foundations and Future Directions" (Albrecht, 2010). For the purposes of this reference series, it is useful to know that the World Health Organization, in the International Classification of Functioning, Disability and Health (ICF), defines disability as "an umbrella term for impairments, activity limitations or participation restrictions" (WHO, 2001, p. 3). ICF also lists environmental factors that interact with all these constructs. Further, the WHO defines impairments as "problems in body function or structure such as significant deviation or loss"; activity limitations as "difficulties an individual may have in executing activities"; participation as "involvement in a life situation"; and environmental factors as those components of "the physical, social and attitudinal environment in which people live and conduct their lives" (WHO, 2001, p. 10). The U.N. Convention on the Rights of Persons with Disabilities, in turn, defines disability as including "those who have long-term physical, mental, intellectual or sensory impairments which in interaction with various barriers may hinder their full and effective participation in society on an equal basis with others." In the introduction to the *Lancet* special issue on disability, Officer and Groce (2009) conclude that "both the ICF and the Convention view disability as the outcome of complex interactions between health conditions and features of an individual's physical, social, and attitudinal environment that hinder their full and effective participation in society" (p. 1795). Hence, disability scholars and activists alike are concerned with breaking down physical, environmental, economic, and social barriers so that disabled people can live independently and participate as fully as possible in society.

Types of Disability

Interest in disability by medical practitioners has traditionally been condition specific (such as spinal cord injury or disabilities due to heart disease), reflecting the medical model approach to training and disease taxonomies. Similarly, disabled people and their families are often most concerned about their particular conditions and how best to deal with them. The SAGE Reference Series on Disability recognizes that there are a broad range of disabilities that can be generally conceived of as falling in the categories of physical, mental, intellectual, and sensory disabilities. In practice, disabled persons may have more than one disability and are often difficult to place in one disability category. For instance, a spinal-cord injured individual might experience depression, and a person with multiple sclerosis may simultaneously deal with physical and sensory disabilities. It is also important to note that disabilities are dynamic. People do experience different rates of onset, progression, remission, and even transition from being disabled at one point in time, to not being disabled at another, to being disabled again. Examples of this change in disability status include disability due to bouts of arthritis, Guillain-Barré Syndrome, and postpartum depression.

Disability Language

The symbols and language used to represent disability have sparked contentious debates over the years. In the *Handbook of Disability Studies* (Albrecht, Seelman, & Bury, 2001) and the *Encyclopedia of Disability* (Albrecht, 2006), authors from different countries were encouraged to use the terms and language of their cultures, but to explain them when necessary. In the present volumes, authors may use "people with disabilities" or "disabled people" to refer to individuals experiencing disability. Scholars in the United States have preferred "people with disabilities" (people-first language), while those in the United Kingdom, Canada, and Australia generally use "disabled people." In languages other than English, scholars typically use some form of the "disabled people" idiom. The U.S. version emphasizes American exceptionalism and the individual, whereas "disabled people" highlights the group and their minority status or state of being different. In my own writing, I have chosen "disabled people" because it stresses human diversity and variation.

In a recent discussion of this issue, DePoy and Gilson (2010) "suggest that maintaining debate and argument on what language is most correct derails a larger and more profound needed change, that of equalizing resources, valuation, and respect. Moreover, . . . locating disability 'with a person' reifies its embodiment and flies in the very face of the social model that person-first language is purported to espouse. . . . We have not heard anyone suggest that beauty, kindness, or even unkindness be located after personhood." While the debate is not likely over, we state why we use the language that we do.

Organization of the Series

These issues were important in conceiving of and organizing the SAGE Reference Series on Disability. Instead of developing the series around specific disabilities resulting from Parkinson's disease or bi-polar disorder, or according to the larger categories of physical, mental, intellectual, and sensory disabilities, we decided to concentrate on the major topics that confront anyone interested in or experiencing disability. Thus, the series consists of eight volumes constructed around the following topics:

- Arts and Humanities
- Assistive Technology and Science
- Disability Through the Life Course
- Education
- Employment and Work
- Ethics, Law, and Policy
- Health and Medicine
- Rehabilitation Interventions

To provide structure, we chose to use a similar organization for each volume. Therefore, each volume contains the following elements:

Series Introduction

Preface

About the Author

About the Series Editor

Chapter 1. Introduction, Background, and History

Chapter 2. Current Issues, Controversies, and Solutions

Chapter 3. Chronology of Critical Events

Chapter 4. Biographies of Key Contributors in the Field

Chapter 5. Annotated Data, Statistics, Tables, and Graphs

Chapter 6. Annotated List of Organizations and Associations

Chapter 7. Selected Print and Electronic Resources

Glossary of Key Terms

Index

The Audience

The eight-volume SAGE Reference Series on Disability targets an audience of undergraduate students and general readers that uses both academic and public libraries. However, the content and depth of the series will also make it attractive to graduate students, researchers, and policymakers. The series has been edited to have a consistent format and accessible style.

The focus in each volume is on providing lay-friendly overviews of broad issues and guideposts for further research and exploration.

The series is innovative in that it will be published and marketed worldwide, with each volume available in electronic format soon after it appears in print. The print version consists of eight bound volumes. The electronic version is available through the SAGE Reference Online platform, which hosts 200 handbooks and encyclopedias across the social sciences, including the *Handbook of Disability Studies* and the *Encyclopedia of Disability*. With access to this platform through college, university, and public libraries, students, the lay public, and scholars can search these interrelated disability and social science sources from their computers or handheld and smart phone devices. The movement to an electronic platform presages the cloud computing revolution coming upon us. Cloud computing "refers to 'everything' a user may reach via the Internet, including services, storage, applications and people" (Hoehl & Sieh, 2010). According to Ray Ozzie (2010), recently Microsoft's chief architect, "We're moving toward a world of (1) cloud-based continuous services that connect us all and do our bidding, and (2) appliance-like connected devices enabling us to interact with those cloud-based services." Literally, information will be available at consumers' fingertips. Given the ample links to other resources in emerging databases, they can pursue any topic of interest in detail. This resource builds on the massive efforts to make information available to decision makers in real time, such as computerizing health and hospital records so that the diagnosis and treatment of chronic diseases and disabilities can be better managed (Celler, Lovell, & Basilakis, 2003). The SAGE Reference Series on Disability provides Internet and Web site addresses which lead the user into a world of social networks clustered around disability in general and specific conditions and issues. Entering and engaging with social networks revolving around health and disability promises to help individuals make more informed decisions and provide support in times of need (Smith & Christakis, 2008). The SAGE Reference Online platform will also be configured and updated to make it increasingly accessible to disabled people.

The SAGE Reference Series on Disability provides an extensive index for each volume. Through its placement on the SAGE Reference Online platform, the series will be fully searchable and cross-referenced, will allow keyword searching, and will be connected to the *Handbook of Disability Studies* and the *Encyclopedia of Disability*.

The authors of the volumes have taken considerable effort to vet the references, data, and resources for accuracy and credibility. The multiple Web sites for current data, information, government and United Nations documents, research findings, expert recommendations, self-help, discussion groups, and social policy are particularly useful, as they are being continuously updated. Examples of current and forthcoming data are the results and analysis of the findings of the U.S. 2010 Census, the ongoing reports of the Centers for Disease Control on disability, the World Health Organization's *World Report on Disability* and its updates, the World Bank reports on disability, poverty, and development, and reports from major foundations like Robert Wood Johnson, Bill and Melinda Gates, Ford, and Hogg. In terms of clinical outcomes, the evaluation of cost-effective interventions, management of disability, and programs that work, enormous attention is being given to evidence-based outcomes (Brownson, Fielding, & Maylahn, 2009; Marcus et al., 2006; Wolinsky et al., 2007) and comparative effectiveness research (Etheredge, 2010; Inglehart, 2010). Such data force a re-examination of policymakers' arguments. For example, there is mounting evidence that demonstrates the beneficial effects of exercise on preventing disability and enhancing function (Marcus et al., 2006). Recent studies also show that some health care reform initiatives may negatively affect disabled people's access to and costs of health care (Burns, Shah, & Smith, 2010). Furthermore, the seemingly inexorable rise in health care spending may not be correlated with desirable health outcomes (Rothberg et al., 2010). In this environment, valid data are the currency of the discussion (Andersen, Lollar, & Meyers, 2000). The authors' hopes are that this reference series will encourage students and the lay public to base their discussions and decisions on valid outcome data. Such an approach tempers the influence of ideologies surrounding health care and misconceptions about disabled people, their lives, and experiences.

SAGE Publications has made considerable effort to make these volumes accessible to disabled people in the printed book version and in the electronic platform format. In turn, SAGE and other publishers and vendors like Amazon are incorporating greater flexibility in the user interface to improve functionality to a broad range of users, such as disabled people. These efforts are important for disabled people as universities, governments, and health service delivery organizations are moving toward a paperless environment.

In the spirit of informed discussion and transparency, may this reference series encourage people from many different walks of life to become knowledgeable and engaged in the disability world. As a consequence, social policies should become better informed and individuals and families should be able to make better decisions regarding the experience of disability in their lives.

Acknowledgments

I would like to recognize the vision of Rolf Janke in developing SAGE Publications' presence in the disability field, as represented by the *Handbook of Disability Studies* (2001), the five-volume *Encyclopedia of Disability* (2006), and now the eight-volume SAGE Reference Series on Disability. These products have helped advance the field and have made critical work accessible to scholars, students, and the general public through books and now the SAGE Reference Online platform. Jim Brace-Thompson at SAGE handled the signing of contracts and kept this complex project coordinated and moving on time. Kevin Hillstrom and Laurie Collier Hillstrom at Northern Lights Writers Group were intrepid in taking the composite pieces of this project and polishing and editing them into a coherent whole that is approachable, consistent in style and form, and rich in content. The authors of the eight volumes—Linda Barrington, Jerome Bickenbach, Cathy Bodine, Brenda Brueggemann, Susanne Bruyère, Lana Collet-Klingenberg, Cheryl Hanley-Maxwell, Sarah Parker Harris, Tamar Heller, Nancy Mudrick, Ross Mullner, and Peggy Turk—are to be commended for their enthusiasm, creativity, and fortitude in delivering high-quality volumes on a tight deadline. I was fortunate to work with such accomplished scholars.

Discussions with Barbara Altman, Colin Barnes, Catherine Barral, Len Barton, Isabelle Baszanger, Peter Blanck, Mary Boulton, David Braddock, Richard Burkhauser, Mike Bury, Ann Caldwell, Lennard Davis, Patrick Devlieger, Ray Fitzpatrick, Lawrence Frey, Carol Gill, Tamar Heller, Gary Kielhofner, Soewarta Kosen, Jo Lebeer, Mitch Loeb, Don Lollar, Paul Longmore, Ros Madden, Maria Martinho, Dennis Mathews, Sophie Mitra, Daniel Mont, Alana Officer, Randall Parker, David Pfeiffer, Jean-François Raveau, James Rimmer, Ed Roberts, Jean-Marie Robine, Joan Rogers, Richard Scotch, Kate Seelman, Tom Shakespeare, Sandor Sipos, Henri-Jacques Stiker, Edna Szymanski, Jutta Traviranus, Bryan Turner, Greg Vanderheiden, Isabelle Ville, Larry Voss, Ann Waldschmidt, and Irving Kenneth Zola over the years contributed to the content, logic, and structure of the series. They also were a wonderful source of suggestions for authors.

I would also like to acknowledge the hospitality and support of the Belgian Academy of Science and the Arts, the University of Leuven, Nuffield College, the University of Oxford, the Fondation Maison des Sciences de l'Homme, Paris, and the Department of Disability and Human Development at the University of Illinois at Chicago, who provided the time and environments to conceive of and develop the project. While none of these people or institutions is responsible for any deficiencies in the work, they all helped enormously in making it better.

Gary L. Albrecht
University of Illinois at Chicago
University of Leuven
Belgian Academy of Science and Arts

References

Albrecht, G. L. (Ed.). (2006). *Encyclopedia of disability* (5 vols.). Thousand Oaks, CA: Sage.

Albrecht, G. L. (2010). The sociology of disability: Historical foundations and future directions. In C. Bird, A. Fremont, S. Timmermans, & P. Conrad (Eds.), *Handbook of medical sociology* (6th ed., pp. 192–209). Nashville, TN: Vanderbilt University Press.

Albrecht, G. L., Seelman, K. D., & Bury, M. (Eds.). (2001). *Handbook of disability studies.* Thousand Oaks, CA: Sage.

Andersen, E. M., Lollar, D. J., & Meyers, A. R. (2000). Disability outcomes research: Why this supplement, on this topic, at this time? *Archives of Physical Medicine and Rehabilitation, 81*, S1–S4.

Banta, H. D., & de Wit, G. A. (2008). Public health services and cost-effectiveness analysis. *Annual Review of Public Health, 29*, 383–397.

Bleich, S., Cutler, D., Murray, C., & Adams, A. (2008). Why is the developed world obese? *Annual Review of Public Health, 29*, 273–295.

Brownson, R. C., Fielding, J. E., & Maylahn, C. M. (2009). Evidence-based public health: A fundamental concept for public health practice. *Annual Review of Public Health, 30*, 175–201.

Burns, M., Shah, N., & Smith, M. (2010). Why some disabled adults in Medicaid face large out-of-pocket expenses. *Health Affairs, 29*, 1517–1522.

Celler, B. G., Lovell, N. H., & Basilakis, J. (2003). Using information technology to improve the management of chronic disease. *Medical Journal of Australia, 179*, 242–246.

Charlton, J. I. (1998). *Nothing about us without us: Disability, oppression and empowerment.* Berkeley: University of California Press.

DePoy, E., & Gilson, S. F. (2010) *Studying disability: Multiple theories and responses.* Thousand Oaks, CA: Sage.

Egede, L. E. (2004). Diabetes, major depression, and functional disability among U.S. adults. *Diabetes Care, 27,* 421–428.

Etheredge, L. M. (2010). Creating a high-performance system for comparative effectiveness research. *Health Affairs, 29,* 1761–1767.

European Disability Forum. (2003). *Disability and social exclusion in the European Union: Time for change, tools for change.* Athens: Greek National Confederation of Disabled People.

European Union. (2000). *Charter of fundamental rights.* Retrieved from http://www.europarll.europa.eu/charter

Gill, T. M., Gahbauer, E. A., Han, L., & Allore, H. G. (2010). Trajectories of disability in the last year of life. *The New England Journal of Medicine, 362*(13), 1173–1180.

Hoehl, A. A., & Sieh, K. A. (2010). *Cloud computing and disability communities: How can cloud computing support a more accessible information age and society?* Boulder, CO: Coleman Institute.

Iezzoni, L. I., & O'Day, B. L. (2006). *More than ramps.* Oxford, UK: Oxford University Press.

Inglehart, J. K. (2010). The political fight over comparative effectiveness research. *Health Affairs, 29,* 1757–1760.

Institute of Medicine. (1991). *Disability in America.* Washington, DC: National Academies Press.

Institute of Medicine. (1997). *Enabling America.* Washington, DC: National Academies Press.

Institute of Medicine. (2001). *Health and behavior: The interplay of biological, behavioral and societal influences.* Washington, DC: National Academies Press.

Institute of Medicine. (2002). *The dynamics of disability: Measuring and monitoring disability for social security programs.* Washington, DC: National Academies Press.

Institute of Medicine. (2007). *The future of disability in America.* Washington, DC: National Academies Press.

Institute of Medicine. (2008). *Improving the presumptive disability decision-making process for veterans.* Washington, DC: National Academies Press.

Kessler, R. C., & Wang, P. S. (2008). The descriptive epidemiology of commonly occurring mental disorders in the United States. *Annual Review of Public Health, 29,* 115–129.

Marcus, B. H., Williams, D. M., Dubbert, P. M., Sallis, J. F., King, A. C., Yancey, A. K., et al. (2006). Physical activity intervention studies. *Circulation, 114,* 2739–2752.

Martin, L. G., Freedman, V. A., Schoeni, R. F., & Andreski, P. M. (2010). Trends in disability and related chronic conditions among people ages 50 to 64. *Health Affairs, 29*(4), 725–731.

Mont, D. (2007). *Measuring disability prevalence* (World Bank working paper). Washington, DC: The World Bank.

Officer, A., & Groce, N. E. (2009). Key concepts in disability. *The Lancet, 374,* 1795–1796.

Ozzie, R. (2010, October 28). *Dawn of a new day.* Ray Ozzie's Blog. Retrieved from http://ozzie.net/docs/dawn-of-a-new-day

Rothberg, M. B., Cohen, J., Lindenauer, P., Masetti, J., & Auerbach, A. (2010). Little evidence of correlation between growth in health care spending and reduced mortality. *Health Affairs, 29,* 1523–1531.

Smith, K. P., & Christakis, N. A. (2008). Social networks and health. *Annual Review of Sociology, 34,* 405–429.

United Nations. (2008). *Convention on the rights of persons with disabilities.* New York: United Nations. Retrieved from http://un.org/disabilities/convention

Whitaker, R. T. (2010). *Anatomy of an epidemic: Magic bullets, psychiatric drugs, and the astonishing rise of mental illness in America.* New York: Crown.

Wolinsky, F. D., Miller, D. K., Andresen, E. M., Malmstrom, T. K., Miller, J. P., & Miller, T. R. (2007). Effect of subclinical status in functional limitation and disability on adverse health outcomes 3 years later. *The Journals of Gerontology: Series A, 62,* 101–106.

World Bank Disability and Development Team. (2004). *Poverty reduction strategies: Their importance for disability.* Washington, DC: World Bank.

World Health Organization. (2001). *International classification of functioning, disability and health.* Geneva: Author.

World Health Organization. (2010). *Community-based rehabilitation guidelines.* Geneva and Washington, DC: Author.

World Health Organization, & World Bank. (2011). *World report on disability.* Geneva: World Health Organization.

Preface

Much of the literature on disability focuses on a specific phase of life. Rarely does the literature on childhood merge with that on adulthood or on older age. Yet there is growing recognition that a life course approach, which addresses disability across generations and through various life stage transitions, informs and furthers our understanding of disability. This approach assumes that, beginning prenatally, events occurring early in life affect later periods in one's life. It recognizes that development does not necessarily proceed in neat stages; rather, in a fluid and dynamic manner, impairments interact with social determinants (e.g., culture and socioeconomic status) and environmental aspects (e.g., services and supports) across the life course, resulting in differing outcomes for people. In this book, the disability studies approach adds to this life course perspective by bringing in the concepts of disability identity and societal attitudes toward disability as important factors throughout the lives of people with disabilities. The disability studies lens further emphasizes the lived experience of people with disabilities and the social and political contexts affecting their lives.

In addition to providing an overall theoretical and historical background, this book addresses disability across the life course through delineation of various age phases and key cross-cutting, lifelong issues that impact the lives of people with disabilities. We discuss disability considerations, challenges, and supports at six life stages: birthrights and early childhood; childhood; youth; adulthood; aging; and death and dying. We also include transition periods, which can often be particularly challenging to individuals with disabilities and their families. The key cross-cutting issues that we highlight are: family; health; policy, legislation, and service; and self-determination and participation. These themes offer a useful contextualization of the lives of people with disabilities.

They also encompass key debates within the field of disabilities that center around the challenges people with disabilities face, the worth and value of human life, and ways to promote and respect human rights for all people.

Chapter 1 provides an introduction to the life course approach. It introduces key concepts, life stages, and important historical developments in approaches to disability. While the medicalization of disability has dominated much of the discussion of disabilities historically, the chapter also covers more recent approaches, such as the human rights approach. It then provides examples of different theoretical approaches to life course studies from various disciplinary traditions, including gerontology, developmental psychology, sociology, and disability studies. The application and limitation of stage theories and theories of "successful aging" to people with disabilities are discussed. Finally, the chapter introduces the cross-cutting issues that affect the lives of people with disabilities throughout the life course, including the role of families, age-related health changes, federal legislation that has had a major impact on people, and the importance of promoting self-determination and community participation as valued goals.

Chapter 2 delves into challenges, debates, and policies and practices that address issues faced by people with disabilities and their families across each generational stage. From the prenatal period to the end of life, debates center around the value of life and ways to obtain and maintain a high quality of life. Many people with disabilities face challenges, including societal discrimination, poverty, inaccessible environments, and lack of opportunities to lead self-determined lives and to meaningfully participate in community life. Inadequate access to health care and to trained health-care professionals and direct-support professionals pose further barriers. Transitions are often particularly difficult, as expectations and roles change and as support networks and systems change. Family involvement and support is critical throughout the life course. People with disabilities not only receive support from their families but also provide support to their families. A key to reducing the challenges and barriers discussed in the chapter is the enactment of effective legislative policies, services, and supports that promote the health, education, employment, and community participation of people with disabilities and their families.

Chapter 3 provides a chronology of events that pertain to disabilities across the life course. The period covered is 1900 to 2010. Key events include discoveries, enactment of important legislation, significant speeches and publications, and the founding of major disability organizations. With each of these landmark events, we provide a synopsis of the event and its implications for people with disabilities. These events illustrate historical developments from the eugenics movement that sought to prevent the procreation of people with disabilities to the enactment of legislation that provided civil rights to people with disabilities. Events such as the growth of the independent living and self-advocacy movement have further helped to foster the self-determination of people with disabilities.

Chapter 4 provides biographies of individuals who have made significant contributions to the study of disability issues. We profile their lives and the impact they have made on the field. Some of these individuals have been leaders in articulating a life course approach to the study of disabilities, while other individuals selected have focused on particular age phases. Many of the individuals have focused on one of the cross-cutting issues addressed in this book.

Chapter 5 comprises annotated data, statistics, tables, and graphs pertinent to disabilities across the life course. It is organized by age phases and covers the key issues embedded in each of these phases. Key statistics pertaining to early childhood through adolescence include data on birthrights, education, peer networks, and sexuality. In adulthood and aging, the data address employment, parenting, retirement, long-term care and support, end-of-life issues, and spirituality.

Chapter 6 provides a listing and description of key governmental and non-governmental organizations that impact the lives of people with disabilities. These include key organizations responsible for funding and administering services, supports, and research regarding people with disabilities and their families. They also include consumer organizations, such as family organizations and self-advocacy organizations, controlled by people with disabilities. Key provider agencies and university centers are also listed as important organizations in the disability field.

The last chapter, Chapter 7, comprises an annotated list of print and electronic resources. The selected resources reflect written publications that have been seminal in articulating various aspects of the life course and disability studies perspectives on the lives of people with disabilities. Some of the publications address specific age phases and others address the cross-cutting issues detailed in Chapters 1 and 2.

A life course perspective helps us understand the developmental trajectories for people with disabilities and their families. The topic of disability across the life course is challenging, as it brings together literature from different disciplines addressing different aspects of the life cycle. It also encompasses various disabilities, including physical, sensory, cognitive, and mental health disabilities. However, understanding disability across the life course is vital if people with disabilities and their families are to achieve a good quality of life and participate in the wider community.

The enormous task of bringing together the disparate literature would not have been possible without the tremendous work of the graduate students in the Department of Disability and Human Development (DHD) at the University of Illinois at Chicago, who worked diligently on this book. DHD has the foremost disability studies graduate program in the United States, including both a master's program in disability and human development and a doctoral program in disability studies. Two students in the master's program were Jeannie Zwick, who compiled the initial readings and did much of the work that went into Chapters 4, 6, and 7, and Robert Gould, who took the lead in compiling Chapters 3 and 5. Abigail Schindler and Lieke van Heumen, doctoral students in disability studies, skillfully contributed major sections to the chapters. Abigail Schindler did a remarkable job of combing through the disparate literature to pull together the various perspectives on life course approaches and cross-cutting issues in Chapters 1 and 2. Lieke van Heumen very thoughtfully brought her expertise in gerontology to sections on aging and on death and dying in Chapter 2.

We would like to acknowledge funding provided, in part, by the National Institute on Disability and Rehabilitation Research, Rehabilitation Research and Training Center on Aging with Developmental Disabilities: Lifespan Health and Function, grant number H133B080009. Finally, we would like to thank our spouses, Robert Heller and Germaine Harris, who supported us throughout this project.

Tamar Heller
Sarah Parker Harris

About the Authors

Tamar Heller, Ph.D., is a professor and head of the Department of Disability and Human Development, University of Illinois at Chicago, and director of its University Center for Excellence in Developmental Disabilities for the State of Illinois. She also directs the Rehabilitation Research and Training Center on Aging with Developmental Disabilities: Lifespan Health and Function and projects on family support and health promotion interventions for individuals with disabilities. One of these projects is the Special Olympics Research Collaborating Center.

Dr. Heller has written over 170 publications and presented numerous papers at major conferences on family support interventions and policies, self-determination, health promotion, and aging of people with disabilities. She is the author or co-editor of five books and has edited special issues of *Technology and Disability, American Journal on Mental Retardation, Journal of Policy and Practice in Intellectual Disabilities,* and *Family Relations.* She is past president of the board of the Association of University Centers on Disabilities. In 2005 she was then Senator Barack Obama's delegate to the White House Conference on Aging. As a co-founder of the national Sibling Leadership Network, she is a member of its executive board.

Dr. Heller's awards include the 2009 Autism Ally for Public Policy Award of The Arc/The Autism Program of Illinois; the 2008 Lifetime Research Achievement Award, International Association for the Scientific Study of Intellectual Disabilities, Special Interest Group on Aging and Intellectual Disabilities; and the 2009 Community Partner Award of Community Support Services.

Sarah Parker Harris, Ph.D., is an assistant professor in the Department of Disability and Human Development, University of Illinois at Chicago. She received her doctoral degree in sociology and social policy from the

University of Sydney in Australia, and has worked in social policy research primarily relating to disability policies and programs. Dr. Parker Harris has published papers and presented at major national and international conferences on international rights, neoliberalism, citizenship, comparative workfare policy, and social entrepreneurship.

Dr. Parker Harris has taught undergraduate and graduate courses in sociological theory, feminist theory, qualitative research methods, and comparative social policy. She currently teaches graduate courses in theories and perspectives of disability studies, and disability policies and legislation. Her research interests include comparative social policy analysis; international and national disability policies and legislation; international human rights; citizenship and social justice; and issues relating to gender, sexuality, and disability. Recent research includes a cross-national project analyzing human rights, neoliberalism, and workfare programs for people with disabilities in three countries; an interdisciplinary study examining the role of social entrepreneurship as an innovative pathway to employment for people with disabilities; and a community-based project on using advocacy and technology to increase civic engagement of people with disabilities.

About the
Series Editor

Gary L. Albrecht is a Fellow of the Royal Belgian Academy of Arts and Sciences, Extraordinary Guest Professor of Social Sciences, University of Leuven, Belgium, and Professor Emeritus of Public Health and of Disability and Human Development at the University of Illinois at Chicago. After receiving his Ph.D. from Emory University, he has served on the faculties of Emory University in Sociology and Psychiatry, Northwestern University in Sociology, Rehabilitation Medicine, and the Kellogg School of Management, and the University of Illinois at Chicago (UIC) in the School of Public Health and in the Department of Disability and Human Development. Since retiring from the UIC in 2005, he has divided his time between Europe and the United States, working in Brussels, Belgium, and Boulder, Colorado. He has served as a Scholar in Residence at the Maison des Sciences de l'Homme (MSH) in Paris, a visiting Fellow at Nuffield College, the University of Oxford, and a Fellow in Residence at the Royal Flemish Academy of Science and Arts, Brussels.

His research has focused on how adults acknowledge, interpret, and respond to unanticipated life events, such as disability onset. His work, supported by over $25 million of funding, has resulted in 16 books and over 140 articles and book chapters. He is currently working on a longitudinal study of disabled Iranian, Moroccan, Turkish, Jewish, and Congolese immigrants to Belgium. Another current project involves working with an international team on "Disability: A Global Picture," Chapter 2 of the *World Report on Disability,* co-sponsored by the World Health Organization and the World Bank, published in 2011.

He is past Chair of the Medical Sociology Section of the American Sociological Association, a past member of the Executive Committee of the

Disability Forum of the American Public Health Association, an early member of the Society for Disability Studies, and an elected member of the Society for Research in Rehabilitation (UK). He has received the Award for the Promotion of Human Welfare and the Eliot Freidson Award for the book *The Disability Business: Rehabilitation in America.* He also has received a Switzer Distinguished Research Fellowship, Schmidt Fellowship, New York State Supreme Court Fellowship, Kellogg Fellowship, National Library of Medicine Fellowship, World Health Organization Fellowship, the Lee Founders Award from the Society for the Study of Social Problems, the Licht Award from the American Congress of Rehabilitation Medicine, the University of Illinois at Chicago Award for Excellence in Teaching, and has been elected Fellow of the American Association for the Advancement of Science (AAAS). He has led scientific delegations in rehabilitation medicine to the Soviet Union and the People's Republic of China and served on study sections, grant review panels, and strategic planning committees on disability in Australia, Canada, the European Community, France, Ireland, Japan, Poland, Sweden, South Africa, the United Kingdom, the United States, and the World Health Organization, Geneva. His most recent books are *The Handbook of Social Studies in Health and Medicine,* edited with Ray Fitzpatrick and Susan Scrimshaw (SAGE, 2000), the *Handbook of Disability Studies,* edited with Katherine D. Seelman and Michael Bury (SAGE, 2001), and the five-volume *Encyclopedia of Disability* (SAGE, 2006).

One

Introduction, Background, and History

Sarah Parker Harris, Tamar Heller, and Abigail Schindler

Historically, people with disabilities of all generations have been iso-lated from general society, which has restricted their opportunities to participate on an equal basis with others. Barriers include environ-ments, attitudes, institutions, discourses, policies, and practices, all of which shape the experiences of people with disabilities throughout the life course (Priestley, 2003). Little research and scholarship specific to a life course approach to disability exists, as much of the work has been grounded in age-related approaches (e.g., birth, youth, adult, or aging) or disciplines (e.g., developmental psychology or gerontology). However, a life course approach that addresses disability issues across generations and through various life stage transitions is useful to inform and further our understanding of disability.

Terms such as "life course" and "lifespan" are often used interchange-ably in the literature to describe the age-related and/or development

1

stages and fluid trajectories of an individual's life. Life course studies meaningfully differ from what developmental psychologists might term the lifespan, which emphasizes the way people develop as compared to a "typical" lifespan (Elder & Giele, 2009). Variation from what is considered the typical life pathway is of key interest within the life course paradigm, which identifies four dynamic factors influencing the individual life course: historical and geographic location, social ties, human agency, and variations in timing of events and social roles (Elder & Giele, 2009). Each of these factors assists in putting the life of individuals and cohorts in meaningful context, which translates into understanding individuals' lived experience. Such an approach is especially pertinent to understanding issues related to disability across the life course, as disability is a fluid and evolving concept.

This chapter provides an introduction to a life course approach to disability. It begins with an overview of key concepts, life stages, and important historical developments of approaches to disability. It then provides examples of different theoretical approaches to disability across and within various life stages. Finally, the chapter highlights key issues that impact a person's livelihood across all generations (family, policy, health, and self-determination). These key themes can offer a useful framework for contextualizing disability across the lifespan.

Key Concepts

Disability in the Life Course

Disability is conceptualized within this volume as a social category that contributes to the exclusion of and prejudice against people with bodily or cognitive variations. This is in contrast to the conventional understanding of disability within much medical and therapeutic literature, which focuses instead on an individual impairment that results in inevitable exclusion. As such, this volume draws heavily on the social model of disability, as originally articulated by Michael Oliver (1990; 1996). This model has been transformative in the lives of many people with disabilities, giving them both a shared identity as disabled as well as a political platform (Thomas, 2004).

There are a number of different factors that contribute to disability within a life course approach. These factors can include age of onset of disability, which is considered to significantly impact an individual's life experience with disability (Kelley-Moore, Schumacher, Kahana, & Kahana, 2006); age at which disability is acquired, which affects long-term health outcomes (Harrison, Umberson, Lin, & Cheng, 2010); identity development (Priestley, 2004); social interactions (Hallberg & Carlsson, 1993); and gender identity (Gutman & Napier-Klemic, 1996), among others. In addition to age of onset, the degree to which the disability is lifelong and the extent to which its manifestations are cyclical can affect outcomes for people with disabilities over the life course. Disability is a condition that can come and go in a person's life and can be experienced differently at different stages in life. Such conditions as episodes of arthritic flare-ups, Guillain Barré syndrome, or depression can occur and then abate. Disability can also occur suddenly or gradually. For example, a person may develop a chronic illness that eventually is experienced as a disability.

Adjustment to disability across the life course may also vary based on individuals' cultural background (Marini, 2001) and social-environmental resources and supports (Heller, 2008). Understanding disability through the life course is a complex area of research that can challenge traditional approaches and understandings of life stages.

Life Course Stages

Traditional approaches to researching human life within the social sciences often separate lives into discrete categories and stages. For instance, both Erikson (1963) and Levinson (1978; Levinson & Levinson, 1996) hypothesized that individuals pass through life stages or cycles sequentially in an order that is both predictable and predetermined. Erikson conceptualized eight distinct psychosocial stages of development, during individuals undergo a "crisis" resulting in either healthy or unhealthy personality traits (1963). Similarly, Levinson argued that men (later revised to include women) go through four life "seasons": preadulthood, early adulthood, middle adulthood, and late adulthood (1978). However, understanding lives as progressing through distinct stages may lead to a reductionist and limited view of humanity (Settersen, 2003). Many studies within the social sciences are "age specific," focusing on one slice of life, instead of recognizing aging as a continuous, dynamic process that occurs throughout life (Elder & Giele, 2009).

A life course approach, in contrast, re-conceptualizes human lives as an ongoing process that cannot be fully captured through a "snapshot" view of individual age groups (Levy et al., 2005). Instead, individuals' life trajectories are the result of a complex interplay between human agency and generational and social forces (Bryman, Bytheway, Allatt, & Keil, 1987; Elder, 2003). As such, life course research designs tend to be longitudinal or cross-sectional in nature, tracking participants' development through time while recognizing various historical and social influences (Elder & Giele, 2009). This is the approach best suited to understanding disability through the life course.

Transitions

The concept of transitions is critical within life course research. Within the life course paradigm, transitions refer to disruptions in individuals' day-to-day lives, which include both proximal (daily hassles and stressors) and distal (major events) changes (Elder, 1985; Rowlinson & Fellner, 1988). The general theory of transitions is a major influence in framing and directing empirical life course research, and is well-accepted within the field (Sackmann & Wingens, 2003). The timing of transitions between various life stages are not merely age-dependent, but take into account factors such as the labor market, social policies, and individual decisions (Heinz, 2009). Major life changes, such as leaving home, changing careers, or renegotiating family relationships, may cause a great deal of stress in individuals' lives, which leads to transitions between life stages (Almeida & Wong, 2009).

People with disabilities and their families may face additional factors that contribute to transitional shifts. They may experience greater obstacles to navigating transitions due not only to their own age-related changes, but also to changes in their supports. One example is the shift from school age, where educational services are legally required in the United States, to adulthood, where there are few mandated services. A person with a disability may move back and forth across traditional life stages, which may be independent of age, or may bridge multiple stages simultaneously. A life course approach, therefore, offers a useful means for understanding such complexities, and for developing whole-of-life policies and services.

Overview of Life Stages

Generational life stage categories tend to shift over time and are shaped by cultural and social influences (Priestley, 2003). For instance, adolescence is a life stage that does not directly translate into many languages and cultures, and its origins may be attributed to the industrialization of Western societies in the early 20th century (Shaffer, 2009). Therefore, it is necessary to critically examine broad, sweeping categories such as childhood, adulthood, and aging, which often project an "ideal" or "normal" life course to which humans are meant to aspire. As such, the lived experience of disability offers valuable insight into the historical and social contexts behind life course stages. For instance, induction into the socially created category of adulthood is often associated with independence and autonomy within Western cultures, to which the experience of disability may create a necessary counterexample. Being considered "dependent" essentially became viewed as a problem with the rise of capitalism, which supplanted previous social systems of interdependence with formalized systems of care (Goble, 2004).

The following sections will provide a background overview of the different broad life stages as related to disability. These stages include birth, childhood, youth, adulthood, aging, and death/dying.

Birth

Even prior to birth, social customs, religious ideology, and socioeconomic status influence prospective parents' experience during pregnancy. In the United States, societal expectations have moved toward pregnant women taking an active role in maintaining the health and development of their children (Hutchison, 2008). This may take the form of childbirth education, prenatal care, and prenatal testing, which are all considered part of a responsible mother's duty (Kail & Cavanaugh, 2007). This attention to prenatal health concerns often directly relates to the prevention of disabling conditions like genetic abnormalities, fetal alcohol syndrome, and other physical and intellectual disabilities. Hence, it is not uncommon for parents of children with disabilities to be blamed or to feel guilty for having a child with disability.

Some disabilities may be apparent at birth or determined through newborn screenings, such as Down syndrome or certain types of deafness (Patient Education Institute, 2009). The majority, however, will be either discovered or acquired later in life, such as autism, spinal cord injury, or traumatic brain injury (Albrecht, Seelman, & Bury, 2003). One survey of 1,505 non-elderly adults with disabilities revealed that the onset of the disability occurred under age 1 in only 9% of the sample, between the ages of 1 and 18 in 10% of the sample, and after the age of 18 in the vast majority (80%) of the respondents (Hanson, Neuman, & Voris, 2003). In the case when disability is discovered at birth, parental reactions have often been described in terms of the stages of grief: shock, denial (refusal to accept the diagnosis), anger, blaming, fear, and acceptance (George, Vickers, Wilkes, & Barton, 2007; Graungaard & Skov, 2007; Wright, 2008). The reaction of parents to the diagnosis of disability has even been described as "chronic sorrow" (Olshansky, 1962), a term coined in the 1960s to describe a grief that is considered a "natural reaction to the tragic fate of having a child who is seriously impaired," lasting throughout life because of the "discrepancy between the child who was dreamed for and the child who actually exists" (Roos, 2002, p. 1). This theory of chronic sorrow remains pervasive in many health professions (Foley, 2006; J. Gordon, 2009). However, the theory is incredibly problematic because it draws upon a "disability as tragedy" discourse, which removes all notions of broader environmental influences (Breen, 2009). This reinforces social, cultural, and economic injustices that families of children with disabilities face (Breen, 2009). Yet the literature shows great variability in family reactions to having a child with disabilities, and that many families adapt well to having a child with disabilities over time (Ha, Hong, Seltzer, & Greenberg, 2008). Also, many families do not experience these distinct phases of reactions to having a child with disabilities at set points in the lifespan, but experience cycles with new demands for accommodation during various transition periods throughout their child's life (Yuan, 2003).

Early Childhood and Childhood

Early childhood is traditionally understood through the lens of major motor and developmental milestones. For instance, Arnold Gesell systematically observed young children at the Yale University Clinic of Child Development in the early 20th century, which led to the establishment of developmental norms for child development (Slee, 2002). While his original theory has undergone a great deal of criticism, the concept of developmental stages remains influential in both developmental psychology and pediatrics (Adolph, Karasik, & Tamis-LeMonda, 2009). Similarly, stages of cognitive, social, and personality development in young children typically imply a universal sequence of skills that must be achieved in a fixed order (Adolph et al., 2009).

However, developmental research within various contexts has tended to contradict this predominant view. For instance, a study of English,

Jamaican, and Indian mothers residing in the same city revealed that mothers from the three cultures had different expectations about when their children would achieve developmental milestones such as walking and crawling, with the Jamaican mothers expecting their children to sit and walk much earlier than English and Indian mothers. Follow-up with these families revealed that the children's attainment of these milestones was more closely related to their mothers' expectations than to any particular age group (Hopkins & Westra, 1989). This observation is of particular relevance for many children who have an identified disability during their early childhood years, since disability can interfere with what are considered the "normal" developmental stages of early childhood.

Children with disabilities and their families may also have extensive interaction with formal disability services. For many families, this entails ongoing involvement with health care professionals, starting with diagnosis and treatment and continuing with ongoing care. For instance, in the United States, children from birth to age 3 who have a disability or are at risk for developing a disability qualify for early intervention services. These services include the delivery of speech, occupational, and physical therapy, as well as case-coordination management. The delivery of these services places a heavy emphasis on family-centered delivery, which includes the involvement of the family in an individualized family service plan (IFSP) and service delivery within the family home (Dunst, 2002). For elementary through high school aged children, the Individuals with Disabilities Education Act (IDEA) also requires families of students with disabilities to have much more extensive interaction with the school system than families of children without disabilities (Harry, 2008). This extensive interaction with formal disability service delivery systems may actually exacerbate existing ethnic, cultural, and financial disadvantages families are already facing (Breen, 2009). For instance, low-income families may be less able to afford disability services, negotiate bureaucracy, and advocate for disability resources than financially advantaged families, impacting the long-term trajectory of the disability (Breen, 2009).

Youth

A predominant mode of understanding youth is by investigating various transitions (e.g., from school to work, from single to married, from living with parents, to living alone). The age at which these transitions occur varies greatly based on social expectations and generational changes (Heinz, 2009). For instance, in the current generation more youth are entering higher education than in previous generations, which delays certain "adult responsibilities" like getting married or buying a house. This trend has given rise to studies of "emerging adulthood," a phase distinct from both adolescence and young adulthood that occurs predominantly in industrialized societies (Arnett, 2000; Arnett & Tanner, 2006). This stage is marked by exploration of social and economic roles without definite commitment, as made evident by factors such as occupational instability and residential mobility (Arnett & Tanner, 2006). In different social contexts, however, this emerging adulthood stage is much less pronounced. For instance, while the age of marriage is rising within developing countries (especially for men), survey data representing about 60% of developing countries reveals that 38% of young women in those countries were married before age 18 years (Lloyd, 2005).

Another way of understanding the stage of life known as youth has been through generations—age groups that share social and historical locations that uniquely influence the way they experience the world (Goodwin & O'Connor, 2009). This theory of generations is attributed to Karl Mannheim (1952), who was attempting to understand the sociology of knowledge through concepts other than social class (Eyerman & Turner, 1998). However, the homogeneity of groups such as Baby Boomers and Generation X remains contested, and the level of interaction between the generational groups largely underestimated (Goodwin & O'Connor, 2009).

Since youth with disabilities often have limited access to peers who have disabilities, they may feel pressured to choose between their identity as a person with a disability and their youth identity (Priestley, 2004). Identity development is generally heightened during adolescence, when individuals develop a sense of self and a personal value system (Muuss, 1996). Disability may complicate this identity development process. A qualitative study of adolescents born with spina bifida revealed that they were able to claim disability as part of their identity in one of three ways: identity as overcoming, identity as objectifying, or identity as integrating disability (Kinavey, 2006). These categories were roughly congruent with Gill's (1997) four types of integration in disability identity development: integrating into society ("coming to feel we belong"), integrating with the disability community ("coming home"), internally integrating sameness and differentness ("coming together"), and integrating how we feel with how we present ourselves ("coming out"). Each model of disability integration "carries risks and rewards, opportunities and loss" (Kinavey, 2006, p. 1103).

Adulthood

Most research and theoretical inquiry into disability is focused on adults of working age, including attention to employment, civil rights, and social inclusion (Priestley, 2003). Ferguson, Gartner, and Lipsky (2000) note that families have a life course of their own, in addition to the life course of each family member. This is a particularly important point for families who have one or more members with a disability, because they may not follow the "typical" family trajectory, wherein children leave the home and become autonomous and independent when they reach adulthood. Modern societies continue to define adulthood through highly gendered and idealized expectations of productivity in the workforce and reproductive capacity, which may ostracize many individuals with disabilities (Priestley, 2004).

In particular, adults with disabilities may feel unfulfilled in adult life because of barriers to participating in employment and parenting, which are socially valued roles on which much of adult identity is built (Priestley, 2004). People with disabilities have consistently held lower rates of employment than the general population. The United States Department of Labor Economic Situation report for April 2011 (U.S. Bureau of Labor Statistics, 2011) shows that for people aged 16–64, 34.5% of people with disability participate in the labor market, compared with 76.4% of people without disabilities. This low rate of employment may be due to factors such as not being offered the same employment benefits as people without disabilities (Lustig, Strauser, & Donnell, 2003), discrimination in the hiring process (McMahon et al., 2008), or pervasive stigma (Scheid, 2005). The issue of employment is particularly important during the adult stage of the life course, as being gainfully employed is a primary signifier of adulthood roles in modern societies (Priestley, 2003).

Many people with disabilities have also faced significant barriers to parenting, another major adulthood role. Professionals, family members, and support staff often implicitly or explicitly discourage individuals with disabilities from having children (Olsen & Clarke, 2003). This is particularly true for parents with mental health issues (Sayce, 2000) and parents with intellectual disabilities (McConnell & Llewellyn, 2002). This prominent view that babies should only be born into genetically "superior" and economically and morally capable families formed the basis of the eugenics movement in the United States (Carey, 2009). The main thrust of the eugenics movement was promoting "genetic purity" by preventing "inferior" people from having children. In addition to facing discrimination, parents with disabilities have barriers related to lack of accessibility and funding for needed assistive technology, training, and/ or social-emotional supports for parenting (Kirshbaum, 2000).

For adults with intellectual disabilities, interaction with the community in which one lives is often regulated and controlled by professionals, making it difficult to break through a paternalistically protected life and experience natural community. This often leads to small and restricted social networks, which may include only those they reside with, paid support workers, and family members (Bigby, 2008; Forrester-Jones et al., 2006; Lippold & Burns, 2009; Verdonschot, De Witte, Reichrath, Buntinx, & Curfs, 2009).

Aging

An estimated 54 million people in the United States have a disability, defined as having one impaired activity of daily living (ADL), such as communication, self-care, or mobility (U.S. Department of Health and Human Services, 2000). However, a high proportion of older adults who are identified within this number do not personally identify themselves as disabled (Langlois et al., 1996; Williamson & Fried, 1996). This may be due to several reasons, including having already experienced life domains such as employment and parenthood as able bodied, perceived independence, and fear of stigma associated with identifying as disabled (Kelley-Moore et al., 2006). A longitudinal study of 662 older adults revealed that subjectively identifying as "disabled" was associated not only with limitations in activities of daily living, but with health anxiety, decline in health, and changing social networks. Regardless of health status, those who had living children and those who were satisfied with their social lives were much less likely to consider themselves disabled (Kelley-Moore et al., 2006).

Life expectancy for individuals who have had lifelong disabilities or disabilities acquired in early age has increased with medical advances (Kemp & Mosqueda, 2004). Physical disability can add complications to the aging process, including the development of additional impairments, and experiencing changes in function earlier than non-disabled peers due to a lower level of reserves and limited economic means (Kemp & Mosqueda, 2004). However, having a lifelong disability may actually facilitate aging well, since these individuals have knowledge of and experience with needed resources, which makes them better able to navigate disability systems (Rothman, 2003).

Ageism may inappropriately limit medical care for elderly individuals, including differential insurance coverage and lack of access to particular treatments or specialists (Kane & Kane, 2005). This ageism is aggravated in the treatment of individuals with disabilities, who may have limits placed on their medical care due to the presence of disability (Sheehan, 2003). Much like elderly individuals, those with disabilities often do not receive adequate treatment because they are considered "irreparably damaged and essentially untreatable," potentially leading to unnecessary and premature mortality (Sheehan, 2003, p. 528).

Death and Dying

Having a lifelong experience with disability can negatively impact individuals' access to quality health care, and end-of-life care in particular (McEnhill, 2004). End-of-life issues are of particular interest to people with disabilities, especially those who identify as part of the disability rights movement. Many disability rights organizations have stood in staunch opposition to legalizing assisted suicide (Gill, 2000). Their argument has been that assisted suicide gives health care professionals "license to treat persons with disabilities less rigorously than 'healthy' individuals in matters of life and death" (Gill, 2000, p. 527). Opponents of assisted suicide find this particularly problematic, given the historical precedent for health professionals to devalue and unjustly treat individuals with disabilities. They argue that in cases where an individual with a disability requests to die, protective safeguards should be put into place just as with non-disabled individuals. To respond otherwise unduly devalues the lives of people with disabilities. Over time, ethicists have faced a number of barriers to fully recognizing the validity of the disability rights position, including intellectual and experiential barriers, as well as defensiveness of a health care system in which many remain socially devalued (Gill, 2010). The disability rights position against assisted suicide has been criticized on a number of grounds, some of which unfairly represent the position (Gill, 2010).

Because individuals with intellectual and developmental disabilities (I/DD) are often perceived as incapable of grief, they are often not invited to attend funerals or participate in other death rituals (Raji & Hollins, 2003). This view that people with I/DD are more vulnerable in situations of death and dying is influenced by a number of erroneous assumptions, and is often the result of attitudinal and societal barriers (Read & Elliott, 2003). Many residential care facilities for people with I/DD are unprepared for supporting individuals in their own process of dying or in their participation in bereavement practices (Todd, 2004). Read and Elliot (2007) developed a bereavement support model for this population that includes all aspects of current and future care delivery.

Theoretical Approaches and Developments

Various theoretical approaches and historical developments provide a framework for understanding disability through the life course. They stem from different disciplines with different areas of focus. Some examples include gerontological, developmental psychology, sociological, and disability studies approaches. These approaches are contextualized within the historical developments of approaches to disability.

Historical Developments

The historical context and wider social context is important for understanding disability. The medicalization of disability has dominated much of our understanding of disability across the life course, including the way it is portrayed throughout history. This perspectives views disability as intrinsic to the individual, and physical and cognitive diversity is considered pathology, something that "needs to be studied, measured, 'fixed,' or altered to match some idealized body" (Ott, 2005, p. 21). This perspective has influenced treatment of, and attitudes toward, people with disabilities across generations, and is a major contributing factor to why children, youth, adults, and elderly people with disabilities often experience exclusion and discrimination.

Throughout American history, disability has been used as a justification for inequality of a number of groups. Claiming that slaves, women, and immigrants are in some way disabled has been a primary mode of establishing that they should justifiably be excluded from citizenship. For instance, women were denied the right to vote because of a perceived lack of "higher order thinking skills," and African Americans were denied full citizenship because of misconceptions around disease, disability, and/or racial inferiority. Typically, these accusations have been countered not with a defense of disability as an acceptable group to belong to, but with a refutation of the claims that the group is indeed disabled. This reveals a dark notion underpinning much of historical American thought: that disability is considered a legitimate reason for inequality (Baynton, 2001). Individuals with disabilities are then denied humanity, which is often judged by "eighteenth-century ideals of rational cognition, physical health, and technological ability" (Siebers, 2008, p. 79). This inevitably devalues those who do not have rational cognitive abilities, physical health, or technical skills, and relegates them to a status of less than human (Siebers, 2008). This historical construction of disability has resulted in exclusionary policies that affect people with disabilities and their families from birth to death.

The roots of understanding bodily and cognitive difference within our Western Judeo-Christian society are biblical texts and religious traditions (Braddock & Parish, 2003). During the period of the Enlightenment, these religious values were challenged by a surge of interest in reason and rationality, which in turn caused medical and scientific knowledge to dominate our understanding of disability. Both of these historical traditions continue to profoundly influence our current understanding of disability within Western societies. These shifts in worldview have been and remain incomplete, with remnants of each combining with a more recent worldview of rights-based understanding of disability. Rehabilitation sciences, for instance, still hold tremendous power in our understanding of disability, and the major tenets of this field bear the marks of previous traditions that emphasized sameness (Stiker, 1999).

While the timeline is contested, the early 1970s gave birth to a worldwide disability rights movement that drew upon earlier successes of the civil rights and women's liberation movements (Charlton, 1998; Fleischer & Zames, 2001). Many attribute the beginning of this movement to Ed Roberts, a wheelchair user who turned disability rights activist when he began to advocate for his own inclusion as a student at the University of California, Berkeley (McCarthy, 2003). Roberts and his compatriots in the "Rolling Quads" group at Berkeley drew on the radical political protests on campus at the time. Simultaneously, disability groups in South America, Southern Africa, Southeast Asia, and around the world were joining what we now know as the disability rights movement, whose rallying call was and is "nothing about us without us" (Charlton, 1998). The shift to a rights-based approach toward people with disabilities significantly altered the approach to disability, and to people with disabilities. Advocates within this movement have been instrumental in passing various disability policies, including Section 504 of the Rehabilitation Act of 1973, the Americans with Disabilities Act of 1990, and the Disability Discrimination Act of 1995 in the United Kingdom (Fleischer & Zames, 2001).

An understanding of the history of disability and society's reaction to it helps us understand the life course of people with disability across generations. For each age cohort, the "zeitgeist" of the time framed their life experience. Hence, comparisons of persons with disabilities across ages need to take into account the experiences and social context of that generation.

Gerontology

Traditionally, gerontology literature has been dominated by an emphasis on aging as a period of decline and loss in function (Achenbaum, 2005). Recognizing the multidirectionality and multidimensionality of aging came primarily as a result of lifespan approaches that emerged from the childhood literature on human development (Baltes, Freund, & Li, 2005). This has led to an approach that takes into account biological and cultural perspectives, lifespan changes in allocation of resources, systematic theory of adaptive psychological aging, and theories of psychological aging in specific domains (Baltes et al., 2005).

Another predominant paradigm within gerontology is "successful aging," which contends that aging well is marked by high cognitive and physical functioning, low incidence of disease and disability, and active engagement with life (Rowe & Kahn, 1998). This paradigm is problematic for individuals with physical disabilities, adding to the marginalization and stigmatization they have experienced throughout the life course (Minkler & Fadem, 2002). Since disability is a socially created condition, a successful approach for understanding aging for people with disabilities will bear in mind the contexts in which the person lives, taking a broader ecological approach to understanding the aging process for these individuals (Minkler & Fadem, 2002).

An adaptation of the successful aging model, which is a better fit for people with disabilities, is the model of "aging well," in which positive outcomes of aging well are (1) maintaining health and function (physical and mental health and independence) and (2) active engagement with life (friendships, contributions to society, and community participation) (T. F. Johnson, 1995). Inherent in this model are the assumptions that aging is a lifelong process and that how well one ages in later life is dependent on events occurring at younger ages. This model emphasizes that aging successfully evolves from exercising the choices that create a successful and productive life (Krain, 1995). In a modification specifically geared to persons with disabilities, the Supports Outcome Model of Aging Well (Heller, 2008), the model is expanded to emphasize the primacy of the environment and individualized supports in influencing outcomes for individuals across the life course.

The fields of aging and disability have typically been distinct both within academic studies and in the service sector. However, acknowledgment of the overlap and shared goals in those fields has led to increased calls for collaboration between the two (Lightfoot, 2007). Both fields have experienced a co-occurring trend toward community-based services and consumer-direction in service delivery, and they share similar goals in regard to accessible transportation, family caregiving, and residential options (Lightfoot, 2007). In recognition of these factors, the Administration on Aging in the United States has funded and expanded Aging and Disability Resource Centers, which are designed to "effectively integrate the full range of long-term supports and services into a single, coordinated system" through a single point of entry (Administration on Aging, 2010, para. 1). More recently, the Aging and Disability Resource Centers have successfully advocated as a coalition for health and long-term care initiatives within the 2010 health care reform bill (the Patient Protection and Affordable Care Act) that would benefit both disabled and elderly individuals. While there has been significant progress in joint policy initiatives between the two networks, the systems largely remain fragmented, with little cross-training and coordination between them.

Developmental Psychology

The study of children's development began in the mid-19th century, at the start of the Industrial Revolution, but the advent of developmental psychology as a field is generally dated around 1882, with the publication of Wilhelm Preyer's seminal work *The Mind of the Child* (Harris & Butterworth, 2002). Modern developmental psychologists differentiate between normative and idiographic development, the latter referring to individual variations in the rate and extent of development (Shaffer & Kipp, 2010). Typically, developmental psychologists rely primarily on normative approaches, which compare individuals and groups along common definitions of psychological constructs. Idiographic approaches, in contrast, gather information that is unique to an individual instead of measuring adherence to or deviance from a common construct (Lee & Tracey, 2005). While idiographic approaches achieve more rich description at the individual level, this is often at the expense of generalizability (Lee & Tracey, 2005).

As mentioned at the beginning of this chapter, developmental psychology has traditionally represented human development through stage theories, which can be problematic for many types of disability. The four primary stage theories promulgated within the field are Sigmund Freud's psychosexual stages, Erik Erikson's psychosocial stages, Jean Piaget's four stages of intellectual development, and Daniel Levinson's life seasons (Lee & Tracey, 2005). Partially due to the stage theories promoted within developmental psychology, individuals with disabilities are often regarded as children well into adulthood (Marshak, Seligman, & Prezant, 1999). Although the field of disability studies does not draw on these theories to frame approaches to disability, they remain a key influence in other fields, and continue to impact ideas about and approaches to disability across different generations and transition stages.

Psychosexual Stages

Freud conceptualized human development in a series of four psychosexual stages. Each stage presents a conflict in a child's life, which when resolved, will allow the child to move on to the next stage. If the conflict during a certain stage remains unresolved, Freud contended, the individual will remain "fixated" at that stage, which will dominate his or her adult personality. The four stages are: oral, anal, phallic, and genital, with a period of latency between the phallic and genital stages (Lerner, 2002). While his theory has been criticized as sexist and culturally biased, it still heavily influences current psychological inquiry (Berzoff, Flanagan, & Hertz, 2008). Freud's theories have had many implications for people with mental illness and their families. These theories tend to blame parents for the mental illness of the offspring and have guided treatment interventions. More recently, researchers have recognized that biological factors play a large causative role in mental illness.

Psychosocial Stages

Erikson, a student of Freud, developed his psychosocial stages in response to what he saw as inadequacy within Freud's theory. Erikson contended that development occurs in eight basic stages, and that development does not end after childhood, but continues throughout adult life. Like Freud, Erikson saw each stage as consisting of a basic conflict that either positively or negatively influenced an individual's personality development. His stages are roughly linked to chronological ages and include: trust versus mistrust; autonomy versus shame and doubt; initiative versus guilt; industry versus inferiority; identity versus role confusion; intimacy versus isolation; generativity versus stagnation; and ego integrity versus despair (Sigelman & Rider, 2009). One of the strengths of this theory is the recognition that development is lifelong. However, there is little research on its applicability to people with disabilities. For example, individuals with severe disabilities may be dependent on families and other carers for longer periods of time than people without disabilities. The theory would not adequately address the fact that autonomy may be an issue much later in the life course for individuals with severe disabilities or with very limited cognitive abilities.

Piaget's Cognitive Stages

Piaget theorized that individuals undergo four stages of cognitive development, which are finalized by the end of adolescence. A developing child, using this theory, is in the process of building cognitive maps and schemas, which assist him or her in understanding and responding to experiences within the environment. As an individual progresses through the stages, cognitive ability increases in sophistication. These stages are: sensorimotor, preoperational, concrete, and formal operational. By the time an individual reaches the formal operational stage, cognitive structures resemble those of a typical adult (Lerner, 2002). Little research exists on the applicability of Piaget's theories to people with cognitive limitations. One might assume that individuals with severe intellectual disabilities would not reach more advanced cognitive stages.

Seasons of Life

Levinson identified five stages of development, which spanned the entire lifespan. These stages were: preadulthood, early adulthood, middle adulthood, late adulthood, and late late adulthood. Each stage involves individual "life structures," which refer to the choices made in partnering, career, having children, and other major life factors. He argued that individuals undergo life cycles, wherein they transition from one life structure to another (Lerner, 2002; Sigelman & Rider, 2009). This developmental model may have greater heuristic value for people with disabilities as they are tied to life roles in different stages. However, many people with disabilities do not have opportunities and do not experience many of the life roles identified, such as getting married and having children.

Overall, stage theories can be problematic for people with and without disabilities. While individuals tended to move through a set of well-timed transitions in the middle part of the last century, much of that regularity has dissolved. The life course has become more individualized, depending on social class, gender, race, and ethnicity (Settersen, 2007). The stage theories are even more problematic when applied to people with disabilities, as we know little about the age-related trajectory for people with various disabilities, and the complexity and fluidity of disability means that not all persons with a disability will "fit" into the structured stage.

Sociology

While there are a number of prominent sociologists who have furthered our understanding of disability in both research and practice, historically sociology as a discipline has not addressed disability across the life course to any great extent. Two approaches that increased our awareness from a sociological perspective are the "sick role" and the biopsychosocial model.

The Sick Role

A prominent sociological approach to disability, particularly related to adulthood, is the historic concept of the "sick role," which relieves unhealthy individuals from complying with social behavioral norms, but also obligates them to be both compliant to and appreciative of medical intervention (Parsons, 1951). This model may be appropriate for acute injuries, but people with disabilities vary in their need for health care, and while some will have frequent health complications, attributing this status to people with disabilities across the board is inappropriate (Hayes & Hannold, 2007). The sick role causes complications for individuals with lifelong disabilities who cannot and/or do not want to be cured, and who are therefore considered deviant (Erkulwater, 2006; Meile, 1986; Quinn, 1998). This attribution turns individuals with disabilities into perpetual patients, stripping them of their rights as citizens, which can prevent them from performing activities of social belonging such as marriage, voting, and participating in education and the workforce (Erkulwater, 2006).

Gerald Gordon (1966) supplemented the concept of the sick role with what he termed the "impaired role," which applies to individuals whose condition is unlikely to change, and who therefore cannot recover as expected for those in the sick role. Individuals within this group are expected to live up to normal societal expectations, within the limitations of their impairment, and to make the most of their situation. Again, the impaired role places people with disabilities at a disadvantage through the expectation that their primary responsibility is to manage their conditions. Reliance on either of these medical interpretations of impairment is often strongly opposed by people with hearing impairments, who consider themselves part of a linguistic minority group and culture, as well as by people with intellectual disabilities and mental health system users (Barnes, Mercer, & Shakespeare, 1999).

Biopsychosocial Model

The World Health Organization (WHO) created the International Classification of Impairments, Disabilities, and Handicaps (ICIDH) in 1980 in order to better evaluate the effectiveness of health care processes for chronic diseases, disorders, and impairments. This classification system was an attempt to move away from a medical model of disability, which proved inappropriate for people whose conditions were not acute and temporary. This revised model viewed disability, impairment, and handicap as distinct entities, taking into account environmental barriers and disadvantages people face based on their limitations (Gray & Hendershot, 2000).

In response to the identified deficiencies of the ICIDH, a new classification, called the International Classification of Functioning, Disability and Health (ICF, sometimes referred to as ICIDH-2) was developed and finalized in 2001. This model is an attempt to identify and measure disability at both individual and population levels (Gray & Hendershot, 2000). The ICF model contends that the experience of disability is a universal human experience, and takes into account the social aspects of disability, especially the person–environment interaction (World Health Organization, 2001). The relevant domains within this model are impairment, activity limitation, and participation restriction. This model was further validated for children and youth in the ICF-CY, which has provided common language and documentation across administrative, clinical, and research settings (Simeonsson, 2009).

More recently, there has been a growing interest in sociological approaches to life course research. Such literature has synthesized trends and developments in the field (e.g., Mayer, 2009) and analyzed the influence of early life experiences on later health outcomes (e.g., Umberson, Crosnoe & Reczek, 2010). While there are other prominent theoretical approaches to disability from a sociological perspective (e.g., Irving Goffman, Michael Foucault), many of the contemporary sociological perspectives on disability are located within the discipline of disability studies. However, little comprehensive work has been done specific to the life course of disability with the exception of Priestley, 2003.

Disability Studies

Disability studies is a diverse interdisciplinary field that examines the social, cultural, and political implications of disability. It emerged directly from the disability rights movement, and continues to be both an academic field as well as an area of political activity (Davis, 2004).

The primary model in disability studies, as articulated by British scholars such as Mike Oliver, has been to differentiate between disability and impairment through the social model. In the United States, disability studies has identified disability as consisting of complex interactions between the biological reality of disability and the social structures that create disability (Mitchell & Snyder, 2006). While there is a large body of work that addresses disability transitions and disability at various generational stages, there is little work specific to the life course approach. However, disability studies is embodied in a critical theoretical approach that seeks to address the whole-of-life of a person and, in this way, provides us with further understanding of the issues facing people with disabilities across their lives.

One issue that transcends generations is that of identity. Because disability is an unstable and ill-defined social category, identity politics within the field of disability studies has been hotly contested (Davis, 2004; Siebers, 2008). Siebers argues that disability studies requires scholars to think more flexibly about what constitutes identity and that the future of the field is in philosophical realism. This position emphasizes identity politics as a form of coalition building for people with disabilities, much like other established forms of political representation (Siebers, 2008). Davis, on the other hand, contends that disability studies has neglected to follow the intellectual trend toward more nuanced understandings of identity. He claims instead that the "malleable view" of the human body and identity that disability studies provides is its greatest strength. He argues instead for a "new ethics" of the body, which he calls "dismodernism." This ethics centers on three components: (1) care *of* the body in a consumerist culture; (2) care *for* the body, as part of the economics of the healthcare industry; and (3) care *about* the body, which subsumes the first two categories. Dismodernism rests on the recognition that the ideal is not the normal, dominant subject, because it acknowledges the interdependent nature of humanity and the universal experiences of bodily limitation (Davis, 2004). For persons with a disability, the issue of identity formation is critical and likely changes throughout the life course and within the social-environmental context they experience. We know very little about how disability identity develops (if at all for some people with disabilities) and how it interacts with not only age but other identities, such as sexual orientation or ethnic/racial group. Little research also exists on changes in disability identity over time and in different contexts.

The following section will more specifically explore key themes from disability studies that impact a person's life, including family, health, policy, and self-determination.

Major Themes

In considering a life-course approach to disability, there are a number of interrelated areas that offer a useful contextualization of the key issues facing people with disabilities in all stages of their life.

Family

Literature within genetics and bioethics often regards having a child with a disability as a necessary hardship for the family, and the parents in particular; yet more recent bodies of literature challenge this assumption (Ferguson et al., 2000). For example, in a study comparing parents of children with Down syndrome, other developmental disabilities, or no disability, Cahill and Glidden (1996) found that all three groups functioned similarly. One longitudinal study of parents of children with developmental disabilities or mental illness revealed that while parents indicated increased negative affect after receiving the diagnosis of disability for their child, over time they tended to adapt well to having a child with disabilities (Ha et al., 2008).

Family Demography

Family demography refers to the study of the family ties that bind people and households together in family units in order to better understand the behavior of both individuals and society (Bianchi & Casper, 2005). These dynamics are considered an indicator of societal well-being, since it is through families that resources are exchanged and "less able members are cared for by those who are more able" (Bianchi & Casper, 2005, p. 93). This concept of families as the natural deliverers of care is particularly important for families who have one or more members with a disability. While parents caring for a minor child is considered natural and socially responsible, caregiving roles become complicated when a son or daughter reaches adulthood and still has support needs (Knox & Bigby, 2007); when a parent with a disability requires support from his or her child (Carretero, Garcés, Ródenas, & Sanjosé, 2009); or when an adult acquires a disability that necessitates support from his or her spouse (Yorgason, Booth, & Johnson, 2008). The literature surrounding family members who care for members of the family beyond the "natural" caregiving cycle for minor children without disability has been dominated by the concept of "caregiver burden."

Caregiver Burden

According to Carretero and colleagues (2009), the concept of caregiver burden first entered the literature in 1963, in reference to the impact of having a family member with a mental illness. The idea has since been adopted by researchers in a wide variety of fields to explore the physical, emotional, and economic consequences of care provision (Carretero et al., 2009, p. 75). The "burden" may refer to primary and secondary stress factors, financial hardship, or perceived inequity in the division of labor. An individual's position within the life course also affects the way that individual responds to providing care for a family member with a disability. Yorgason, Booth, and Johnson contend that the negative impact of disability on marriages is greater in younger cohorts, where disability is less expected and assistance with activities of daily living is more likely to interfere with child rearing and careers (2008). Similarly, research has focused on the "sandwich generation" of women who provide care to both their children and their aging parents, which is expected to increase their stress (Pierret, 2006). However, the study of caregiver burden often fails to account for the false binary of "carer" and "cared for," and the fact that those who are receiving care are an active part of the caring relationship (Heller, Miller, & Factor, 1997; Knox & Bigby, 2007; Y. Williams & Robinson, 2001).

Family Systems Health Model

Families almost universally deal with the experiences of illness and disability at some point in the family life cycle. Rolland (1994) developed a normative, preventative model called the "family systems health model" for the assessment and intervention of families who face chronic disorders. This model outlines three dimensions: psychosocial types, major phases in their natural history, and family systems variables. These dimensions are part of an interactive process that determines the goodness of fit of a family's individual style and the caregiving demands of chronic disorders over time, which means that no one family pattern is inherently healthy or unhealthy.

The impact of disability on the family and the family's role in facilitating participation of children or adults with a disability is a well-researched area that provides a good understanding of complex disability issues and transitions though life stages. The following chapter will discuss the role of the family in more detail.

Health

A life course perspective on health provides a framework for examining changes in health status for persons with disabilities as they age. Its premise is that health is a developmental process occurring throughout the lifespan, starting with the prenatal stage. Many population-based studies have shown that early life events influence the occurrence of many chronic diseases that appear in adulthood (Kuh & Ben-Shlomo, 2004). Early events can influence the development of immune, neurological, endocrine, and other systems. For example, malnutrition of the fetus can lead to later-life diabetes, heart disease, hypertension, and obesity. In addition to biological factors, determinants of health status include socioeconomic and environmental factors, access to health care, and behavior factors (Tarlov, 1996). We know that poverty, discrimination, and inadequate health insurance often experienced by people with disabilities can lead to health disparities (Albrecht, 2010). Hence, environmental factors can interact with genetic predispositions, resulting in varied health outcomes. For example, genetic variations in serotonin levels in the brain are associated with greater depression in the face of high stress associated with poverty (Halfon, 2009).

Many adults with disabilities experience age-related health conditions and secondary conditions associated with the primary disability earlier than the general population. For example, for people with intellectual disabilities, some genetic conditions, such as Down syndrome, result in earlier aging and earlier onset of Alzheimer's disease (Prasher & Janicki, 2002). Adults with disabilities may also experience an increase in conditions related to altered postures, immobility, and long-term use of psychotropic medication. Poor health habits, such as lack of physical activity and poor nutrition, contribute to higher rates of obesity reported for adolescents and adults with disabilities (Rimmer & Wang, 2005). Individuals with disabilities also face obstacles to receiving adequate health care due to access barriers and inadequate professional education regarding disability issues (Marks, Sisirak, & Heller, 2010). Continuity and coordination of health care is particularly challenging during transition periods, such as the transition from adolescence to adulthood.

Although many people associate disability with poor health, one can have a disability and be healthy. Due to differences in physical, social, cognitive, or emotional abilities, people with disabilities may harbor different conceptualizations of health than do people without disabilities (Marks, et al., 2010). Health across the life course will be discussed in more detail in the following chapter.

Policy, Legislation, and Services

As noted earlier in this chapter, people with disabilities often have extensive interactions with formal disability service systems. While all people will have experiences with state agency structures across their lifetimes, these interactions are only considered normative when used rarely and for short time periods. The consistent expectation for "normal" individuals is that they will be able to recover to the point that such structures will no longer be required (McNair & Schindler, in press). This normative expectation often leaves people with disabilities stigmatized for what is considered excessive dependency.

A few pieces of legislation are essential to people with disabilities in the United States throughout the life course. These include the Individuals with Disabilities Education Improvement Act (IDEIA), Section 504 of the

Rehabilitation Act, the Fair Housing Act, the Air Carrier Access Act, and finally the Americans with Disabilities Act (ADA).

Individuals with Disabilities Education Improvement Act

Public Law 94-142, the Education for the Handicapped Act, was enacted in 1975 in response to a growing awareness that many children with disabilities were being denied education (Pierangelo & Giuliani, 2007). Now known as the IDEA or H.R. 1350 (2004), this law is instrumental in securing access to primary and secondary education for children with learning or educational disabilities. The IDEA gives children with disabilities the right to a free and appropriate public education in the least restrictive environment. Qualifying children receive an individualized education program that caters to their educational needs. Part C of the IDEA mandates that all states also implement programs for early intervention. This intervention refers to health, educational, and therapeutic services for children ages 0 to 3 who have a developmental delay or are at risk for developmental delays (National Information Center for Children with Disabilities, 2010).

Section 504

Section 504 of the Rehabilitation Act of 1973 is considered the first civil rights legislation for people with disabilities in the United States. The section states that no qualified individuals with disabilities could be excluded from, denied the benefits of, or subjected to discrimination under any programs receiving federal financial assistance. The language of this section was modeled after the Civil Rights Act of 1964, and its enactment was spurred on by protests by disability rights activists in the 1970s (Fleischer & Zames, 2001).

Fair Housing Act

An amendment to the Fair Housing Act in 1988 provided individuals with disabilities with protection against discrimination in housing (Steven Winter Associates, 2001). In addition, this law gives individuals with disabilities the right to make reasonable modifications to rented housing (for instance, installing grab bars in a bathroom), and the right to accommodations in housing rules, policies, and practices (for instance, allowing a seeing-eye dog in a house where pets are typically banned). Lastly, the law requires that all multifamily housing consisting of four or more units be designed and constructed to be accessible, including accessible entrances, common areas, and bathrooms.

The Americans with Disabilities Act

The Americans with Disabilities Act of 1990 (ADA) is a broad, sweeping law that prohibits discrimination against people with disabilities in employment, public transportation, public accommodations (e.g., hotels), and telecommunications. Under Title 1 of this law, individuals are considered to have a disability if they have a "physical or mental impairment that substantially limits one or more major life activities" or "is regarded as having such an impairment." Over time, courts narrowed the scope of the ADA, denying protection to individuals with such diverse disabilities as intellectual disabilities, HIV, breast cancer, and bipolar disorder (Sweeney, 2009). In response to this narrowing of scope, the ADA Amendments Act of 2008 reestablishes the broad range of impairments that qualify as a disability under the law. The 2008 amendments acknowledge that mitigating measures (for instance, using assistive devices like canes, wheelchairs, or medicine) should not be considered in determining whether a person's impairment qualifies as a disability. This act also states that individuals with episodic impairments such as epilepsy should be covered under the law.

Policies and legislative structures play a significant role in shaping approaches to disability across the life course. Many policymakers now seek to address social barriers to inclusion, rather than focusing efforts only on individualized issues of impairments for people with disabilities (Bickenbach, 2001). However, neoliberal trends in approaches to disability policy, law, and services are having a significant and adverse effect on people with disabilities across all generations. The influence of policy will be further discussed in the following chapter.

Self-Determination and Participation

Promoting self-determination has emerged as a valued goal for people with disabilities over the last two decades and underpins much of the legislation and many of the practices in the field. The construct of self-determination can be described as "volitional actions that enable one to act as the primary causal agent in one's life and to maintain or improve one's quality of life" (Wehmeyer, 2005, p. 117). It is a central construct in the burgeoning independent living and consumer movement across disabilities, in which advocates strive for greater autonomy, choice, and personal control of their lives.

Though self-determination has been primarily viewed as relevant to adolescence and adulthood, the process of becoming self-determined begins in early childhood and continues across the life course. At each stage in life, differences exist in age-related abilities and in societal and cultural expectations for individuals. To promote self-determination within a social-ecological approach, a lifespan perspective is essential, as it takes into account the changing roles of families, friends, and the community/environment in supporting and expanding opportunities for people with disabilities at different ages. This model emphasizes the complex and dynamic interaction that occurs between the person and the environment over time.

Self-determination of people with disabilities has been associated with a variety of positive outcomes for children and adults with disabilities. These benefits include better employment outcomes (e.g., Fornes, Rocco, & Rosenberg, 2008; Madaus, Gerber, & Price, 2008); greater inclusion in general education settings (Agran, Blanchard, Wehmeyer, & Hughes, 2001); improved physical and psycho-social well-being (e.g., W. Johnson & Krueger, 2005); and greater independence (Sowers & Powers, 1995; Wehmeyer & Palmer, 2003; Wehmeyer & Schwartz, 1997). Despite these benefits, youth and adults with disabilities typically are less self-determined than their non-disabled peers, with fewer opportunities to make choices in their daily lives (Chambers et al., 2007).

Self-determination is essential for families and for people with disabilities. It is a core discourse within disability studies, and will be addressed in more detail across each life stage in the following chapter.

Conclusion

There are a number of interrelated factors that impact people with disabilities as they transition through life stages. Many people with disabilities continue to experience exclusion and discrimination from birth and childhood, through adulthood, to aging and dying. As a result, increasing effectiveness of support and policies across the life course becomes vital if people with disabilities and their families are to achieve a good quality of life and participate in the wider community.

This chapter has introduced key concepts, life stages, and historical developments in approaches to disability. While little specific work exists on life course and disability, a number of theoretical approaches have been used to frame our understanding of disability issues. These include gerontology, development psychology, sociology, and disability studies.

A life course perspective helps us understand the developmental trajectories for people with disabilities and their families. This approach assumes that what happens earlier in life (including prenatally) affects subsequent periods in one's life. In addition, it recognizes the great variability in people, and the fact that development does not necessarily proceed in neat stages. Impairments interact with social determinants and environmental aspects across the lifespan to result in differing outcomes for people. Finally, this approach acknowledges the important role that culture, socioeconomic status, and environmental factors (including services and supports) have on the well-being of people with disabilities and their families. The disability studies approach adds to this life course perspective by bringing in the concepts of disability identity and societal attitudes toward disability as important factors throughout the lives of people with disabilities.

Core themes that stem from a critical disability studies approach, such as the role of the family, the influence of policy and legislation, and the ability to enact self-determination, are all significant in furthering our understanding of disability across the life course.

The following chapter will address each of these themes across each generational stage as it relates to disability.

References

Achenbaum, W. A. (2005). Ageing and changing: International historical perspectives on ageing. In M. L. Johnson, V. L. Bengtson, P. G. Coleman, & T. B. L. Kirkwood (Eds.), *The Cambridge handbook of age and ageing* (pp. 21–29). Cambridge, UK: Cambridge University Press.

Administration on Aging. (2010). Aging and disability resource centers. Retrieved from http://www.aoa.gov/AoAroot/AoA_Programs/HCLTC/ADRC/index.aspx

Adolph, K. E., Karasik, L. B., & Tamis-LeMonda, C. S. (2009). Motor skill. In M. Bornstein (Ed.), *Handbook of cross-cultural developmental science: Vol. 1. Domains of development across cultures* (pp. 61–87). Mahwah, NJ: Lawrence Erlbaum.

Agran, M., Blanchard, C., Wehmeyer, M. L., & Hughes, C. (2001). Teaching students to self-regulate their behavior: The differential effects of student vs. teacher-delivered reinforcement. *Research in Developmental Disabilities, 22*(4), 319–332.

Albrecht, G. L. (2010). The sociology of disability: Historical foundations and future directions. In C. Bird, P. Conrad, A. Fremont, & S. Timmerman (Eds.), *Handbook of sociology* (pp. 192–209). Nashville, TN: Vanderbilt University Press.

Albrecht, G. L., Seelman, K. D., & Bury, M. (2003). Introduction: The formation of disability studies. In G. L. Albrecht, K. D. Seelman, & M. Bury (Eds.), *Handbook of disability studies* (pp. 1–10). Thousand Oaks, CA: Sage.

Almeida, D. M., & Wong, J. D. (2009). Life transitions and daily stress processes. In G. H. Elder & J. Z. Giele (Eds.), *The craft of life course research* (pp. 11–162). New York: Guilford Press.

Americans with Disabilities Act of 1990. (1991). P.L. 101-336, § 1, 104 Stat. 328.

Arnett, J. J. (2000). Emerging adulthood: A theory of development from late teens through early twenties. *American Psychologist, 55*(5), 469–480.

Arnett, J. J., & Tanner, J. L. (Eds.). (2006). *Emerging adults in America: Coming of age in the 21st century.* Washington, DC: American Psychological Association.

Baltes, P. B., Freund, A. M., & Li, S. (2005). The psychological science of human aging. In M. L. Johnson, V. L. Bengtson, P. G. Coleman, & T. B. L. Kirkwood (Eds.), *The Cambridge handbook of age and ageing* (pp. 47–71). Cambridge, UK: Cambridge University Press.

Barnes, C., Mercer, G., & Shakespeare, T. (1999). *Exploring disability: A sociological introduction.* Cambridge, UK: Polity Press.

Baynton, D. (2001). Disability and the justification of inequality in American history. In P. Longmore & L. Umansky (Eds.), *The new disability history: American perspectives* (pp. 33–57). New York: New York University Press.

Berzoff, J., & Flanagan, L. M., & Hertz, P. (2008). *Inside out and outside in: Psychodynamic clinical theory and psychopathology in contemporary multicultural contexts* (2nd ed.). New York: Jason Aronson.

Bianchi, S. M., & Casper, L. M. (2005). Explanations of family change. In V. L. Bengtson, A. C. Acock, K. R. Allen, P. Dilworth-Anderson, & D. M. Klein (Eds.), *Sourcebook of family theory and research* (pp. 93–117). Thousand Oaks, CA: Sage.

Bickenbach, J. (2001). Disability human rights, law, and policy. In G. L. Albrecht, K. D. Seelman, & M. Bury (Eds.), *Handbook of disability studies* (pp. 565–584). Thousand Oaks, CA: Sage.

Bigby, C. (2008). Known well by no-one: Trends in the informal social networks of middle-aged and older people with intellectual disability five years after moving to the community. *Journal of Intellectual & Developmental Disability, 33*(2), 148–158.

Braddock, D. L., & Parish, S. L. (2003). An institutional history of disability. In G. L. Albrecht, K. D. Seelman, & M. Bury (Eds.), *Handbook of disability studies* (pp. 11–68). Thousand Oaks, CA: Sage.

Breen, J. (2009). Early childhood service delivery for families living with childhood disability: Disabling families through problematic implicit ideology. *Australasian Journal of Early Childhood, 34*(4), 14–21.

Bryman, A., Bytheway, B., Allatt, P., & Keil, T. (Eds.). (1987). *Rethinking the life cycle.* Basingstoke, UK: Macmillan.

Cahill, B. M., & Glidden, L. M. (1996). Influence of child diagnosis on family and parental functioning: Down syndrome versus other disabilities. *American Journal of Mental Retardation, 101*, 149–160.

Carey, A. C. (2009). The feebleminded versus the nation: 1900s to 1930s. In A. C. Carey, *On the margins of citizenship: Intellectual disability and civil rights in twentieth century America* (pp. 52–82). Philadelphia: Temple University Press.

Carretero, S., Garcés, J., Ródenas, F., & Sanjosé, V. (2009). The informal caregiver's burden of dependent people: Theory and empirical review. *Archives of Gerontology and Geriatrics, 49*(1), 74–79.

Chambers, C. R., Wehmeyer, M. L., Saito, Y., Lida, K. M., Lee, Y., & Singh, V. (2007). Self-determination: What do we know? Where do we go? *Exceptionality, 15*, 3–15.

Charlton, J. (1998). *Nothing about us without us: Disability oppression and empowerment.* Berkeley: University of California Press.

Davis, L. J. (2004). The end of identity politics and the beginning of dismodernism: On disability as an unstable category. In L. J. Davis (Ed.), *The disability studies reader* (pp. 231–242). New York: Routledge.

Dunst, G. J. (2002). Family-centered practices: Birth through high school. *The Journal of Special Education, 36*(3), 139–147.

Elder, G. H. (1985). Perspectives on the life course. In G. H. Elder (Ed.), *Life-course dynamics: Trajectories and transitions* (pp. 23–49). Ithaca, NY: Cornell University Press.

Elder, G. H. (2003). The life course in time and place. In W. R. Heinz & V. W. Marshall (Eds.), *Social dynamics of the life course* (pp. 57–71). New York: Walter de Gruyter.

Elder, G. H., & Giele, J. Z. (2009). *The craft of life course research.* New York: Guilford Press.

Erikson, E. H. (1963). *Childhood and society* (2nd ed.) New York: Norton.

Erkulwater, J. L. (2006). *Disability rights and the American social safety net.* New York: Cornell University Press.

Eyerman, R., & Turner, B. S. (1998). Outline of a theory of generations. *European Journal of Social Theory, 1*(1), 91–106.

Fair Housing Act. (1968). 42 U.S.C. § 3601 *et seq.*

Ferguson, P. M., Gartner, A., & Lipsky, D. K. (2000). The experience of disability in families: A synthesis of research and parent narratives. In E. Parens & A. Asch (Eds.), *Prenatal testing and disability rights.* Washington, DC: Georgetown University Press.

Fleischer, D. Z., & Zames, F. (2001). *The disability rights movement: From charity to confrontation.* Philadelphia: Temple University Press.

Foley, G. M. (2006). The loss-grief cycle: Coming to terms with the birth of a child with a disability. In G. M. Foley & J. Hochman (Eds.), *Mental health in early intervention: Achieving unity in principles and practice* (pp. 227–243). Baltimore: Paul H. Brookes.

Fornes, S., Rocco, T. S., & Rosenberg H. (2008). Improving outcomes for workers with mental retardation. *Human Resource Development Quarterly, 19*(4), 373–395.

Forrester-Jones, R., Carpenter, J., Coolen-Schrijner, P., Cambridge, P., Tate, A., & Beecham, J. (2006). The social networks of people with intellectual disability living in the community 12 years after resettlement from long-stay hospitals. *Journal of Applied Research in Intellectual Disabilities, 19*, 285–295.

George, A., Vickers, M. H., Wilkes, L., & Barton, B. (2007). Chronic grief: Experiences of working parents of children with chronic illness. *Contemporary Nurse, 23*(2), 228–242.

Gill, C. J. (1997). Four types of integration in disability identity development. *Journal of Vocational Rehabilitation, 9*, 39–46.

Gill, C. J. (2000). Health professionals, disability, and assisted suicide: An examination of relevant empirical evidence and reply to Batavia. *Psychology, Public Policy, and Law, 6*(2), 526–545.

Gill, C. J. (2010). No, we don't think our doctors are out to get us: Responding to the straw man distortions of disability rights arguments against assisted suicide. *Disability and Health Journal, 3*(1), 31–38.

Goble, C. (2004). Dependence, independence, and normality. In J. Swain, S. French, C. Barnes, & C. Thomas (Eds.), *Disabling barriers–enabling environments* (pp. 41–46). London: Sage.

Goodwin, J., & O'Connor, H. (2009). Youth and generation: In the midst of an adult world. In A. Furlong (Ed.), *Handbook of youth and young adulthood: New perspectives and agendas* (pp. 22–30). New York: Routledge.

Gordon, G. (1966). *Role theory and illness: A sociological perspective.* New Haven, CT: College and University Press.

Gordon, J. (2009). An evidence-based approach for supporting parents experiencing chronic sorrow: What is chronic sorrow? *Pediatric Nursing, 35*(2), 115–119.

Graungaard, A. H., & Skov, L. (2007). Why do we need a diagnosis? A qualitative study of parents' experiences, coping and needs, when the newborn child is severely disabled. *Child: Care, Health & Development, 33*(3), 296–307.

Gray, D. B., & Hendershot, G. E. (2000). The ICIDH-2: Developments for a new era of outcomes research. *Archives of Physical Medicine and Rehabilitation, 81*(Suppl. 2), S10–S14.

Gutman, S. A., & Napier-Klemic, J. (1996). The experience of head injury on the impairment of gender identity and gender role. *American Journal of Occupational Therapy, 50*(7), 535–544.

Ha, J., Hong, J., Seltzer, M. M., & Greenberg, J. S. (2008). Age and gender differences in the well-being of midlife and aging parents with children with mental health problems or developmental disorders: Report of a national study. *Journal of Health and Social Behavior, 49*, 301–316.

Halfon, N. (2009, February). Life course health development: A new approach for addressing upstream determinants of health and spending. *Expert Voices.* Washington, DC: NIHCM Foundation.

Hallberg, L. R. M., & Carlsson, S. G. (1993). A qualitative study of situations turning a hearing disability into a handicap. *Disability, Handicap & Society, 8*(1), 71–86.

Hanson, K., Neuman, T., & Voris, M. (2003). *Understanding the health-care needs and experiences of people with disabilities: Findings from a 2003 Survey.* Washington, DC: Kaiser Family Foundation.

Harris, M., & Butterworth, G. (2002). *Developmental psychology: A student's handbook.* New York: Taylor and Francis.

Harrison, T. C., Umberson, D., Lin, L., & Cheng, H. (2010). Timing of impairment and health-promoting lifestyles in women with disabilities. *Qualitative Health Research, 20,* 816–829.

Harry, B. (2008). Collaboration with culturally and linguistically diverse families: Ideal versus reality. *Exceptional Children, 74,* 372–388.

Hayes, J., & Hannold, E. M. (2007). The road to empowerment: A historical perspective on the medicalization of disability. *Journal of Health and Human Services Administration, 30*(3), 352–377.

Heinz, W. R. (2009). Youth transitions in an age of uncertainty. In A. Furlong (Ed.), *Handbook of youth and young adulthood: New perspectives and agendas* (pp. 3–13). New York: Routledge.

Heller, T. (2008). Report of the state of the science in aging with developmental disabilities: Charting lifespan trajectories and supportive environments for health community living symposium. *Disability and Health Journal, 1*(3), 127–130.

Heller, T., Miller, A., & Factor, A. (1997). Adult children with mental retardation as supports to their parents: Effects on parental caregiving appraisal. *Mental Retardation, 35,* 338–346.

Hopkins, B., & Westra, T. (1989). Maternal expectations of their infants' development: Some cultural differences. *Developmental Neuroscience and Child Neurology, 31,* 384–390.

Hutchison, E. D. (2008). *Dimensions of human behavior: The changing life course* (3rd ed.). Thousand Oaks, CA: Sage.

Individuals with Disabilities Education Improvement Act of 2004. (2004). P.L. 108-446, § 20, 1400 Stat. 2647.

Johnson, T. F. (1995). Aging well in contemporary society: Introduction. *American Behavioral Scientist, 9*(2), 120–130.

Johnson, W., & Krueger, R. F. (2005). Higher perceived life control decreases genetic variance in physical health: Evidence from a national twin study. *Journal of Personality and Social Psychology, 88*(1), 165–173.

Kail, R. V., & Cavanaugh, J. C. (2007). *Human development: A lifespan view* (4th ed.). Belmont, CA: Thomson Wadsworth.

Kane, R. L., & Kane, R. A. (2005). Ageism in healthcare and long-term care. *Generations, 29*(3), 49–54.

Kelley-Moore, J. A., Schumacher, J. G., Kahana, B., & Kahana, E. (2006). When do older adults become "disabled"? Social and health antecedents of perceived disability in a panel study of the oldest old. *Journal of Health and Social Behavior, 47,* 126–141.

Kemp, B. J., & Mosqueda, L. (2004). Introduction. In B. J. Kemp & L. Mosqueda (Eds.), *Aging with a disability: What the clinician needs to know.* Baltimore: Johns Hopkins University Press.

Kinavey, C. (2006). Explanatory models of self-understanding in adolescents born with spina bifida. *Qualitative Health Research, 16*(8), 1091–1107.

Kirshbaum, M. (2000). A disability culture perspective on early intervention with parents with physical or cognitive disabilities and their infants. *Infants and Young Children, 13*(2), 9–20.

Knox, M., & Bigby, C. (2007). Moving towards midlife care as negotiated family business: Accounts of people with intellectual disabilities and their families "just getting along with their lives together." *International Journal of Disability, Development and Education, 54*(3), 287–304.

Krain, M. A. (1995). Policy implications for a society aging well: Employment, retirement, education, and leisure policies for the 21st century. *American Behavioral Scientist, 39*(2),131–151.

Kuh, D., & Ben-Shlomo, Y. (Eds.). (2004). *A life course approach to chronic disease epidemiology* (2nd ed.). Oxford, UK: Oxford University Press.

Langlois, J. A., Maggi, S., Harris, T., Simonsick, E. M., Ferrucci, L., Pavan, M., et al. (1996). Self-report of difficulty in performing functional activities identifies a broad range of disability in old age. *Journal of the American Geriatrics Society, 44*(12), 1421–1428.

Lee, D., & Tracey, T. J. G. (2005). Incorporating idiographic approaches into multicultural counseling research and practice. *Journal of Multicultural Counseling and Development, 33*(2), 66–80.

Lerner, R. M. (2002). *Concepts and theories of human development.* Mahwah, NJ: Lawrence Erlbaum Associates.

Levinson, D. J. (1978). *The seasons of man's life.* New York: Alfred A. Knopf.

Levinson, D. J., & Levinson, J. D. (1996). *The seasons of a woman's life.* New York: Alfred A. Knopf.

Levy, R., Ghisletta, P., Le Goff, J., Spini, D., & Widmer, E. (Eds.). (2005). *Towards an interdisciplinary perspective on the life course: Vol. 10. Advances in life course research.* Amsterdam: Elsevier.

Lightfoot, E. (2007). Disability. In J. A. Blackburn & C. D. Dulmus (Eds.), *Handbook of gerontology: Evidence-based approaches to theory, practice, and policy* (pp. 201–229). Hoboken, NJ: John Wiley & Sons.

Lippold, T., & Burns, J. (2009). Social support and intellectual disabilities: A comparison between social networks of adults with intellectual disability and those with physical disability. *Journal of Intellectual Disability Research, 53*(5), 463–474.

Lloyd, C. B. (2005). *Growing up global: The changing transitions to adulthood in developing countries.* Washington, DC: National Academies Press.

Lustig, D. C., Strauser, D. R., & Donnell, C. (2003). Quality employment outcomes: Benefits for individuals with disabilities. *Rehabilitation Counseling Bulletin, 47*(1), 5–14.

Madaus, J. W., Gerber, P. J., & Price, L. A. (2008). Adults with learning disabilities in the workforce: Lessons for secondary transition programs. *Learning Disabilities Research & Practice, 23*(3), 148–153.

Mannheim, K. (1952). The problem of generations. In K. Mannheim (Ed.), *Essays on the sociology of knowledge* (pp. 276–320). London: Routledge & Kegan Paul.

Marini, I. (2001). Cross cultural counseling issues of males who sustain a disability. *Journal of Applied Rehabilitation Counseling, 32*(1), 36–44.

Marks, B., Sisirak, J., & Heller, T. (2010). *Health matters for people with developmental disabilities: Creating a sustainable health promotion program.* Baltimore: Paul H. Brookes.

Marshak, L. E., Seligman, M., & Prezant, F. (1999). *Disability and the family life cycle: Recognizing and treating developmental challenges.* New York: Basic Books.

Mayer, K. U. (2009). New directions in life course research. *Annual Review of Sociology, 35*, 413–433.

McCarthy, H. (2003). The disability rights movement: Experiences and perspectives of selected leaders in the disability community. *Rehabilitation Counseling Bulletin, 46*(4), 209–223.

McConnell, D., & Llewellyn, G. (2002). Stereotypes, parents with intellectual disability, and child protection. *Journal of Social Welfare and Family Law, 24*(3), 297–317.

McEnhill, L. (2004). Disability. In D. Oliviere & B. Monroe (Eds.), *Death, dying and social differences* (pp. 97–118). Oxford, UK: Oxford University Press.

McMahon, B. T., Rumrill, P. T., Jr., Roessler, R., Hurley, J. E., West, S. L., Chan, F., et al. (2008). Hiring discrimination against people with disabilities under the ADA: Characteristics of employers. *Journal of Occupational Rehabilitation, 18*(2), 112–122.

McNair, J., & Schindler, A. (in press). A secular case for religious inclusion of individuals with intellectual and developmental disabilities. In D. Schumm & M. Stoltzfus (Eds.), *World religions and disability.* New York: Palgrave MacMillan.

Meile, R. L. (1986). Pathways to patienthood: Sick role and labeling perspectives. *Social Science Medicine, 22*(1), 35–40.

Minkler, M., & Fadem, P. (2002). Successful aging: A disability perspective. *Journal of Disability Policy Studies, 12*(4), 229–235.

Mitchell, D. T., & Snyder, S. L. (2006). Introduction. In D. T. Mitchell & S. L. Snyder (Eds.), *Cultural locations of disability.* Chicago: University of Chicago Press.

Muuss, R. E. (1996). *Theories of adolescence* (6th ed.). New York: McGraw-Hill.

National Information Center for Children with Disabilities. (2010). *Overview of early intervention.* Retrieved from http://www.nichcy.org/babies/overview/Pages/default.aspx

Oliver, M. (1990). *The politics of disablement.* Basingstoke, UK: Macmillan.

Oliver, M. (1996). *Understanding disability: From theory to practice.* Basingstoke, UK: Macmillan.

Olsen, R., & Clarke, H. (2003). *Parenting and disability: Disabled parents' experiences of raising children.* Bristol, UK: Policy Press.

Olshansky, S. (1962). Chronic sorrow: A response to having a mentally defective child. *Social Casework, 43*(4), 190–193.

Ott, K. (2005). Disability and the practice of public history: An introduction. *The Public Historian, 27*(2), 11–24.

Parsons, T. (1951). *The social system.* London: Routledge & Kegan Paul.

Patient Education Institute. (2009). *Newborn screening.* Retrieved from http://www.nlm.nih.gov/medlineplus/tutorials/newbornscreening/htm/_no_50_no_0.htm

Pierangelo, R., & Giuliani, G. (2007). *Special education eligibility.* Thousand Oaks, CA: Corwin.

Pierret, C. R. (2006). The "sandwich generation": Women caring for parents and children. *Monthly Labor Review, 129*(9), 3–10.

Prasher, V. P., & Janicki, M. P. (Eds.). (2002). *Physical health of adults with intellectual disabilities.* Oxford, UK: Blackwell.

Priestley, M. (2003). *Disability: A life course approach.* Cambridge, UK: Polity Press.

Priestley, M. (2004). Generating debates: Why we need a life course approach to disability. In J. Swain, S. French, C. Barnes, & C. Thomas (Eds.), *Disabling barriers–enabling environments* (pp. 94–98). London: Sage.

Quinn, P. (1998). *Understanding disability: A lifespan approach.* Thousand Oaks, CA: Sage.

Raji, O., & Hollins, S. (2003). How far are people with learning disabilities involved in funeral rites? *British Journal of Learning Disabilities, 31,* 42–45.

Read, S., & Elliott, D. (2003). Death and learning disability: A vulnerability perspective. *Journal of Adult Protection, 5*(1), 5–14.

Read, S., & Elliott, D. (2007). Exploring a continuum of support for bereaved people with intellectual disabilities. *Journal of Intellectual Disabilities, 11*(2), 167–181.

Rehabilitation Act of 1973. P.L. 93-112, § 87, Stat. 394.

Rimmer, J. H., & Wang, E. (2005). Obesity prevalence among a group of Chicago residents with disabilities. *Archives of Physical Medicine and Rehabilitation, 86*(7), 1461–1464.

Rolland, J. S. (1994). *Families, illness, and disability.* New York: Basic Books.

Roos, S. (2002). *Chronic sorrow: A living loss.* New York: Brunner-Routledge.

Rothman, J. C. (2003). *Social work practice across disability.* Boston: Allyn & Bacon.

Rowe, J., & Kahn, R. (1998). *Successful aging.* New York: Random House.

Rowlinson, R. T., & Fellner, R. D. (1988). Major life events, hassles, and adaptation in adolescence: Confounding in the conceptualization and measurement of life stress and adjustment revisited. *Journal of Personality and Social Psychology, 55*(3), 432–444.

Sackman, R., & Wingens, M. (2003). From transitions to trajectories: Sequence types. In W. R. Heinz & V. W. Marshall (Eds.), *Social dynamics of the life course: Transitions, institutions, and interrelations* (pp. 93–115). New York: Walter de Gruyter.

Sayce, L. (2000). The illusion of citizenship. In L. Sayce (Ed.), *From psychiatric patient to citizen: Overcoming discrimination and social exclusion* (pp. 56–83). New York: St. Martin's Press.

Scheid, T. L. (2005). Stigma as a barrier to employment: Mental disability and the Americans with Disabilities Act. *International Journal of Law and Psychiatry, 28,* 670–690.

Settersen, R. A. (2003). Propositions and controversies in life-course scholarship. In R. A. Settersen (Ed.), *Invitation to the life course: Toward new understandings of later life* (pp. 15–45). Amityville, NY: Baywood.

Settersen, R. A. (2007). 10 reasons why shake-ups in the life course should change approaches to old-age policies. *Public Policy and Aging Report, 17*(3), 21–27.

Shaffer, D. R. (2009). *Social and personality development* (6th ed.). Belmont, CA: Wadsworth.

Shaffer, D. R., & Kipp, K. (2010). *Developmental psychology: Childhood and adolescence* (8th ed.). Belmont, CA: Wadsworth.

Sheehan, M. N. (2003). Disabilities and aging. *Theoretical Medicine, 24,* 525–533.

Siebers, T. (2008). Disability studies and the future of identity politics. In T. Siebers, *Disability theory* (pp. 70–95). Ann Arbor: University of Michigan Press.

Sigelman, C. K., & Rider, E. A. (2009). *Life-span human development.* Belmont, CA: Wadsworth.

Simeonsson, R. J. (2009). ICF-CY: A universal tool for documentation of disability. *Journal of Policy and Practice in Intellectual Disabilities, 6*(2), 70–72.

Slee, P. T. (2002). *Child, adolescent, and family development* (2nd ed.). Cambridge, UK: Cambridge University Press.

Sowers, J., & Powers, L. (1995). Enhancing the participation and independence of students with severe physical and multiple disabilities in performing community activities. *Mental Retardation, 33,* 209–220.

Steven Winter Associates. (2001). *A basic guide to fair housing accessibility: Everything architects and builders need to know about the fair housing accessibility guidelines.* New York: John Wiley & Sons.

Stiker, H. J. (1999). *A history of disability.* Ann Arbor: University of Michigan Press.

Sweeney, N. J. (2009). *Construction law update 2009.* New York: Aspen.

Tarlov, A. R. (1996). Social determinants of health: The sociological translation. In D. Blane, E. Bruner, & R. Wilkinson (Eds.), *Health and social organization: Towards a health policy for the twenty-first century* (pp. 71–93). New York: Routledge.

Thomas, C. (2004). Disability and impairment. In J. Swain, S. French, C. Barnes, & C. Thomas (Eds.), *Disabling barriers—enabling environments* (pp. 21–27). London: Sage.

Todd, S. (2004). Death counts: The challenge of death and dying in learning disability services. *Learning Disability in Practice, 7*(10), 12–15.

Umberson, D., Crosnoe, R., & Reczek, C. (2010). Social relationships and health behavior across the life course. *Annual Review of Sociology, 36,* 139–157.

U.S. Bureau of Labor Statistics. (2011, May). Employment situation—April 2011. Retrieved May 20, 2011, from http://www.bls.gov/news.release/empsit.nr0 .htm

U.S. Department of Health and Human Services. (2000). Disability and secondary conditions. In *Healthy people 2010: Understanding and improving health* (Sec. 6, pp. 1–28). Washington, DC: U.S. Government Printing Office. Retrieved from http://healthypeople.gov/2010/document/HTML/Volume1/06Disability.htm

Verdonschot, M. M. L., De Witte, L. P., Reichrath, E., Buntinx, W. H. E., & Curfs, L. M. G. (2009). Community participation of people with an intellectual disability: A review of empirical findings. *Journal of Intellectual Disability Research, 53*(4), 303–319.

Wehmeyer, M. L. (2005). Self-determination and individuals with severe disabilities: Reexamining meanings and misinterpretations. *Research and Practice in Severe Disabilities, 30,* 113–120.

Wehmeyer, M. L., & Palmer, S. B. (2003). Adult outcomes for students with cognitive disabilities three years after high school: The impact of self-determination. *Education and Training in Developmental Disabilities, 38,* 131–144.

Wehmeyer, M. L., & Schwartz, M. (1997). Self-determination and positive adult outcomes: A follow-up study of youth with mental retardation or learning disabilities. *Exceptional Children, 63,* 245–255.

Williams, V., & Robinson, C. (2001). More than one wavelength: Identifying, understanding and resolving conflicts of interest between people with intellectual disabilities and their family carers. *Journal of Applied Research in Intellectual Disabilities, 14,* 30–46.

Williamson, J. D., & Fried, L. P. (1996). Characterization of older adults who attribute functional decrements to "old age." *Journal of the American Geriatrics Society, 44*(12), 1429–1434.

World Health Organization. (2001). *International classification of functioning, disability and health.* Geneva: Author.

Wright, J. A. (2008). Prenatal and postnatal diagnosis of infant disability: Breaking the news to mothers. *Journal of Perinatal Education, 17*(3), 27–32.

Yorgason, J. B., Booth, A., & Johnson, D. (2008). Health, disability, and marital quality: Is the association different for younger versus older cohorts? *Research on Aging, 30,* 623–648.

Yuan, S. (2003). Seeing with new eyes: Metaphors of family experience. *Mental Retardation, 1*(3), 207–211.

Two

Current Issues, Controversies, and Solutions

*Sarah Parker Harris, Tamar Heller,
Abigail Schindler, and Lieke van Heumen*

A life course approach to disability involves a number of interrelated issues and debates across each generational stage. Key debates that stem from a critical disability studies perspective focus on the role of the family and health, the influence of policy and legislation, and the ability to enact self-determination, all of which are critical to furthering our understanding of a disability across the life course.

One of the most ubiquitous and controversial debates in a life course approach to disability centers on questions about the "worth" or "value" of a life. Such questions are underpinned by medicine, culture, religion, and/or moral beliefs. These varying approaches all have a significant role in valuing and determining what should guide decisions about the worth of a life. Compounding this issue is an ongoing challenge that people with disabilities face in transitioning though generational stages, especially when the markers of success focus on autonomy and independence.

Factors such as the type of disability, the availability of informal and formal supports, and economic resources influence concepts around "normal" transitions through life stages. Additionally, as medical advances change the level of information and knowledge about disability, and as the population of persons with a disability increases at birth and in aging, the issues become more complex. At times, there may be competing perspectives on what is "best" at any given life stage among families; individuals; medical, health care, and other service professionals; disability rights activists and scholars; and government.

This chapter is divided into six life stages: Birthrights and Early Childhood; Disability and Childhood; Disability and Youth; Disability and Adulthood; Disability and Aging; and Death and Dying. Within each of these generational life stages, the core themes (as introduced in the previous chapter) are discussed in relation to disability. These themes include: family; health; policy, legislation, and services; and self-determination and participation. Further understanding of the major debates, controversies, and solutions within each of the core domains contributes to achieving a good of quality life of people with disabilities.

Birthrights and Early Childhood

The life stages during which most genetic screening for disability and disease occurs are the first month after birth and during an individual's reproductive period (preconception/prenatal screening) (Grosse, McBride, Evans, & Khoury, 2009). Because of this early screening, disability is a factor that determines the worth of a life even before it begins. Determinations of the worth of a life have led to a number of controversial debates, particularly in relation to health and policy. These debates are contextualized by the influence of inequality and poverty, not only in developed countries but in emerging economies, where daily life is a struggle and decisions on the value or worth of a life are shaped by our contexts and resources (de Blij, 2009). The role of the family is a critical area in which some of these debates have played out.

Family

Prenatal Care

The current state of health care in Western countries sets up an expectation for a pregnant woman to self-regulate her pregnancy in order to provide the best outcomes for her child. This includes an expectation that the pregnant woman will take prenatal vitamins, abstain from alcohol and drugs, control weight gain, and other factors. These practices reveal a complex relationship between a woman's self-determined choice and medical practitioners' expectations, even extending to social expectations for compliance with medical authority (Alderson, 2002). Part of the expectation for these prenatal practices is that, by following them, the woman will significantly reduce her risk of having a child with a disability or chronic health problem. This is a contentious issue within the disability field, as the presence of disability becomes equated with a "problem" that needs to be fixed or prevented through medical intervention.

Pregnant women are also expected to prevent disability by being aware of the risk their own health conditions may place on having a child with a disability. H. Leonard et al. (2006), for instance, determined that expectant mothers with renal or urinary conditions, asthma, and diabetes had a slightly increased risk for having a child with mild to moderate intellectual disability. They concluded that "this information is still important for women affected by these particular conditions and those involved in their clinical management. . . . They provide opportunities for prevention in an area for which we currently have few strategies" (pp. 452–453). The type of prevention expected here is ambiguous, but suggests a moral obligation for women carrying risk factors to take measures against conceiving in order to prevent more disability from entering the world (Alderson, 2002). The health care information a pregnant woman receives regarding her child's risk of having a disability varies based on the discipline of the health care practitioner, with obstetricians and pediatric specialists giving conflicting information about the best interests of the fetus and the expectant mother (Bijma et al., 2004).

Some feminist counterarguments to the prevalent expectation that a woman has a moral obligation to her fetus contend that a pregnant woman's right to self-determination and bodily autonomy outweighs the interests of the unborn child. Ruhl (1999, p. 95) critiques these contemporary methods of regulating pregnancy, arguing that they rely on liberal governance, setting up a dynamic of the "responsible" pregnant woman versus the "irresponsible" pregnant woman who is seen to endanger the health and well-being of her fetus. She refers to the medical imperatives of prenatal care as risk discourses, which place an individual moral responsibility on pregnant women, although the realities of pregnancy are that it is both individual and collective in nature. Such debates have no easy solution, as the issues are complicated by competing interests from a variety of different groups involved in prenatal care, including individuals, families, health care practitioners, and disability rights groups.

Receiving a Diagnosis

A key debate in disability across the life course centers on diagnosis of disability, and the level and quality of information that families receive during this process. Parental satisfaction with the disclosure or diagnosis of disability has been investigated across disability categories, including autism, cerebral palsy, blindness, and deafness (Baird, McConachie, & Scrutton, 2000; Cole-Hamilton & McBride, 1996; Goin-Kochel, Mackintosh, & Myers, 2006; Lavi & Rosenburg, 2005; Osborne & Reed, 2008; Tattersall & Young, 2006; Wright, 2008). The reaction of parents varies based not only on the type of disability but on the severity of the disability, the age at which a diagnosis is made, and especially the professional communication through which the diagnosis is made.

In the case of autism, for instance, there is no simple biological test, so the diagnosis is made through behavioral assessments and historical reports, a process that many parents feel is slow and chaotic (Goin-Kochel, Mackintosh, & Myers, 2006; Mansell & Morris, 2004). Because parents often report high levels of dissatisfaction with the disclosure of their child's disability, some studies have attempted to set out best practice guidelines for medical professionals who make a diagnosis of infant or early childhood disability. Wright (2008), for example, contends that a private setting, a sensitive and compassionate manner, and up-to-date information are the most crucial factors in conveying a diagnosis of disability.

Another solution that has been offered for providing more effective and disability-positive support to families comes from a popular anecdote for sharing an early diagnosis of disability, called "Welcome to Holland" by Emily Pearl Kingsley. In this anecdote, Kingsley likens having a child with a disability to preparing for a trip to Italy, only to find out you will be arriving in Holland instead. She explains that while a trip to Holland might not be what you planned, "if you spend your life mourning the fact that you didn't get to Italy, you may never be free to enjoy the very special, the very lovely things . . . about Holland" (Kingsley, 1987, p. 71).

Health

Traditionally, the role of public health in disability has been to reduce its incidence, which has influenced ideas that equate disability with a failure of the public health system. This focus on prevention (for instance, encouraging expectant mothers to consume folic acid during pregnancy to prevent neural tube defects) had been to the exclusion of other crucial public health activities for people with disabilities that go outside the realm of prevention (Lollar & Crews, 2003). One key issue related to approaches to disability during early life stages is the "worth" of babies with health conditions, especially as it relates to low birth weight.

Low Birth Weight

Individuals within the medical community have debated the use of resources for low birth weight and extremely preterm infants, in part because the survival rate of these infants may reach as high as 90% (Chan et al., 2001; Tyson et al., 1996). In addition, the families of these infants often require substantial supports in the months and years following birth, regardless of the child's impairment level, in the form of re-hospitalizations, early intervention, and special outpatient services (Hintz et al., 2008). This high resource utilization is also accompanied by the high likelihood that the child will have moderate to severe disability in later life, including chronic conditions, functional limitations, and poor cognition (Hack et al., 2005). These factors have led to a number of controversial issues and solutions in the health care field.

Neonatal bioethics, for example, sets out specific guidelines for which extremely preterm babies should not receive resuscitation, which may set different moral standards than those laid down for older individuals (Janvier et al., 2008). In fact, while the American Academy of Pediatrics recommends that the "ethical principles regarding resuscitation of newborns should be no different from those followed in resuscitating an older child or adult," in practice the resuscitation of an extremely preterm infant requires full parental informed consent, while the resuscitation of an older patient would be carried out without such consent (Janvier et al., 2008, p. 403).

This differential treatment may be due in part to a feeling that extremely preterm infants have a different moral status than older children and adults. Another reason for the differential medical treatment of preterm infants may be the perception that the child will face lifelong disabling conditions. This approach is part of a wider contentious issue regarding the "worth" of people with disabilities. J. A. Blackman (1991) notes that using resources to sustain the lives of preterm infants has sometimes been seen as unjustified, especially if the result is an increase in the number of children with a disability, though he claims that these outcomes are not well documented. Such debates are played out in the broader policy context.

Policy, Legislation, and Services

Policy and legislation provides structure to, or mediates debates among, approaches to disability, which are contextualized within the influence of the broader economy. Households in which there is at least one person with a disability are significantly more likely to fall below the poverty line than households without a person with a disability, 28% as compared with 8.3% (Fujiura, Yamaki, & Czechowicz, 1998). If these estimates take into account the increased costs of living for individuals with disabilities, the economic disparities become even more striking. She and Livermore (2007) contend that material hardship is likely to be more prevalent among people with disabilities. Furthermore, the official poverty measure is likely to understate the magnitude of hardship among people with disabilities.

Disability and poverty often co-occur, with those in poverty more likely to have such wide-ranging health conditions as cancer, children's asthma, coronary heart disease, adolescent depression, obesity, and pediatric trauma hospitalizations (Lustig & Strauser, 2007). A number of specific policies directed to families with children with disabilities are intended to ameliorate, in part, some of the additional costs of disability and to provide effective supports.

Title V of the Social Security Act

Title V of the Social Security Act of 1934 allows for federal grants to individual states that support the provision of a wide range of maternal and child health services. These grant funds continue to be provided to states through the Maternal and Child Health Bureau, and typically focus on underserved areas and low-income families (Barusch, 2009). While not all Title V programs specifically target children with disabilities, many are vitally important to this population and their families, including programs providing rehabilitative services, case management, care coordination, and other critical services for children with special health care needs (Health Resources and Services Administration, 2000).

Katie Beckett Waivers

Ordinarily, Medicaid services and health care are provided only to those who meet strict income requirements. However, the Tax Equity and Fiscal Responsibility Act of 1982 included a provision that allowed states to provide Medicaid benefits to children with disabilities who would not ordinarily qualify for Medicaid because of parents' income or resources. These waivers, often referred to as "Katie Beckett waivers" after the daughter of parent advocates who helped to pass the law, offer families the means to provide care for children with medically complex needs at home, as opposed to placing them in an institution (Semansky & Koyanagi, 2004). This has been an effective solution for many families who required additional financial support in raising a child with a disability.

Early Intervention

As noted in Chapter 1, Part C of the Individuals with Disabilities Education Act (IDEA) mandates state implementation of early intervention programs. This intervention includes health, educational, and therapeutic services for children ages 0 to 3 with a developmental delay or at risk for developmental delays (National Dissemination Center for Children with Disabilities, 2010). This early intervention system heavily emphasizes the involvement of the family in planning and service delivery, and it consistently focuses on family-centered practices as a critical factor in the delivery of high-quality and effective services. This family-centeredness refers to "a set of interconnected beliefs and attitudes that shape directions of program philosophy and behavior of personnel as they organize and deliver services" (Pletcher & McBride, 2000, p. 1). The belief that family should be actively included in early childhood/school services is grounded in historical educational practices in the United States (Dunst, 2002), and is considered to be an effective means of better supporting young children with disabilities.

Immunization Policies

In the United States, the Advisory Committee on Immunization Practices (ACIP), a group of experts selected by the Secretary of the U.S. Department of Health and Human Services, develops recommendations regarding which vaccines children and adolescents should receive, and their dosing intervals. These recommendations take into account scientific data, safety and efficacy, and cost-effectiveness (J. C. Smith et al., 2009). Schools require all children to be immunized before entering, except in rare cases of medical or religious exemption (Opel, Diekema, & Marcuse, 2008). While these compulsory vaccinations are considered one of the greatest achievements of the public health system, some argue that the benefits are not outweighed by the ethical drawbacks. Debates center around two main approaches. One side argues that compulsory vaccination diminishes autonomy for the person receiving the vaccine and/or for the parents making this decision on their children's behalf. However, others argue that the choice not to vaccinate a child puts undue pressure on other families to vaccinate their own children, in order to maintain "herd immunity." Herd immunity refers to the fact that unvaccinated individuals indirectly benefit from vaccinated individuals, because those who are vaccinated prevent the transmission of disease within the entire population. If the number of vaccinated children reaches a critical mass, all others are indirectly protected (Salmon et al., 2008).

The debate surrounding immunization has become particularly relevant within recent years, as public consensus for compulsory vaccination has declined (Feudtner & Marcuse, 2001). This declining public consensus is due to an upsurge in anti-vaccination sentiment, largely sparked by the allegation that immunizations are directly related to autism (Calandrillo, 2004). While the scientific evidence for this link is for the most part discredited, the concept has been widely perpetuated on the Internet and endorsed by celebrities (Offit, 2008). One study revealed that an Internet search on the term "vaccination" returned 43% anti-vaccination Web sites among the top ten hits across search engines, and that one search engine (Google) returned 100% anti-vaccination sites among the top ten hits (Davies, Chapman, & Leask, 2002). Such debates are ongoing in public discourse.

Self-Determination and Participation

Genetic Engineering

Interest in genetic engineering, which is known to critics as "new eugenics," has been steadily increasing in recent years due to major advancements in prenatal screening as well as biomedical interventions (Rembis, 2009). The social and ethical implications of the Human Genome Project, in particular, have garnered much criticism, with critics voicing concern that altering human genomes is "playing God," with serious moral consequences (Crook, 2008). Disability scholars have voiced alarm about this new eugenics, since our culture's ideals of bodily and mental perfection are a result of a complex interplay of social and cultural processes that typically devalue disabled bodies (Kerr & Shakespeare, 2002). Some of the most contentious issues in genetic engineering relate to prenatal screening.

Genetic Counseling and Prenatal Screening

Prenatal screening, abortion, and disability are issues that interrelate in complex and paradoxical ways (Shakespeare, 1998), as such issues embrace ideas of science, culture, religion, and morality. While many within the disability rights movement agree with a feminist argument that women have a right to choose to terminate an unwanted pregnancy, they also contend that terminating a pregnancy based on the fact that the future child will have a disability is a form of "weak eugenics" (Shakespeare, 1998). Although the disability rights movement includes a diversity of perspectives, this understanding has come to be known as the disability rights critique of abortion (Sharp & Earle, 2002), and it remains a highly controversial debate within the field of disability studies.

Disability rights activists contend that prenatal testing for disability is morally problematic for several reasons. The first of those reasons is that selective abortion conveys discriminatory attitudes about both the disabling trait itself and those who carry it, thus disparaging the lives of existing and future disabled people (Asch, 1989, p. 81). Another contention is that women make reproductive decisions in the context of a medical establishment that understands having a disability to necessarily involve unacceptable suffering, thus limiting a woman's capacity to make a truly free choice (Shakespeare, 1998). According to this argument, genetic counseling and reproductive intervention for parents can never truly fulfill the mandate of being "nondirective" because of the inherent eugenic assumptions of modern Western societies (King, 2001). Such debates are also linked to the limited awareness of disability rights by the medical profession, and to the negative information about disability that is provided to the parents during a diagnosis of disability.

Summary: Birthrights and Early Childhood

There are a number of complex and interrelated debates facing parents during prenatal and early life stages of children with disabilities, the most prevalent being related to health and the perceived "worth" of people with disabilities. Such controversies have no easy solutions, as there are competing, and at times conflicting, interests among mothers, families, and medical professions, which are contextualized within broader debates by feminist and disability rights scholars. As medical advances change the level of information about disability, new approaches to diagnosis, immunization, and genetic screening are needed.

In addition, families require a greater level of financial and other supports to ameliorate the additional health care costs of having a child with a disability.

Disability and Childhood

As children with disabilities move into school age, they face issues of both social acceptance and academic achievement. Often a learning disability is only diagnosed once children are in school and having difficulty learning to read or experiencing behavioral challenges. At this stage, children with diagnosed disabilities qualify for special education services, which could include inclusive (integrated), segregated, or mixed classes and activities with children without disabilities. Children with disabilities are likely to experience more bullying and social isolation than their peers (Bourke & Burgman, 2010; Connors & Stalker, 2007; Nadeau & Tessier, 2006). During the school years, families of children with disabilities benefit from the legal mandates for free and appropriate public education for all children, though the degree of preparedness of the school systems to provide adequate education and adjunct services for children with a disability varies widely.

In addition to school and educational debates, a key issue for families is the increased role and knowledge they are expected to have in order to be effective advocates for their children.

Family

Family Advocates

Families of children with disabilities are often expected to have a higher degree of involvement in their children's lives than families of children without disabilities. This increased involvement includes activities such as serving on boards and committees (Caldwell, Hauss, & Stark, 2009), making and keeping medical appointments (Leonard, Brust, & Sapienza, 1992), and advocating for the child in the school system (Trainor, 2010). These experiences in advocating for their children may be both in collaboration with supportive professionals within service systems, and in conflict with non-supportive professionals. One study of female caregivers revealed that those who had non-supportive interactions with professionals experienced lack of trust, lack of power, and challenges in their caregiving situations.

However, these feelings often inclined them to become advocates for their own care recipient, and to improve the situation of other caregivers in similar situations (Nuefeld et al., 2008). The additional knowledge families are required to have to effectively advocate for their children in professional and medical settings is often not well supported by broader policies and services. The "expertise" oftentimes comes from informal networks of advocates, which may exclude families that are not in well-supported communities or disability networks.

Family Impacts

Families of children with disabilities often face greater challenges than other families do. These challenges can include additional physical demands, social isolation, and emotional reactions, as well as financial difficulties (Shattuck & Parish, 2008). These multiple demands can lead to greater parenting stress and higher rates of divorce among these families (Hartley et al., 2010; Taanila et al., 2002; Wallander & Noojin, 1995). Generally, the impact of having a child with disabilities is greater on the mother than on the father, as he is likely to spend less time caregiving (Beckman, 1991). Mothers of children with disabilities are expected to have a "special competence" due to their complex caring role (Ryan & Runswick-Cole, 2008).

However, there is great variability in parental reactions, depending not only on the disability characteristics of the child but also on the context of care, including the availability of support and the socio-cultural context. For example, child characteristics associated with poorer maternal well-being include the diagnosis of autism (Abbeduto et al., 2004; Blacher & McIntyre, 2006; Singer, 2006) and the presence of challenging behaviors (Orsmond et al., 2006). Divorce or separation is more likely in families of children with more severe and impacting types of disabilities, including autism (Hartley et al., 2010; Hodapp & Krasner, 1995). Social resources, including friends and families, support groups, and family support services, can serve as protective factors (Blacher et al., 1997). Many families of children with disabilities report factors of resilience, such as making positive meaning of disability, mobilizing resources, becoming united and closer as a family, finding greater appreciation of life in general, and gaining spiritual strength (Bayat, 2007). Examination of family narratives and the cultural construction of disability further add to our understanding of family experiences and highlight the great variability in families (Ferguson, 2001).

Siblings

The entrance of a child with disabilities into the family affects not only parents but also other members of the family, particularly siblings. The sibling relationship is the longest-lasting relationship encompassing shared memories and experiences. Since siblings are often the closest peer relationships, children with disabilities learn many social skills from their sibling interactions and their siblings have a major long-term influence on their development (Cicirelli, 1995).

Research results on the impact of having a brother or sister with disabilities are mixed. Early research on children who had siblings with disabilities focused on the negative consequences of the relationship, with the assumption that the non-disabled siblings would be at risk for poorer social adjustment and depression (Stoneman, 2001). The relationships were often described as unhealthy, with the non-disabled siblings experiencing shame and guilt because they did not have a disability or because parents paid more attention to the child with a disability. However, more recent research has found that generally non-disabled siblings report affection and positive regard for their sibling with a disability, as well as such positive impacts as possessing higher levels of empathy and altruism that they attributed to their experience of having a sibling with a disability (Rossiter & Sharpe, 2001; Stoneman, 2005). Generally, they are as well-adjusted as other children who do not have a sibling with a disability.

There is some variability in outcomes depending on the type of disability, as non-disabled children who have brothers or sisters with mental health conditions, with autism, or with other severe behavior disorders are more likely to experience problems in the early relationship and to exhibit symptoms of depression or less positive adjustment in later life (Orsmond & Seltzer, 2007). The very limited research on support provided to siblings during childhood suggests that psychoeducational groups, such as "sib-shops" that provide opportunities to meet other siblings and to discuss concerns about disability and family issues, can have long-lasting positive benefits (Heller et al., 2008).

Health

Childhood disability and health problems often compel parents to spend increased time in caring for the affected child in comparison to children without disabilities. This increased time expenditure includes involvement with the health care system and additional investment in both therapeutic and non-therapeutic activities to enhance development (Leonard, Brust, & Sapienza, 1992). For children with intellectual disabilities, these time demands tend to decrease throughout the life cycle, averaging 31 to 60 hours per week in early childhood, and 15 to 30 hours per week in adulthood (Haveman et al., 1997).

Chronic Health Conditions and Child Development

The frequent hospitalization of individuals with chronic illnesses in childhood and early childhood may have a long-term impact on their future health and psychosocial outcomes. The hospital environment may be distressing and even traumatic for young children, which can in turn affect the way they will interact with and trust the medical system for the remainder of their lives (Turkel & Pao, 2007). Having a lifelong chronic illness has also been associated with less permanent employment and delayed independence (Gledhill, Rangel, & Garralda, 2000; Kokkonen, 1995). In the words of Jim Ferris (2004), a poet with disabilities who frequented hospitals in his childhood:

Orphaned for the first time

at five—no one died—

Mom just took me to the hospital.

And left. At once I am waif

. . . All orphans are equal—all need fixing.

This poem, titled "Child of No One," describes the isolation and abandonment he felt as a young child experiencing frequent hospitalization.

Because there is a high degree of variation in outcomes of childhood hospitalization based on factors such as missed days of school and severity of impairment, intervention approaches should be catered to both the individual child and his or her type of impairment (Turkel & Pao, 2007). A review of various psychological interventions for chronic pediatric illness revealed that there was little evidence for cross-disability efficacy in psychological interventions (Beale, 2006). This is an ongoing area of concern for families.

Health Disparities

While health disparity models are widely referenced within research literature, these models seldom explicitly address disability. Lewis (2009) describes a disability disparity as the differential treatment individuals from underserved ethnic and racial minority groups may receive when trying to access formal rehabilitation and disability services. She contends that this disparity results in a higher incidence of disability in these groups, less participation in formal disability service systems, and fewer successful outcomes than are achieved by those in the majority culture group (Lewis, 2009). All these factors impact health and disability in the early life stages.

Policy, Legislation, and Services

Children with disabilities have historically been excluded from mainstream educational opportunities. Educational provisions for young people with disabilities started with the 1965 Elementary and Secondary Education Act (ESEA), which required states to monitor and assess the educational progress of students and sought to provide compensatory educational programs for culturally disadvantaged students.

In 1975 the Individuals with Disabilities Education Act (IDEA) was passed, which shifted the discourse of education from segregation to integration. Other contemporary education legislation and initiatives include Section 504 of the Rehabilitation Act of 1973, and the Americans with Disabilities Act.

Section 504 covers qualified students with disabilities who attend schools receiving federal financial assistance. Section 504 requires that school districts provide a free and appropriate public education to qualified students in their jurisdictions who have a physical or mental impairment that substantially limits one or more major life activities. As noted previously, the IDEA requires that children ages 0 to 21 receive free and appropriate public education regardless of disability or ability to pay for specialized services. A core guideline is that children be taught in the least restrictive environment, which entails inclusive and mainstreamed education. This guideline remains controversial, as some advocates are concerned that children with disabilities miss out on specific educational services when they are primarily taught in regular classrooms. A greater balance between mainstreaming and acknowledging different educational needs of some children with disabilities is needed.

Compounding the issue of mainstreaming is the considerable pressure that has been put on school officials to increase the academic performance of students and schools. Such efforts are contextualized within a tightening of state funds for education. This emphasis on academic standards targets children with disabilities who may not be performing at equal levels to their peers. The 2001 No Child Left Behind Act funds education programs aimed at increasing standards, aids schools in improving their test scores, and increases state accountability. There are ongoing debates on how to provide equitable education for children with different learning needs in a policy environment of standardized testing.

Self-Determination and Participation

Early Identity Formation

While few studies have focused on the identity of children with disabilities, a two-year longitudinal study of the bullying experiences of children with disabilities (ages 7 to 15) revealed that they viewed themselves as being similar to their non-disabled counterparts, suggesting a social relational model of disability (Connors & Stalker, 2007). Thus, they understand their own disability in terms of an unequal social relationship, akin to the barriers people face because of racism or sexism. These barriers to participation occur both in one-to-one relationships with peers and in institutional policies and practices. Children within this study tended to emphasize that they were the same as other children, while simultaneously expressing frustration with barriers such as other people's reactions to their disability, lack of access to leisure facilities, and transportation difficulties.

Another study of retrospective accounts of young individuals with autism gives some insight into the early identity formation of children with autism (Huws & Jones, 2008). Participants within this study found that learning of their diagnosis of autism (which parents often did not disclose to them until many years later) actually assisted them in explaining previous life events.

Promotion of Self-Determination

The foundation for self-determination starts in childhood, as parents, families, and teachers support essential elements of self-determination; these include self-regulation of behaviors, choice-making, problem-solving, decision-making, and self-advocacy. Each of the elements of self-determination has a unique developmental course or is acquired through specific learning experiences. Some elements have greater applicability for secondary education, transition, and beyond, while others focus more on elementary years. Development of these skills early on sets the groundwork for an individual's self-determination at a later age (Wehmeyer & Palmer, 2003).

Structuring the home and school environments to support opportunities for children with disabilities to gain capacity in these skills also promotes their self-determination. Each of these skills has a unique developmental course and requires different types of supports depending on the age of the child. In early childhood these supports may include matching activities to a child's desires. Hauser-Cram, Bronson, and Upshur (1993) found that children with disabilities who exercised more choices in their activities were more sociable with their peers and more persistent and focused on tasks. Mithaug et al. (1998) demonstrated the importance of self-regulation in task performance of children as young as 6 to 8 years. When these children received instructions in selecting work tasks and recording data on tasks completed, their task performance increased.

One positive solution to developing and enhancing self-determination of children with disabilities is through school. During elementary and middle school years, students can begin to attend their Individual Education Program (IEP) meetings and assert their needs, opinions, and preferences for activities. One example of a program developed to encourage self-regulated problem-solving is *The Self-Determined Learning Model of Instruction*, which was effective for both adolescents and younger children (Palmer & Wehmeyer, 2003).

Summary: Disability and Childhood

A key challenge facing families of children with disabilities concerns the need for parents to be advocates. Having a child with a disability affects all family members, including siblings, as greater attention and resources are needed, particularly if a child has increased hospitalization and health needs. Once children begin school, there are additional issues facing families. They can at times be caught between policies of mainstreaming and full integration, and more controversial approaches to standardized testing and increasing test scores. However, it is within the school system that children with a disability can also begin to develop their capacity for making choices and self-regulating behavior. This important early life stage is a critical period for developing self-determination both in the family and within broader structural settings.

Disability and Youth

The definition of "youth" within this volume refers to the period of transition from childhood to adulthood, which typically occurs between the ages of 16 and 25 within Western contexts. While this age category may be a relatively recent phenomenon, it is increasingly significant to the lives of individuals in industrialized societies (Priestley, 2003). This period of transition differs between societies according to their respective cultural traditions, education, employment, and welfare systems (Heinz, 2009, p. 5). Sociological research on entering adulthood has typically focused on educational attainment, entering the full-time labor force, marriage, and childbearing (Danziger & Ratner, 2010; Settersten & Ray, 2010). More recent studies, however, have shown that while the majority of Americans still see completing school, establishing an independent household, and being employed full-time as important markers of becoming an adult, many young people no longer see marriage and parenthood as prerequisites for adulthood (Arnett, 2004; Settersten & Ray, 2010).

Regardless of these changing markers of adulthood, people with disabilities often face challenges in their transition to adulthood, especially when the markers focus on autonomy and independence.

Family

Family and Psychiatric Disabilities in Early Adulthood

Young adults are the least likely age group to receive appropriate care for depression and anxiety, putting those youth with psychiatric disabilities at risk of self-harm, suicide, and trauma (Arcelus & Vostanis, 2005; Young et al., 2001). Since young adulthood also marks the onset of many major mental illnesses, this lack of mental health care is critical (Öngür, Lin, & Cohen, 2009). With the majority of mental health care now taking place in the community, the care of people with mental health needs and psychiatric disability typically falls on the family. Often, however, family members feel untrained and unsupported to meet these complex support needs (Doornbos, 2002). Despite the stress and complexity of caring for a family member with a mental illness, family members who do so also report that this experience has helped them to identify personal strengths, gain new insight about their lives, and achieve greater intimacy with others (Chen & Greenberg, 2004).

Transition to Adult Services

The transition from childhood to adult disability services may also complicate the transition to adulthood in the lives of people with various types of disability. Because childhood and adult services are often dissimilar, there has been an increasing emphasis on multiagency collaboration and specialist approaches to transitions in order to facilitate better outcomes for young adults (Galambos, 2004; Hudson, 2006). Hudson (2006) suggests that a "whole systems" approach would better facilitate the transition of individuals with disabilities. This approach consists of a shared vision, comprehensive range of services, and individual guidance through the system. Families, in partnership with professionals and the individual with disabilities, play a critical role in the transition process and have a great influence on outcomes of transition planning (Morningstar, Turnbull, & Turnbull, 1995).

This period of adolescence and young adulthood is challenging for families as they negotiate a balance between the child's need for independence and autonomy with their support needs and with parents' own feelings of protectiveness. In addition, families confront the reality that access to publicly supported services, such as post-secondary education and vocational services, may be lacking once the child leaves the special education system. Many public service systems in which children with disabilities are involved have eligibility criteria only up to the age of 18 or 21, and the dramatic change from childhood to adult services is not always well facilitated (Osgood, Foster, & Courtney, 2010). A longitudinal study that followed students from eighth grade through approximately age 25 revealed that those with visual, speech, and hearing disabilities were less likely than their non-disabled counterparts to find full-time employment, establish an independent residence, marry, and have children (Janus, 2009). Those with learning disabilities were also more likely than those without disabilities to fall into the "just workers" category— still living with parents, but working full-time.

Health

Transition From Pediatric to Adult Health Care

For children with disabilities and chronic health conditions, the transition from pediatric to adult health care may pose particular challenges. It is complicated by the lack of provider guidelines for the transfer of children with disabilities at the primary-care level to adult services (Sherifali, Ciliska, & O'Mara, 2009). While pediatric services are typically comprehensive and developmentally appropriate, adult services are often more fragmented (Kennedy & Sawyer, 2008). Adult services, in contrast to pediatric services, typically hold the expectation that the individual receiving health care services will remain autonomous and self-directing (Sawyer & Aroni, 2005). Yet transition programs generally fail to incorporate health care goals in IEPs.

In a review of 149 peer-reviewed publications on transition from child-centered to adult-centered health care for people with cerebral palsy and spina bifida, Binks et al. (2007) found that (1) individuals were reluctant to transfer from child-centered services, which had provided care all their lives; (2) parents were reluctant to relinquish control over their child's health care; and (3) service providers were distrustful of adult-centered health providers' knowledge about how to treat this population. In addition, adult-centered health providers acknowledged being ill-prepared and ill-trained to meet the needs of these groups. A number of studies have attempted to meet the need for practice guidelines for transitioning people with disabilities into adult health care. However, much of this literature uses small cohorts, often with only one disorder or disease group (Kennedy & Sawyer, 2008).

These findings demonstrate the need for better solutions in transitioning from childhood to adulthood in the area of health.

Disability and Sexuality

For individuals with disabilities, expressions of sexuality have been both denied and heavily regulated (Priestley, 2003), and remain highly controversial. Although some disability-related government departments (i.e., human services, health, education), as well as disability service providers and health-related professionals, have guidelines/policies to address issues pertaining to the sexuality of people with disabilities, such policies remain inconsistent, underutilized, and predominantly focused on being "crisis reactive" rather than preventative/rights-oriented (Ward, Trigler, & Pfeiffer, 2001). There are many debates around how to effectively teach young people with disabilities about sexuality. Youth with disabilities are often excluded from processes of defining, developing, and disseminating information around healthy sexual practices, and this exclusion affects the empowerment and rights of all persons with a disability. The current national, state, and local guidelines/policies that address sexuality among people with disabilities are very few, and remain inconsistent and underutilized.

In many states across the nation, sexual and reproductive policies and practices focus solely on protection from abuse and do not address rights to sexual citizenship or sexual agency, particularly for high-risk groups such as young girls and women with disabilities. This is part of a broader socio-cultural and political problem wherein people with disabilities (and in particular people with intellectual and developmental disabilities) are highly stigmatized, considered as either asexual or in need of "protection" from accessing sexual activity (Swango-Wilson, 1995).

The problem is compounded by a lack of education, information, and knowledge about sexuality and disability, with many service providers and families unaware of what to do when issues arise. Furthermore, educational materials and/or training resources are often inaccessible, which puts women and young girls with disabilities at an even higher risk of sexual abuse, sexually transmitted diseases, or unplanned pregnancies (Ailey et al., 2003). There are a number of different and often circular policy issues in this area. Ultimately, young people with disabilities do not have the same basic rights and opportunities in the areas of sexual and reproductive health as their non-disabled peers.

Policy, Legislation, and Services

Many of the policies discussed in the previous section (Disability and Childhood) also apply here. In addition, youth with disabilities have particular needs in training and employment transitions. Youth with disabilities who are transitioning out of school settings often have poor post-secondary outcomes and express little hope of achieving meaningful competitive employment (Winn & Hay, 2009). Their low rate of employment can be attributed to internal factors, such as physical health problems and side-effects of medication, as well as to external factors, such as negative attitudes of employers (Winn & Hay, 2009). Because of these factors, most special education systems have transition planning built into the students' high school educational plan (Wells, Sandefur, & Hogan, 2003). However, there remains debate over the full effectiveness of such plans.

In regard to health care, the Patient Protection and Affordable Care Act (PPACA), passed in 2010, has several provisions that impact Americans with disabilities, including the Community Living Assistance Services and Supports (CLASS) Act and the Community First Choice Option (CFC). The CLASS Act establishes national voluntary insurance for purchasing community living assistance services and supports. Monthly premiums, taken as payroll deductions, are deposited in a federal fund and given lockbox protection. Once an individual is determined eligible, they may begin to withdraw cash from their account on a monthly basis for the purchase of non-medical long-term care services and supports, such as home modifications, adaptive technology, home care services, transportation, or compensation to family and other caregivers. This provision is intended to allow people who become disabled to live and work in their community, without having to become impoverished in order to qualify for Medicaid benefits (Caldwell, 2010).

The second provision of the PPACA that impacts people with disabilities, the CFC, is available to states as a waiver option. Participation in it requires that home- and community-based attendant services and supports are made available to all eligible individuals for assistance with activities of daily living. Eligible persons are those individuals who would otherwise require an institutional level of care and meet income requirements. The CFC is significant for people with disabilities in that it allows states greater flexibility in their Medicaid waiver programs, and will likely result in increased support for Olmstead community integration plans by offering services in the least restrictive setting appropriate to an individual's needs (Caldwell, 2010). These policy initiatives offer effective solutions to ameliorate some of the health and service needs of people with disabilities.

Self-Determination and Participation

Transition to Adulthood

Individuals with chronic disease and disability may face a number of challenges in the transition to adulthood, including difficulty caused by not meeting developmental milestones related to adulthood (DiNapoli & Murphy, 2002; Stam et al., 2006). Interviews with adolescents with juvenile idiopathic arthritis revealed that they felt they were in a constant, dynamic process of struggle and adjustment to their disability. While they struggled to overcome the disease to be more like their peers, they simultaneously coped with being dependent on personal assistance (Östlie, Johansson, & Möller, 2009).

Identity Development

Personal identity refers to an individual's core characteristics, whereas social identity is a definition of oneself in relation to others. The process of developing a social identity involves identification with others based on group characteristics, shared enjoyment, language, dress, and customs (Duszak, 2002). For people with disabilities, identity development is complicated by an effort to achieve "normality" as defined by medical standards, the redefinition of such standards of normality, and an emphasis on marginality in the depiction of positive disability identity (Bridgens, 2009). These issues continue to pose significant problems for young people with disabilities as they seek to interact with their peers.

Promotion of Self-Determination

During the process of transitioning from childhood to adulthood, youth with disabilities face planning tasks related to current and future vocational choices, residential options, post-secondary education and training, and leisure-time activities. This process provides an opportunity for youth to develop and assert their self-determination skills. Parents, teachers, and community members play an essential role in building and supporting the decision-making capacity of these youth. Through leadership training, youth can also develop self-advocacy skills and learn to advocate not only for themselves but also for others with disabilities.

Reviews of research have shown that adolescents with disabilities, including those with intellectual and developmental disabilities, can become more self-determined through various interventions and instructional strategies, and can acquire skills for involvement with educational planning (Wehmeyer et al., 2007). In addition, these studies show that students with greater self-determination have more positive adult outcomes, including enhanced quality of life and better employment outcomes.

Summary: Disability and Youth

Transitioning from youth to adulthood is the main area of concern at this life stage, and it impacts a number of life domains, including education, health, sexuality, and identity. The role of the family in assisting young people can be challenging, as many families seek to support growing independence within a context of protection. Young people attempting to make the transition from education to employment often lack necessary financial and social supports to enable access to the labor market. A key controversial area that begins in this life stage, and can be an ongoing debate for certain individuals (i.e., those with an intellectual disability), is that of sexuality and sexual expression, with young people receiving conflicting information or no information at all. More promising solutions for supporting young people as they transition to adulthood can be found in new health policies, which offer new approaches to health, services, and community support.

Disability and Adulthood

The salient developmental tasks as one turns 18 years old typically are moving away from home to live on one's own, beginning post-secondary education, choosing a career, and choosing a romantic partner. Further into adulthood, typical roles include getting married or choosing a life partner, having children, and becoming economically self-sufficient. As noted earlier, adults with disabilities face many barriers in assuming these roles. Priestley (2003) notes the danger of focusing on these "normal" transitions and suggests looking at broader social issues that influence timing of events in people's lives. Many adults do not achieve these milestones at the same time or to the same degree as other people. The type and extent of disability and the available supports can affect the degree to which people can fulfill their desired adult roles. Often people with disabilities experience the greatest gap in meeting adulthood goals of self-sufficiency, community inclusion, and productivity. There are also greater gaps in services in adulthood than in childhood, wherein educational services are federally mandated.

Family

Support From Families

Many adults with disabilities continue living with their parents into adulthood. Over 60% of adults with developmental disabilities live with family (Braddock, Hemp, & Rizzolo, 2008). As many as one-third of adults with mental illness live with parents (Lefly, 1987). Individuals with disabilities often report a preference for remaining at home, a preference family members typically share (Johnson, Kastner, & Committee on Children with Disabilities, 2005). Whether or not individuals with disabilities live in the family home, their family members provide most of their socio-emotional and instrumental supports. Benefits of these informal supports for the adult with disabilities include higher morale, decreased loneliness and worry, feelings of usefulness, lower mortality, better survival and recovery rates from acute conditions, and reduced institutionalization (Hooyman, 1983; Mendes de Leon et al., 1999, 2001). In a U.S. nationwide survey, Thompson (2004) found that 78% of adults with all types of disabilities who receive long-term care at home receive their care exclusively from unpaid family and friends. Yet funding for family support is woefully inadequate across disabilities.

Long-Term Impact on Families

Family members who provide care over a period of many years to a relative with disabilities often experience an impact on their economic, health, and psychosocial well-being. In two large population-based samples, the Midlife Development in the U.S. (MIDUS) and the Wisconsin Longitudinal Study, mothers of adults with intellectual disabilities reported increased negative affect after receiving their child's diagnosis of intellectual disabilities, but over time they adapted well to having a child with disabilities. However, these mothers did have fewer visits with friends, lower rates of employment, lower family savings, and greater family-related work role strain (Ha et al., 2008; Seltzer et al., 2001). Parents who had a child with a serious mental health problem had normative patterns of educational and occupational attainment and marriage, but elevated levels of physical symptoms, depression, and alcoholism at mid-life. Such studies demonstrate the challenges that families continue to face across the life course when supporting a child, of any age, with a disability.

One solution that has shown some success in improving outcomes for families is the availability of formal services and support. For families of adults with developmental disabilities, greater unmet needs for services have contributed to poorer mental health (Caldwell, 2006), increased caregiving burden (Heller & Factor, 1993), and the desire for an out-of-home placement (Heller & Factor, 1993). Key service needs reported by families include respite services; case coordination; transportation; recreation services; and information regarding housing, financial plans, and guardianship (Heller, Miller, & Hsieh, 1999; Pruchno & McMullen, 2004). Major needs reported by families of persons with severe mental illness include information, coping strategies support, understanding of conditions, and assistance with problem-solving (Drapalski et al., 2008). Such interventions as psychoeducational and support groups, cash subsidies, and support brokerage are examples of practices and policies that enhance family capacity to continue providing care and promote family well-being (Heller & Schindler, 2009; Pekkala & Merinder, 2002).

Parenting With a Disability

Often overlooked in the literature on families and "caregiving" is the role of people with disabilities in caring for others. Yet there are over 10 million households in the United States, which comprise about 11% of American families, in which children live with a parent with disabilities (Kirshbaum & Olkin, 2002). Assumptions framing much of the research on parents with disabilities presuppose negative effects on the children due to the disability of the parent. Also, many of the studies focus on populations in clinical settings or in the child welfare system. In addition to their disability, these parents face many challenges, including prejudice and discrimination about their rights or abilities to parent, social isolation, and poverty (Kirshbaum & Olkin, 2002; Llewellyn & McConnell, 2002; Sands, 1995). There are also critical distinctions by type and level of disability. For example, parents with intellectual disabilities face additional key challenges, including understanding their child's developmental needs, illiteracy, and increased risk of having a child with intellectual disabilities. Parents with physical disabilities encounter barriers in obtaining adaptive equipment and universally designed environments enabling baby care. Parents with severe mental illness often face challenges in their recovery process, including difficulties in managing stress and harsh self-judgment, that can affect their parenting.

Such programs as "Through the Looking Glass," a national resource center for parents with disabilities, have reframed the focus of research and services for this population using a non-pathological disability culture perspective. Kirshbaum and Olkin (2002) argue that problems attributed to the disability are often caused by important contextual factors, such as poverty, history of abuse in childhood, substance abuse, or lack of adequate supports. They and other researchers have demonstrated the effectiveness of changes in policies and practices—such as legislation allowing for publicly funded assistive technology; training in child care, safety, and health practices; and housing, vocational, and financial supports—in helping parents with disabilities overcome these problems.

Health

Health is a large area of concern during this life stage, as adults with disabilities are more likely than the general population to experience disparities in health. While many people with disabilities have good health, only 27% of persons with disabilities report their health to be excellent or very good, versus 60% of persons without disabilities (Centers for Disease Control and Prevention, 2008). Those with disabilities face a greater risk for secondary and chronic conditions, preventable complications, and premature death. In addition, they tend to have poorer and riskier health habits, and they have less access to appropriate health care, early disease identification or preventive screening, or health promotion activities (Drum, Horner-Johnson, & Krahn, 2008; Havercamp, Scandlin, & Roth, 2004).

Key secondary conditions include pain, fatigue, depression, and obesity (Nosek et al., 2006). Other key conditions that people with disabilities experience to a greater degree than the general population include diabetes, heart disease, and osteoporosis (Rimmer, 2006). These are often preventable conditions that arise out of the confluence of the impairment, the health behaviors, and the access to services. For example, mobility limitations, use of psychotropic and anti-seizure medication, and poor absorption of nutrients can contribute to some of these conditions.

A key factor is poor health habits, including higher rates of obesity, sedentary behavior, and smoking among adults with disabilities compared to other adults. A recent analysis of the 2008 Behavioral Risk Factor Surveillance Study found that adults (18 years and older) with disabilities were more likely than those without disabilities to be obese (37% versus 24%) and to smoke (27% versus 17%) (Rehabilitation Research and Training Center on Disability Statistics and Demography, 2010). Researchers have also documented low rates of physical activity in persons with disabilities (Rimmer, 2006). Inadequate levels of physical activity may decrease the muscle strength, aerobic capacity, and flexibility of people with disabilities, leading to chronic health conditions. Various health-promotion programs have been developed to improve the fitness and health of people with disabilities. These programs have resulted in improved physical fitness for people with disabilities overall (Rimmer et al., 2010), and in improved fitness and psychosocial outcomes for people with intellectual disabilities (Heller, McCubbin, Drum, & Peterson, in press).

Environmental factors, such as policy and the built environment, can also influence health behaviors in a community (Rimmer, 2005). For example, inaccessible fitness facilities can prevent people with disabilities from participating in exercise activities. In addition, societal attitudes can be barriers to health-promoting behaviors. Research has found that health care professionals recommend health-promotion behaviors less often to people with disabilities than to the general population (Harris et al., 2004).

Policy, Legislation, and Services

The main policy domains that impact adults with a disability relate to employment and income support. There is significant policy concern about the increasing numbers of working-age people reliant on disability benefits, and the low levels of economic and social participation of these people. Current research demonstrates that low rates of labor market participation by people with disability have an effect on the overall economy (Ozawa & Yeo, 2006). Moreover, qualified people with disability continue to be directed to sheltered and non-integrated jobs, further limiting their opportunity for economic self-sufficiency, independence, and social inclusion (Blanck & Schartz, 2001).

Employment rates of people with disability in the United States are extremely low at 17.7%, compared to 79.7% for working-age people without disabilities (Bjelland, Burkhauser, & Houtenville, 2008). This disparity is partly attributed to the historically low levels of federal funding allocated specifically to disability education, training, and/or employment transition programs (Goodman & Stapleton, 2007). Disability benefits remain the main source of income for jobless people with disabilities, and even comprise half of the income for employed persons with disabilities. In addition, people with disabilities often find it difficult, if not impossible, to combine labor-market earnings with benefit payments. Furthermore, they face considerable barriers to employment when secondary benefits (e.g., medical care) are linked with disability benefit entitlements (Organisation for Economic Co-operation and Development, 2009). Access to health care should not be a disincentive to work and should not stand in the way of any medical treatment needed to return to work (Stapleton, Livermore, & Gregory, 2007). This is especially pertinent for adults with disabilities, given their increased health needs (as discussed above).

Disability policy for working-age people is an amalgamation of different policy approaches and the result of ongoing reforms to the welfare system. In the United States, the trend toward "active" disability policy for working-age people stems from neoliberal policy ideals, where the role of the state has been diminished so that the mechanisms of the free market take a bigger role in public policy and service provision. These shifts have resulted in draconian cuts to welfare policies, programs, and services, which are having an adverse effect on the rights of people with disabilities.

Policy reform efforts have included the introduction of the Personal Responsibility and Work Opportunity Reconciliation Act (PRWORA) in 1996. A key policy under this act is the Temporary Assistance to Needy Families (TANF), a means-tested cash-assistance program run by individual states involving work requirements (e.g., job search or job readiness, work experience and on-the-job training, or community service). Most efforts to encourage labor-market participation for people with disability are associated with the Social Security Administration's Ticket to Work Program. This program is designed to promote work by providing Supplemental Security Income (SSI) and Disability Insurance (DI) recipients with a "ticket" to purchase services from state vocational rehabilitation (VR) agencies, as well as other agencies that provide employment and rehabilitation services (Wittenburg & Loprest, 2004). The objectives of this legislation were to provide more opportunities for people with disabilities to participate in employment, to reduce disincentives and inherent risks in transitioning from income support to employment, and to increase financial well-being while simultaneously decreasing dependence on welfare benefits (National Council on Disability, 2005; Stapleton et al., 2007).

Other relevant policies include the Vocational Rehabilitation Act, various tax credits, and medical care coverage extensions. A core policy is the Americans with Disabilities Act of 1990 (ADA), federal antidiscrimination legislation that protects people with disability. Evidence shows that although disability antidiscrimination laws are critical for protecting the rights and raising the profile of people with disability, in the past they have not always had the envisaged outcomes. The National Council on Disability found some evidence of people with disability experiencing less discrimination and receiving more accommodations, but those improvements have not been accompanied by increases in hiring or the employment rate.

The success of the ADA continues to be controversial, and the many attempts to evaluate its impact on the employment rates of people with disability have returned mixed results. Some studies (Acemoglu & Angrist, 2001; DeLeire, 2000) indicate that the ADA actually decreased the employment rate of people with disability. Other studies (Blanck et al., 2003; Goodman & Waidmann, 2003) argue that while the employment of people with disability may be decreasing, the ADA is not to blame, as broader economic, political, and cultural contexts influence employment outcomes.

Policy reform efforts are complicated by debates over the definition of disability, both in policy discourse and in practice. Silverstein (2000) notes that the definitions of disability are constructed to meet the goals of the policy, wherein the policy focus is not about "what is disability," but about "what is disability for the purpose of this legislation." It is within these systemic goals that an individual is located and defined.

Self-Determination and Participation

Adulthood provides the greatest potential and expectations for enhanced self-determination. Although adults with disabilities clearly value self-determination, and it contributes significantly to their quality of life, they experience many barriers in exercising it (Lachappelle et al., 2005; Nota et al., 2007). They often have limited opportunities for autonomy and decision-making due to public attitudes, restrictive settings, and lack of accessibility. For example, persons who support adults with significant disabilities tend to view self-determination as less important than do individuals with disabilities themselves (Wehmeyer, Agran, & Hughes, 2000). Unlike most young adults, those with disabilities often continue to live with parents through adulthood, or they may live in congregate settings with rules that restrict choices and staff who may not honor or know their desires (e.g., Heller, Miller, & Hsieh, 2002; Stancliffe, 2001). Furthermore, low employment rates, poverty, and lack of transportation can contribute to restricted opportunities for pursuing desired activities.

Several trends have helped facilitate the greater self-determination and participation of adults with disabilities. These include deinstitutionalization, the advent of the consumer movement, and the growth of the self-advocacy movement. For example, in the United States the population of people with developmental disabilities living in large congregate settings dropped from nearly 500,000 in the late 1960s to less than 100,000 by 2006 (Braddock, Hemp, & Rizzolo, 2008). Instead, the majority of adults with developmental disabilities living in residential placements out of the family home now live in small, community-based settings, which are much more likely to foster autonomy and community participation.

With the advent of the consumer movement, beginning in the 1970s, adults with disabilities have increasingly demanded more control of their lives, including the services and supports they receive. While the consumer movement first focused on people with physical disabilities, over the years it has expanded to include people with developmental disabilities and mental health disabilities (Cook, 2005). The consumer movement has spurred an increase in consumer controlled and delivered services that emphasize individual preferences. Many of the independent living centers and mental health providers are controlled and/or staffed by people with disabilities. The Association of Persons with Disabilities, Self-Advocates Becoming Empowered (SABE), and the National Mental Health Consumers' Self-Help Clearinghouse are examples of peer-led national self-advocacy organizations that give voice to people with disabilities in the national policy front. For people with mental illness, the consumer movement has also been associated with the concept of recovery, which emphasizes not only symptom abatement but self-determination, dignity, hopefulness, and a high level of role functioning (Cook, 2005).

In addition to changes in the disability movements that promote self-determination, various training programs have been developed to promote the development of self-determination skills. These programs include training of persons with disabilities and their families in person-centered planning, self-advocacy, and methods of directing one's personal support. Studies are beginning to empirically test the effectiveness of these programs for adults (Heller et al., in press).

Summary: Disability and Adulthood

As many individuals with a disability continue to live with their families into adulthood, there is increased need for formalized supports and services to assist both the individuals and their families. Parents with a disability may require additional supports and services, particularly as they face a number of structural and attitudinal barriers in parenting with a disability. Health needs are an ongoing area of concern through the life course for people with disabilities, as adults face poorer outcomes in health and wellness that are compounded by a lack of information, funding, and support. There are some promising strengths-based approaches to health and disability, and these offer useful solutions to poor diet and activity levels that many adults with a disability experience. In terms of employment, there are a number of different disability policies and laws in place. However, these have not been effective in increasing participation in the labor market, and working-age people with disabilities continue to experience high rates of unemployment. Constraints to full and equal participation are also evident in areas of self-determination, although this situation is rapidly changing with the advent of the consumer movement and other self-advocacy movements.

Disability and Aging

The prevalence of disability among people over age 65 has rapidly increased during the 20th century in the United States and other industrialized nations. According to the U.S. Census, 54.7% of people over age 65 had a disability in 2000, or approximately 18 million people (McNeil, 2001). The growing number of people with disabilities over age 65 includes both people with lifelong disabilities who are living into their later years (Ansello & Janicki, 2000; Heller & Marks, 2006; Kemp & Mosqueda, 2004; Priestley, 2003), and people who are living longer and acquiring disabilities in their later years (Lightfoot, 2007; Priestley, 2003).

These trends suggest a convergence in disability status in later life between older people who grew up with impairments and those who acquired them later. However, an ongoing debate in aging and disability fields is that older people with impairments are less likely than younger people to be perceived, or to perceive themselves, as being disabled, because aging processes are commonly associated with the onset of impairment, and hence impairment is seen as "normal" (Priestley, 2003). People with early-onset disabilities are said to "age with disability," while those with mid- or late-life onsets are said to have "disability with aging." Verbrugge and Yang (2002) caution that this view is stereotypic, since disability and aging are processes that interweave across the whole life course. However, it is important to give attention to the unique experiences of people aging with a disability.

Family

One of the issues facing people aging with disabilities is that their need for assistance with daily activities may increase as they get older (McColl, 2004). Families have a pivotal role in meeting the increased needs for care by persons with disabilities as they age (Heller & Caldwell, 2006; Kemp, 2004; Mosqueda, 2004). It often becomes difficult for family caregivers to meet these needs, however, as the caregivers themselves get older. In the United States, the majority of adults with intellectual and developmental disabilities live at home with family caregivers, and 25% of these caregivers are over 60 years of age (Braddock, Hemp, & Rizzolo, 2008; Fujiura, 1998). In addition, a National Alliance on Mental Illness (NAMI) survey found that over 40% of persons with mental illness lived with parents, many of whom were elderly (G. C. Smith, Hatfield, & Miller, 2000). The number of aging caregivers providing care to relatives with disabilities will continue to increase in the coming decades.

With longer life expectancy, parents of persons with a long-term disability have a longer period of responsibility. As a result, these parents often must deal with their own aging in addition to the aging of their adult children (Heller & Marks, 2006; G. C. Smith et al., 2000). Even though the term "family caregiving" primarily refers to support provided to the adult with disabilities, adults with disabilities may also provide support to their aging family members because of their increased life expectancy (Heller, Caldwell, & Factor, 2007). There is a greater likelihood of the family member with a disability outliving his or her parents as well (Heller & Caldwell, 2006; G. C. Smith et al., 2000). Aging persons with intellectual disabilities in particular, unlike most elderly individuals, generally do not have children or a spouse on whom they can depend for support (Seltzer, 1985). Hence, when parents die, siblings of the person with disabilities often take over caregiving responsibilities. For those without siblings or other interested relatives and friends, there is a high risk of social isolation (Hogg, Moss, & Cooke, 1988).

Future Planning

Planning for the future is a task encountered by all people as they age. People with intellectual and developmental disabilities and severe mental illness may need lifelong support and face major life transitions when primary caregivers pass away or become unable to continue providing care (Heller & Caldwell, 2006). Therefore, planning for the future is particularly important for these individuals and their families (Freedman, Krauss, & Seltzer, 1997; Heller & Caldwell, 2006; G. C. Smith et al., 2000). Without adequate plans and supports in place, these individuals have a greater chance of facing emergency placements in inappropriate settings and inadequate or inflexible financial and legal safeguards when primary caregivers can no longer provide care (Freedman et al., 1997; Heller & Factor, 1993; G. C. Smith et al., 2000). Yet many families fail to make residential or financial plans. Frequently identified barriers to planning include lack of information, availability of services, difficulty affording attorneys, benefits resulting from the caregiving role, reciprocity of caregiving, and emotional issues concerning mortality (Heller & Caldwell, 2006; G. C. Smith et al., 2000).

Siblings

The relationships among siblings often become closer as other family members age and their extended family begins to shrink (White, 2001). Siblings tend to have long-lasting close relationships with their sibling with a disability. Generally, the siblings of adults with mental illness or with autism report a less positive impact of the relationship and less involvement with their siblings than the siblings of adults with intellectual disabilities. Women are more likely to be involved with their sibling. Brothers are more likely to be involved with brothers, indicating a preference for same-sex dyads (Heller & Arnold, 2010). Horwitz (1994) notes the importance of reciprocity as a predictor of current and projected social support from the non-disabled sibling to the sibling with disabilities.

As a result of the longer lifespan of this population and the aging of their parents, siblings play an increasing role in the lives of people with disabilities and anticipate taking on a greater supportive role in the future (Greenberg et al., 1999; Heller & Arnold, 2010). One study found that almost 60% of siblings of adults with intellectual disabilities expected to assume primary caregiving responsibility in the future, although only one-third of siblings of adults with mental illness held this expectation (Greenberg et al., 1999). Despite the likelihood of siblings assuming caregiving responsibility, many parents do not discuss future plans with siblings (Bigby, 2000; Heller & Factor, 1994). One solution is psychoeducational programs that involve siblings and families in future planning, which may help promote planning activities and reduce worries about the future for families (Heller & Caldwell, 2006).

Health

Aging With a Disability

People who are aging with disabilities often experience a multitude of age-related functional, medical, and psychological problems that tend to occur earlier than in people without disabilities (Heller & Marks, 2006; Kemp & Mosqueda, 2004). Several chronic conditions seem to be more prevalent among individuals with disabilities than in the general population, including non-atherosclerotic heart disease, hypertension, hypercholesteremia, obesity, heart disease, diabetes, respiratory illness, osteoporosis, and pressure sores. Mobility impairment, thyroid disease, psychotropic drug polypharmacy, and deaths due to pneumonia, gastrointestinal cancer, bowel obstruction, and intestinal perforation also have a higher prevalence among groups of people with various disabilities (Heller & Marks, 2006; Thompson, 2004).

There is still limited knowledge about age-related health conditions for people with developmental disabilities (Evenhuis et al., 2001; Haveman et al., 2010). People with developmental disabilities have some age-related health conditions similar to those of people without disabilities, but they also have unique health concerns (Lightfoot, 2007). They have, on average, twice as many health problems as the general public (van Schrojenstein Lantman-de Valk & Walsh, 2008). Syndrome-specific effects link to special risk factors. People with Down syndrome, for example, have an earlier onset of Alzheimer's disease (Strydom et al., 2009). Persons aging with cerebral palsy may experience earlier-onset arthritis related to excessive joint wear and tear, chronic pain, gastroesophageal reflux, contractures, and bowel and bladder problems (Heller & Marks, 2006; Thompson, 2004).

Many older people with intellectual disabilities manifest mental disorders and associated severe behavioral problems that may extend into later life (Jacobson, 2003; Tyrell & Dodd, 2003). For the oldest age cohorts, behavior disorders and alterations in psychosocial functioning tend to be associated with the onset of dementia (Jacobson, 2003). The increased prevalence of psychiatric disorders in this population is associated with social, biological, and medical factors, life events, and specific syndromes (Tyrell & Dodd, 2003). Among social factors are lack of education, institutionalization at an early age, limited social networks, loss of close and confiding relationships, bereavement, lack of valued roles, low income and relative poverty, service breaks and transitions, and shifting patterns of interdependence with parents during the life course. All these factors predispose individuals to mental health problems later in life (Grant, 2005).

People aging with spinal cord injury have a greater risk for pressure ulcers, decreased muscular strength, decline in immune system function and increase in incidence of infection, decreased flexibility of soft tissues, osteoarthritis, osteoporosis, diminished sensation, and spasticity. They may also experience overuse, degenerative changes, and nerve entrapment in the shoulders and lower extremities due to repetitive use from wheeling their wheelchairs (Thompson, 2004). An estimated 25% to 50% of polio survivors develop post-polio syndrome, causing the reappearance of some of the initial problems 10 to 40 years after the paralytic attack. New symptoms such as increased muscle weakness, fatigue, swallowing difficulties, breathing difficulty, and muscle or joint pain can appear later in life as well, after years of stable functioning (Thompson, 2004). Because people with disabilities often experience premature aging-related functional and health problems by middle age, the issue of how to maintain a positive quality of life becomes important. For those who have a difficult time coping with such changes, depression can result (Kemp, 2004).

There are a growing number of elderly persons with severe mental illness, including those with lifelong disabilities and those who develop mental illness in later life (Smyer & Qualls, 1999). Improvements in mental health care combined with advancements in general medical care have resulted in more individuals with schizophrenia surviving into old age than ever before (Moak, 1996). Remarkably little is known about the course and treatment of severe mental illness in later life (Light & Lebowitz, 1991).

Because this is the first time in history that large numbers of people with disabilities are living into middle age and beyond, it is unknown what to expect and what to accept. Based on the understanding of normal aging, new diseases and new disability should not be accepted as an inevitable consequence of aging with a disability. Although there is a tendency to accept these functional changes as inevitable outcomes of aging, many of the common consequences are not inevitable (Mosqueda, 2004).

In addition to age-related biological changes, lifestyle and environmental issues have a significant impact. People with disabilities also face accessibility barriers to receiving appropriate health care, including health care providers' lack of knowledge (Ansello & Janicki, 2000; van Schrojenstein Lantman-de Valk, 2009), complex bureaucracy, and physical and societal attitudinal barriers (Heller & Marks, 2006; Lightfoot, 2007). There is a need for more evidence-based practice standards in the area of health care for older people with disabilities, as well as for more well-trained medical professionals who specialize in providing health care services to this population (Lightfoot, 2007).

Dementia

An estimated 5.1 million Americans age 65 and older, or 13% of the population in this age group, have dementia of the Alzheimer's type (Alzheimer's Association, 2010). One disability group that develops

Alzheimer's disease earlier than the general population is people with Down syndrome. Approximately 50% to 60% of adults with Down syndrome may develop dementia of the Alzheimer's type by the time they reach 60 to 70 years of age, which is a much higher rate than in the general population.

In people with intellectual disabilities, early symptoms of dementia are often not very noticeable. The disease process can evolve more rapidly as well. The mean time to death may be as short as 3 to 4 years after the diagnosis (Strydom et al., 2009). The occurrence of dementia among individuals with intellectual disabilities has a profound impact on the quality of life of affected individuals and on their families, friends, and caregivers (Janicki, McCallion, & Dalton, 2000). Because dementia is a progressive condition, care needs and caregiver demands increase slowly. Increased caregiving time is associated with difficulty experienced by staff and families, and they may experience increased emotional exhaustion (Lloyd, Kalsy, & Gatherer, 2008). Another important factor is the presence of challenging behavior, which was found to be negatively correlated with staff well-being in those who cared for people with Down syndrome and dementia (Donaldson, 2002).

There are several interventions that may be effective in slowing decline, improving quality of life, and reducing caregiver stress. These include interventions with caregivers or co-residents in the form of education, training, and support groups (Acton & Kang, 2001), or pharmacological treatments, exercise, and other psychosocial interventions with the person with dementia (Strydom et al., 2009).

Assistive Technology and Environmental Modifications

As individuals with long-term disabilities and other older adults face declines in health and function, there is a greater need for assistive technology and environmental interventions to help them maintain their independence and community participation. Assistive technology commonly includes seating and mobility, communication, access, environmental control, and daily living technologies. Other technologies include telemonitoring, telehealth, telemedicine and information, and communication technologies that are intended to improve the aging or care experience. Environmental modifications such as grab bars, ramps, lifts, and modifications to building interiors and exteriors target the same goals and are often delivered in conjunction with assistive technology. Despite the potential benefits, only a small percentage of older adults with disabilities use assistive technology and environmental modifications. Many older individuals and their caregivers are unaware of these interventions or unable to access or pay for them (Carlson et al., 2005; Hammel, Lai, & Heller, 2002; Mirza & Hammel, 2009). Another barrier is the shortage of outcome studies demonstrating the value of the technologies and their cost effectiveness and efficiency. Making these technologies available and accessible to the growing number of people who need them entails simultaneous investment in organizational changes, innovative business strategies, and human capital (Vimarlund & Olve, 2005).

Policy, Legislation, and Services

Consumer Direction and Family Support

In the United States, Medicaid provides national health insurance for persons with disabilities that covers both acute and long-term services. Over 75% of Medicaid expenditures are allocated toward institutional care (Heller & Marks, 2006); hence there is a clear institutional bias in spending. For example, even though most adults with developmental disabilities live with families, only about 5% of developmental disabilities funding is allocated for family support (Braddock, Hemp, & Rizzolo, 2008). Aging populations and increasing demand for long-term services are influencing policymakers to consider policies that support families to avoid more costly institutional placements of persons with disabilities and to increase consumer satisfaction (Heller et al., 2007; Simon-Rusinowitz et al., 2000). The trend over the past couple of decades has been the development of consumer-directed programs.

Medicaid has expanded to include the Personal Care Program and the Home and Community-Based Services Program. The Personal Care Program includes home health care and assistance with personal care, activities of daily living, and housekeeping chores. The Home and Community-Based Services Program includes home modification, case management, pre-vocational and educational habilitation, and supported employment. These consumer-directed programs offer people with disabilities monthly cash subsidies or individualized budgets, potentially fostering greater autonomy and choice. This approach, also known as Cash and Counseling, involves disbursing funds through a cash allowance and at the same time providing counseling services

(Heller et al., 2007; Simon-Rusinowitz et al., 2000). The Home and Community-Based Services Program is the major source of funding for community living for older people with disabilities who receive subsidies for residential care (Lightfoot, 2007). A trend within the recent consumer-directed supports has been to allow family caregivers to become paid employees (Heller et al., 2007).

Comparison studies have found that consumer-directed services resulted in greater service satisfaction and fewer unmet service needs than agency-directed services. In general, studies have reported no significant differences in health status or safety. Individuals with disabilities experience benefits in community participation and employment in consumer-directed programs (Heller, Miller, & Hsieh, 1999). Some studies have reported psychological benefits concerning feelings of empowerment and perceived quality of life of individuals with disabilities (Foster et al., 2003). Caregivers have reported reduced feelings of stress and burden, greater self-efficacy, better access to health care, more opportunities for employment, and improved social and leisure opportunities (Caldwell, 2006; Caldwell & Heller, 2003; Heller et al., 1999). Findings from a longitudinal study also indicated that consumer-directed supports resulted in decreased institutional placements over a period of eight years (Heller & Caldwell, 2005).

Integrating Disability and Aging Services

Historically there have been different approaches to services for older adults and for people with disabilities. Aging programs aim to assist and compensate elderly persons who experience age-related declines in function. Services tend to focus on financial support, disease management, assistance with adaptive functioning, and promotion of social well-being. Disability programs focus on education, job training, and residential services (Heller & Marks, 2006). As more people live longer and potentially develop disabilities, and more persons with long-term disabilities live into older age, greater attention is being given to the overlapping needs and constituencies of elderly persons and those with disabilities. Many of the key issues of concern to older people and people with disabilities of all ages are similar; for example, family caregiving, residential options, consumer-directed services, and accessible transportation (Lightfoot, 2007).

Federal and state initiatives address issues of family support through both disability services and aging services. In 2003, the Administration on Aging and the Centers for Medicare and Medicaid jointly developed the Aging and Disabilities Resource Centers (ADRCs), a network of coordinated informational centers designed to streamline access to long-term care. ADRC programs provide information and assistance to individuals needing either public or private resources, to professionals seeking assistance on behalf of their clients, and to individuals planning for their future long-term care needs. The programs also serve as the entry point to publicly administered long-term supports, including those funded under Medicaid, the Older Americans Act, and state revenue programs (Administration on Aging, 2010). To date, nearly every state has an ADRC, though many limit the scope of the type of disabilities they serve.

Self-Determination and Participation

Older adults with lifelong disabilities have the same rights to personal growth as do others without such disabilities (Nowak, 1999). Integral to personal growth is the exercise of choice and self-determination (Dybwad, 1999; Levitz, 1999). Choice needs to be informed, so aging adults can define, when it is appropriate, what long-range planning can be most useful to them. This planning may emphasize skills acquisition, promote independent self-care, and introduce rewarding use of leisure time, as well as help sustain current skills. Individuals with lifelong disabilities may require lifelong assistance. However, such assistance does not need to subordinate the individual or eliminate the exercise of choice. Consistent with autonomy are initiatives on Cash and Counseling, modifying home environments, planning for later life and retirement, and promoting health and preventing disease (Ansello & Janicki, 2000).

Older adults with developmental disabilities typically have had few opportunities to exercise self-determination in their lives (Heller, Factor, Sterns, & Sutton, 1996) and hence often have little understanding of, and few skills to express, their desires. Later-life planning interventions have been developed to provide individuals with intellectual and developmental disabilities with knowledge and opportunities to make choices as they age (Heller & Caldwell, 2006). These interventions give persons with intellectual and developmental disabilities increased knowledge of later-life options, access to leisure activities for individuals living with families, and opportunities for choice making (Heller et al., 1996, 2000).

Retirement

As people are living longer, there are different challenges facing older people with a disability. Aging people with lifelong disabilities move beyond the traditional skills development or job programs (Bigby, 1997), and retirement from these work experiences becomes a more common expectation (Ansello & Janicki, 2000). Similar to many older adults in the general population, many older adults with disabilities prefer to continue working as long as possible and desire to obtain better-paying jobs in the community (Heller, 1999). A major ongoing concern is that despite aspirations for continuing inclusion, older people with disabilities experience few opportunities to participate in meaningful day and leisure activities of their choice (Bigby, 2005).

Summary: Disability and Aging

There has been a significant increase in numbers of people aging with a disability, as well as people acquiring a disability in later life. While these two groups may have different support needs, a number of similar challenges remain. For families, there are ongoing and increased support needs as caregivers age, or as adult children live longer in the family home. Future planning and the role of siblings in the care of older people with a disability are essential areas of concern for many families. There are a number of specific disability health-related issues and problems that tend to occur earlier than in people without disabilities, and there remains limited knowledge about age-related health conditions for people with disabilities. Policies are not well developed to support aging people with a disability in the community, and further integration between aging policies and disability policies is needed. Issues around choice and self-determination become even more prevalent as people age, especially for those individuals who have had limited opportunities across their lifespan to learn self-determination skills.

Death and Dying

The fact that people with disabilities are reaching older adulthood in greater numbers has resulted in a multitude of new challenges and debates in both the aging and disability fields. The natural processes of aging may be more stressful for some people with disabilities because of a greater dependence on others for everyday support. As more middle-age individuals with various types of disabilities live into older adulthood, and many times outlive parents and siblings, they might face their own mortality alone.

Death should be viewed as unique to individuals, but occurring within particular social contexts, which suggests that the process of dying involves both an objective biological fact and a socially negotiated construction (Corr, Doka, & Kastenbaum, 1999). For people with disabilities, death is often constructed as less tragic, timelier, more expedient, or more merciful than it is for people without disabilities. It is less likely to be considered premature or untimely, which may reflect the low social and economic value attributed to the lives of people with disabilities (Priestley, 2003). There are new controversies facing families, health professionals, and policymakers in the area of death and dying. These debates embody science, culture, religion, and moral beliefs—all of which play a significant, and at times conflicting, role in valuing and determining what should guide end of life decisions, and what should be done as general principles and in individual cases.

Family

The life expectancy of people with disabilities has increased, although it is still shorter overall than for people without disabilities. Therefore, the experience of death among their contemporaries is also much more common. Despite this, there can be an overprotection of some people with a disability from knowledge of death or impending death (Hollins & Tuffrey-Wijne, 2005). The role of the family is critical in helping people with disabilities, across all generational stages, understand what death and dying means. However, the literature notes how many families are concerned about the capacity of the person with a disability to understand and cope with the finality of death, or alternatively do not recognize their need to be informed and included, and to grieve (Blackman, 2003).

Although not specific to disability, families may be unfamiliar with talking openly about illness and death, and feel very anxious about discussing such topics with other family members. In cases of an illness of the person with a disability, health professionals may not have the skill or familiarity to effectively communicate about death, dying, and other serious health concerns, especially with people who use different modes of communication. Oftentimes, health professionals leave it up to the family to discuss, as it is usually the families that have developed the most effective ways of communicating with the member with disabilities (Hollins & Tuffrey-Wijne, 2005).

The need for appropriate death education and bereavement counseling for individuals with intellectual disabilities has been recognized by many in the applied field (Sterns et al., 2000). One of the challenges in dealing with death and dying for people with a developmental disability is that it is still considered to be a "taboo." Family members may feel inadequate or uncomfortable discussing the subject. Parents may be reluctant to address the issues of their own death or may not know how to discuss death openly and appropriately with their son or daughter. Staff and other caregivers may believe that death experiences are too stressful for individuals with developmental disabilities, whose ability to cope with everyday stressors may be compromised. Staff and caregivers may not see the need to include, educate, or support aging adults with intellectual disabilities who may face death, dying, and loss experiences (Sterns et al., 2000). A common belief is that individuals with intellectual disabilities do not possess or are not capable of a mature understanding of the concept of death (Yanok & Beifus, 1993). However, there is little supporting evidence for this belief.

Although families and professionals alike are too often tempted to protect older people with developmental disabilities from the necessity of coping with the losses associated with aging, such interference denies them important opportunities to learn and grow (Ludlow, 1999). Families may withhold information or give incomplete or inappropriate information in an attempt to protect the individual. They may also attempt to limit the person's response or expressions of grief, or not allow him or her time to deal with and adjust to loss. Staff in residential and day care settings also want and need education, emotional support, and assistance in dealing with end-of-life issues, in order to better prepare people with disabilities in their care to deal with end-of-life issues (Botsford, 2000a).

Health

End-of-Life Care and Advance Medical Directives

A controversial issue for people with disabilities in terms of end-of-life care is the strong push for encouraging older people to file advance directives for health care. There are ongoing debates among families, health care professionals, and people with disabilities about whether advance directives support autonomy of the individuals or represent a form of "rationing." One debate centers on how older people are encouraged to sign away their rights to future care on the presumption that living in a state of "dependency" would be intolerable (Kane & Kane, 2005). These debates are evident in both the disability and aging fields.

Another challenging area is the aging of carers of adult children with disabilities, in particular adults with an intellectual disability who may be living with parents who have a decline in cognitive functioning (i.e., Alzheimer's). A process of surrogate medical decision making may be needed for individuals with an intellectual disability requiring medical care in cases where parents are unavailable. An effective solution is establishing a proxy directive, if a close family member or friend is available. The research has shown that many older adults with intellectual disabilities, if provided with adequate and timely counseling, are capable of choosing someone they know to serve in a proxy role (Kapp, 1999). The right to control medical decisions, personally or through a surrogate, allows people with disabilities to make meaningful choices in terms of their health care as they or their primary carers age.

End-of-life decision making means making choices that are likely to affect the quality of someone's remaining life, how long someone will live, and where they will live and be cared for. In terms of end-of-life palliative care, disability-specific services and support are lacking. Community care systems, for instance, have been focused on increasing independence, and on serving younger adults. Therefore, the transition to providing increased support and end-of-life care may be difficult (Todd, 2005). Furthermore, palliative health care professionals have had restricted exposure to disability, which has resulted in limited training and information on best practices in terms of end-of-life care for people with disabilities (Tuffrey-Wijne, Hogg, & Curfs, 2007). This lack of information results in ongoing debates around the "value" of the lives of people with disabilities.

Disability-Adjusted Life Years

The use of disability-adjusted life years (DALY) has significant implications on the value of life for people with disabilities, and on the approach taken by health care professionals. Developed by the World Health Organization (WHO) in 1993, the DALY measures the impact of premature death, impairment, and disease in terms of years of healthy life lost. It relies on the idea that "years of life" of people with certain kinds of impairment can be regarded as "years of life lost," even though the person may still be living.

The use of DALY calculations has been subject to much debate and controversy. Disability rights scholars have argued that impairment diagnosis alone tells us very little about the expectancy of quality of life for people with disabilities. The real barriers to dignity and quality of life stem from broader cultural and social constructs. While there is evidence that people with certain impairments are more likely to die at a younger age, differential access to medical treatment, health care, healthy environments, and welfare resources play a large part in the lowered life expectancy of people with disabilities. Therefore, the labeling in the DALY of specific impairments as equivalent to "years of life lost" perpetuates an approach to policy and resource allocation that places a lower value on the life of people with disabilities (Priestley, 2003).

Policy, Legislation, and Services

The most significant policy issue that impacts different generational stages of disability, but is most prevalent within later life, concerns physician-assisted suicide and euthanasia. Within these debates, there are two key questions: whether people have the right to die by refusing medical treatment, and whether people have the right to die by acting positively to cause death. Dworkin, Frey, and Bok (1998) note the important role of both science and morality in framing these controversial debates, and provide strong arguments both for and against euthanasia and physician-assisted suicide. Proponents argue that it is both morally and legally permissible for physicians to provide the knowledge and means by which patients can take their own lives; whereas opponents call for caution in moving forward with such measures, particularly in a risk-laden context of inadequate health insurance.

Disability issues have figured prominently in these debates, since many of the most contested legal cases and legislative debates have involved people whose impairments limit their functional capacity to take their own lives without assistance. The issues surrounding euthanasia have been strongly contested by legal, medical, and religious establishments, as well as by disability activists. The debates center on fears that euthanasia procedures may be open to abuse and that people with disabilities, and older people with disabilities in particular, may be more heavily targeted for "voluntary" deaths.

Advocates of assisted death for people with disabilities have often based their arguments on calls for "death with dignity." The controversial assumptions that underpin these arguments concern the perceived poor quality of life that results from having an impairment. Furthermore, disability is often confused with terminal illness by some ethicists and physicians, in judicial rulings, by assisted suicide advocates, and in news media (Longmore, 2003). These perceptions can support practices of encouraging death via assisted suicide and other means for people who, although vulnerable, are not at the end of their lives (Schwartz & Lutfiyya, 2009).

There is an increase in the number of physician-assisted suicide cases in which people with disabilities are assisted to die. The main difference between physician-assisted suicide and euthanasia is that in assisted suicide, the patient is in complete control of the process that leads to death, because the patient actually performs the act of suicide. The other person simply helps (for example, by providing the means for carrying out the action). Disability groups have been active in campaigning on right-to-life issues, and in protesting eugenic abuses in cases of child killing, euthanasia, and assisted death (Priestley, 2003). Disability advocates argue that many people with disabilities who request assisted suicide worry about being a "burden" on their family, or lack adequate financial, health care, and social supports. With better supports and improved palliative care, they argue, the desire to terminate one's life would be reduced. However, the arguments that disability rights advocates present in opposition to legalized assisted suicide are frequently misconstrued as restricting choice and autonomy of people with terminal illness at the end of life (Gill, 2010), which has contributed to ongoing highly controversial and public debates within and across disability and aging fields.

Self-Determination and Participation

In the late 1960s, the hospice care movement introduced death as an issue for public discussion, professional training, and re-examination of care practices. The values of death with dignity, respect for the individuality of the dying person, and empowerment of the dying person to make decisions about her or his care, death, and funeral emerged from this period. The focus was on the needs, preferences, and wishes of the dying individual and the need to support the survivors through their grief and bereavement (Botsford, 2000a).

However, many people with disabilities lack access to appropriate and usable information concerning dying, which puts them at a disadvantage (Priestley, 2003). The availability of choices regarding end-of-life issues, such as what treatment or care is to be provided and where, is crucial for the achievement of an optimal quality of life; yet this is difficult to achieve if the person concerned is not informed and involved. Providing appropriate and sensitive end-of-life support, regardless of the age of the dying person, presents a significant challenge to family, support networks, and services (Hollins & Tuffrey-Wijne, 2005).

People with disabilities have often been excluded from supportive rituals and education about the end of life. There is an ongoing need to help older people with disabilities to understand that changes may occur in their environment as a result of the death of friends, loved ones, and caregivers, and to assist them in expressing their losses. Some of the more positive strategies in assisting people with developmental disabilities include death education, grief counseling, support groups, bereavement services, crisis teams, certified staff, and end-of-life committees (Botsford, 2000a, 2000b).

Summary: Death and Dying

Issues around death and dying are highly controversial for people both with and without disabilities. However, for people with disabilities and their families, aging is associated with many additional aspects of loss, and raises further debates on the value of life. Talking about dying, death, and serious illness can be difficult for anyone; however, there are additional supports needed for families and health/disability support professionals dealing with such critical issues concerning people with an intellectual or developmental disability. End-of-life care and advance medical directives continue to feature prominently in the aging and disability field, and further education is needed for both families and medical professionals on what these mean for people with disabilities. The most significant controversy in this life stage has to do with physician-assisted suicide and euthanasia, debates that touch on legal, moral, ethical, and medical dilemmas. For individuals to exercise self-determination in the domain of death and dying, it requires a shift in broader notions of the value of life. Ongoing challenges remain as the population of aging people with a disability increases.

Conclusion

There are a number of complex and interrelated debates in a life course approach to disability. Many people with disabilities continue to experience exclusion and discrimination from birth and childhood, through adulthood, to aging and dying. As a result, increasing the effectiveness of support and policies across the life course becomes critical if people with disabilities and their families are to achieve a good quality of life and meaningful participation in the wider community.

One controversial issue that cuts across generational stages concerns the quality of life, the value of life, and the worth of a person with a disability. This important issue impacts socio-cultural understandings of disability; creates new legislative and policy responses; challenges medical approaches to disability; and raises moral and ethical debates that involve individuals, families, health professionals, disability scholars and activists, and government. Notions on the value of a life for disability begin with conception and continue to end of life.

A related challenge in this area centers on development of capacity, skill, and opportunities in self-determination. This is an ongoing process, prevalent from a young age and continuing well into later adulthood. Issues around choice and self-determination become even more ubiquitous as people age, especially for those individuals who have had limited opportunities across their lifespan to learn self-determination skills. People with disabilities can sometimes be caught between what the family wants and what they want, and this problem can be compounded by broader structural barriers and influences. Constraints to equal participation and self-determination have been ameliorated to some extent with the consumer movement and an increase in self-advocacy. Policies and practices that provide greater control of one's life, such as deinstitutionalization, disability-friendly accessible environments, and consumer-directed services, also contribute to the self-determination of persons with disabilities across the life course.

The importance of family involvement and support is critical at all stages, and is essential in a life course approach to disabilities. The role of the family in assisting young people as they move to adulthood can be fraught with challenges, as many families seek to support growing independence within a context of protection. As many people with a disability continue to live with their families into adulthood, there is increased need for formalized supports and services to support both individuals with disabilities and their families. Future planning and the role of siblings in the care of older people with a disability is a major area of concern for many families. What is often missing in the discussion of family caregiving is the realization that people with disabilities are not only recipients of care, but also provide care and support to other family members. A major issue for debate is the extent to which families should receive payment for the provision of care to a member with disabilities.

The role of health and medical professionals at times enhances a life course approach to disabilities and, at other times, can be in conflict with individuals and their families. Medical advances have changed approaches to disability from birth to death, increased knowledge and awareness, and provided better quality of life. However, medical advances have also led to a number of new controversies related to genetic screening and diagnoses, as well as end-of-life choices including medical directives, physician-assisted suicide, and euthanasia. There needs to be greater emphasis on the additional health-care costs of having a disability across the life course, as many people with disabilities face significant financial challenges due to poorer outcomes in health and wellness. As people with disabilities live much longer, there is also a growing problem related to the limited knowledge of health professionals, service providers, families, and people with disabilities about age-related health conditions. Furthermore, there is a growing recognition of the social determinants of health and the role that earlier environmental and behavioral risk factors play in later-life health. Hence, we need greater education regarding the interaction of disability with these social determinants of health, as well as more effective screening, health promotion, and health access interventions across the life course.

Transitions among generational stages are significant areas that require greater support and policies, particularly in domains of education, employment, health, and sexuality. Oftentimes, children with disabilities can be caught between policies of mainstreaming and specialization, which creates significant barriers to full participation. As young people transition into adulthood, conflicts around sexual expression arise, and there is a lack of consistent information available for families, policymakers, or in the education system. People making the transition into adulthood also face challenges in the areas of employment, housing, welfare, and health. Working-age people with a disability experience high rates of unemployment, and this leads to a significant number of people with disabilities living in poverty. In later life, policies are not well developed to support aging people with a disability in the community, and further integration between aging policies and disability policies is needed.

A life course perspective helps us understand the developmental trajectories for people with disabilities and their families. This approach assumes that what happens earlier in life affects subsequent periods in one's life. In addition, it recognizes the great variability in people, and the fact that development does not necessarily proceed in clear stages. The disability studies approach adds to this life course perspective by bringing in the concepts of disability identity and societal attitudes toward disability as important factors throughout the lives of people with disabilities. Core themes that stem from a critical disability studies approach, such as the role of the family, the influence of policy and legislation, and the ability and opportunities to enact self-determination, are all significant in furthering our understanding of disability across the life course.

References

Abbeduto, L., Seltzer, M. M., Shattuck, P., Krauss, M. W., Orsmond, G., & Murphy, M. M. (2004). Psychological well-being and coping in mothers of youths with autism, Down syndrome, or fragile X syndrome. *American Journal on Mental Retardation, 109*(3), 237–254.

Acemoglu, D., & Angrist, J. (2001). Consequences of employment protection? The case of the Americans with Disabilities Act. *Journal of Political Economy, 109*(5), 915–957.

Acton G. J., & Kang, J. (2001). Interventions to reduce the burden of caregiving for an adult with dementia: A meta-analysis. *Research in Nursing & Health, 24*(5), 349–360.

Administration on Aging. (2010). *ADRC factsheet*. Retrieved from http://www.aoa.gov/AoAroot/Press_Room/Products_Materials/fact/pdf/ADRC.pdf

Ailey, S., Mark, B., Crisp, C., & Hahn, J. (2003). Promoting sexuality across the lifespan for individuals with intellectual and developmental disabilities. *Nursing Clinics of North America, 38*(2), 229–252.

Alderson, P. (2002). Prenatal counseling and images of disability. In D. L. Dickenson (Ed.), *Ethical issues in maternal fetal medicine*. Cambridge, UK: Cambridge University Press.

Alzheimer's Association. (2010). *Alzheimer's disease facts and figures*. Retrieved from http://www.alz.org/documents_custom/report_alzfactsfigures2010.pdf

Ansello, E. F., & Janicki, M. P. (2000). The aging of nations: Impact on the community, the family and the individual. In M. P. Janicki & E. F. Ansello (Eds.), *Community supports for aging adults with lifelong disabilities*. Baltimore: Paul H. Brookes.

Arcelus, J., & Vostanis, P. (2005). Psychiatric comorbidity in children and adolescents. *Current Opinion in Psychiatry, 18*, 429–434.

Arnett, J. J. (2004). *Emerging adulthood: The winding road from the late teens through the twenties*. Oxford, UK: Oxford University Press.

Asch, A. (1989). Reproductive technology and disability. In S. Cohen & N. Taub (Eds.), *Reproductive laws for the 1990s*. Clifton, NJ: Humana Press.

Baird, G., McConachie, H., & Scrutton, D. (2000). Parents' perception of disclosure of the diagnosis of cerebral palsy. *Archives of Disease in Childhood, 83*, 475–480.

Barusch, A. S. (2009). *Foundations of social policy: Social justice in human perspective*. Belmont, CA: Brooks-Cole.

Bayat, M. (2007). Evidence of resilience in families of children with autism. *Journal of Intellectual Disability Research, 51*(9), 702–714.

Beale, I. L. (2006). Scholarly literature review: Efficacy of psychological interventions for pediatric chronic illnesses. *Journal of Pediatric Psychology, 31*(5), 437–451.

Beckman, P. J. (1991). Comparison of mothers' and fathers' perceptions of the effect of young children with and without disabilities. *American Journal on Mental Retardation, 95*, 585–595.

Bigby, C. (1997). Later life for adults with intellectual disability: A time of opportunity and vulnerability. *Journal of Intellectual and Developmental Disabilities, 22*, 97–108.

Bigby, C. (2000). *Moving on without parents: Planning, transitions and sources of support for middle aged and older adults with intellectual disability.* Baltimore: Paul H. Brookes.

Bigby, C. (2005). Growing old: Adapting to change and realizing a sense of belonging, continuity and purpose. In G. Grant, P. Goward, M. Richardson, & P. Ramcharan (Eds.), *Learning disability: A life cycle approach to valuing people.* New York: Open University Press.

Bijma, H. H., Schoonderwaldt, E. M., van der Heide, A., Wildschut, H. I., van der Maas, P. J., & Wladimiroff, J. W. (2004). Ultrasound diagnosis of fetal anomalies: An analysis of perinatal management of 318 consecutive pregnancies in a multidisciplinary setting. *Prenatal Diagnosis, 24*, 890–895.

Binks, J., Barden, W., Burke, T., & Young, N. (2007). What do we really know about the transition to adult-centered health care? A focus on cerebral palsy and spina bifida. *Archives of Physical Medicine and Rehabilitation, 88*, 1064–1073.

Bjelland, M., Burkhauser, R., & Houtenville, A. (2008). *2008 progress report on the economic well-being of working age people with disabilities* [Electronic version]. Ithaca, NY: Rehabilitation Research and Training Center for Economic Research on Employment Policy for Persons with Disabilities.

Blacher, J., & McIntyre, L. L. (2006). Syndrome specificity and behavioural disorders in young adults with intellectual disability: Cultural differences in family impact. *Journal of Intellectual Disability Research, 50*(3), 184–198.

Blacher, J., Shapiro, J., Lopez, S., Diaz, L., & Fusco, J. (1997). Depression in Latina mothers of children with mental retardation: A neglected concern. *American Journal on Mental Retardation, 101*, 483–496.

Blackman, J. A. (1991). Neonatal intensive care: Is it worth it? Developmental sequelae of very low birthweight. *Pediatric Clinics of North America, 38*(6), 1497–1511.

Blackman, N. (2003). *Loss and learning disability.* London: Worth.

Blanck, P., & Schartz, H. (2001). *Towards researching a national employment policy for persons with disabilities.* Law, Health Policy & Disability Center, University of Iowa. Retrieved from http://disability.law.uiowa.edu/lhpdc/publications/blanckpubs.html

Blanck, P., Schur, L., Kruse, D., Schwochau, S., & Song, C. (2003). Calibrating the impact of the ADA's employment provisions. *Stanford Law and Policy Review, 14*(2), 267–290.

Botsford, A. (2000a). Dealing with the end of life. In M. P. Janicki & E. F. Ansello (Eds.), *Community supports for aging adults with lifelong disabilities.* Baltimore: Paul H. Brookes.

Botsford, A. (2000b). Integrating end of life care into services for people with an intellectual disability. *Social Work in Health Care, 31*(1), 35–48.

Bourke, S., & Burgman, I. (2010). Coping with bullying in Australian schools: How children with disabilities experience support from friends, parents and teachers. *Disability and Society, 25*(3), 359–371.

Braddock, D., Hemp, R., & Rizzolo, M. C. (2008). *The state of the states in developmental disabilities: 2008.* Boulder: University of Colorado, Coleman Institute for Cognitive Disabilities and Department of Psychiatry.

Bridgens, R. (2009). Disability and being "normal": A response to McLaughlin and Goodley. *Sociology, 43*(4), 753–761.

Calandrillo, S. P. (2004). Vanishing vaccinations: Why are so many Americans opting out of vaccinating their children? *University of Michigan Journal of Law Reform, 37*(2), 353.

Caldwell, J. (2006). Consumer-directed supports: Economic, health, and social outcomes for families. *Mental Retardation, 44*, 405–417.

Caldwell, J. (2010). Perspectives. Implications of health care reform for individuals with disabilities. *Intellectual and Developmental Disabilities, 48*(3), 216–219.

Caldwell, J., Hauss, S., & Stark, B. (2009). Participation of individuals with disabilities and families on advisory boards and committees. *Journal of Disability Policy Studies, 20*(2), 101–109.

Caldwell, J., & Heller, T. (2003). Management of respite and personal assistance services in a consumer-directed family support programme. *Journal of Intellectual Disability Research, 47*, 352–366.

Carlson, B., Dale, S., Foster, L., Brown, R., Phillips, B., & Schore, J. (2005). *Effect of consumer direction on adults' personal care and well-being in Arkansas, New Jersey, and Florida.* Washington, DC: U.S. Department of Health and Human Services, Office of Disability, Aging, and Long-Term Care Policy. Retrieved from http://aspe.hhs.gov/daltcp/reports/adultpcw.htm

Centers for Disease Control and Prevention. (2008). Racial/ethnic disparities in self-rated health status among adults with and without disabilities—United States, 2004–2006. *MMWR, 57*(39), 1069–1073.

Chan, K., Ohlsson, A., Synnes, A., Lee, D. S., Chien, L. Y., & Lee, S. K. (2001). Survival, morbidity, and resource use of infants of 25 weeks' gestational age or less. *American Journal of Obstetrics and Gynecology, 185*(1), 220–226.

Chen, F. P., & Greenberg, J. S. (2004). Caregiving gains in family care for people with mental illness. *Community Mental Health, 40*, 423–435.

Cicirelli, V. G. (1995). *Sibling relationships across the life span.* New York: Plenum Press.

Cole-Hamilton, I., & McBride, S. (1996). *Taking the time: Telling parents their child is blind or partially sighted.* London: Royal National Institute for the Blind.

Connors, C., & Stalker, K. (2007). Children's experiences of disability: Pointers to a social model of childhood disability. *Disability & Society, 22,* 19–33.

Cook, J. A. (2005). *"Patient-centered" and "consumer-directed" mental health services.* Washington, DC: Institute on Medicine.

Corr, C. A., Doka, K. J., & Kastenbaum, R. (1999). Dying and its interpreters: A review of selected literature and some comments on the state of the field. *Omega-Journal of Death and Dying, 39*(4), 239–259.

Crook, P. (2008). The new eugenics? The ethics of bio-technology. *Journal of Politics and History, 54*(1), 135–143.

Danziger, S., & Ratner, D. (2010). Labor market outcomes and the transition to adulthood. *The Future of Children, 20*(1), 133–158.

Davies, P., Chapman, S., & Leask, J. (2002). Antivacccination activists on the World Wide Web. *Archives of Disease in Childhood, 87,* 22–25.

de Blij, H. (2009). *The power of place: Geography, destiny, and globalizations's rough landscape.* New York: Oxford University Press.

DeLeire, T. (2000). The unintended consequences of the Americans with Disabilities Act. *Regulation, 23*(1), 21–24.

DiNapoli, P. P., & Murphy, D. (2002). The marginalization of chronically ill adolescents. *Nursing Clinics of North America, 37,* 565–572.

Donaldson, S. (2002). Work stress and people with Down syndrome and dementia. *Down Syndrome: Research and Practice, 8*(2), 74–78.

Doornbos, M. M. (2002). Family caregivers and the mental health care system: Reality or dreams. *Archives of Psychiatric Nursing, 16*(1), 39–46.

Drapalski, A., Marshall, T., Seybolt, D., Medoff, D., Peer, J., Leith, J., et al. (2008). Unmet need of families of adults with mental illness and preferences regarding family services. *Psychiatric Services, 59*(6), 655–662.

Drum, C. E., Horner-Johnson, W., & Krahn, G. L. (2008). Self-rated health and healthy days: Examining the "disability paradox." *Disability Health Journal, 1,* 71–78.

Dunst, C. J. (2002). Family-centered practices: Birth through high school. *The Journal of Special Education, 36,* 139–147.

Duszak, A. (2002). *Us and others: Social identities across languages, discourses and cultures.* Philadelphia: John Benjamin.

Dworkin, G., Frey, R. G., & Bok, S. (1998). *Euthanasia and physician-assisted suicide: For and against.* Cambridge, UK: Cambridge University Press.

Dybwad, G. (1999). Foreword. In S. S. Herr & G. Weber (Eds.), *Aging, rights and quality of life: Prospects for older people with developmental disabilities.* Baltimore: Paul H. Brookes.

Evenhuis, H., Henderson, C., Beange, H., Lennox, N., & Chicoine, B. (2001). Healthy aging–adults with intellectual disabilities: Physical health issues. *Journal of Applied Research in Intellectual Disabilities, 14*(3), 175–194.

Ferguson, P. M. (2001). Mapping the family: Disability studies and the exploration of parental response to disability. In G. L. Albrecht, K. D. Seelman, & M. Bury (Eds.), *Handbook of disability studies* (pp. 373–395). Thousand Oaks, CA: Sage.

Ferris, J. (2004). Child of no one. In *The hospital poems*. Charlotte, NC: Main Street Rag. Retrieved from http://www.mainstreetrag.com/JFerris.html

Feudtner, C., & Marcuse, E. K. (2001). Ethics and immunization policy: Promoting dialogue to sustain consensus. *Pediatrics, 107*(5), 1158–1164.

Foster, L., Brown, R., Phillips, B., Schore, J., & Carlson, B. L. (2003). Improving the quality of Medicaid personal assistance through consumer direction. *Health Affairs, 22,* 162–175.

Freedman, R. I., Krauss, M. W., & Seltzer, M. M. (1997). Aging parents' residential plans for adult children with mental retardation. *Mental Retardation, 35*(2), 114–123.

Fujiura, G. T. (1998). Demography of family households. *Mental Retardation, 103*(3), 225–235.

Fujiura, G. T., Yamaki, K., & Czechowicz, S. (1998). Disability among ethnic and racial minorities in the United States. *Journal of Disability Policy Studies, 9,* 111–130.

Galambos, N. L. (2004). On the road to nowhere? Young disabled people and transition. *Child Care, Health and Development, 30,* 581–587.

Gill, C. J. (2010). No, we don't think our doctors are out to get us: Responding to the straw man distortions of disability rights arguments against assisted suicide. *Disability and Health Journal, 3,* 31–38.

Gledhill, J., Rangel, L., & Garralda, E. (2000). Surviving chronic physical illness: Psychosocial outcome in adult life. *Archives of Disease in Childhood, 83,* 104–110.

Goin-Kochel, R. P., Mackintosh, V. H., & Myers, B. J. (2006). How many doctors does it take to make an autism spectrum diagnosis? *Autism, 10*(5), 439–451.

Goodman, N. J., & Stapleton, D. C. (2007). Federal program expenditures for working-age people with disabilities. *Journal of Disability Policy Studies, 18*(2), 66–78.

Goodman, N. J., & Waidmann, T. (2003). Social Security Disability Insurance and the recent decline in the employment rate of people with disabilities. In D. C. Stapleton & R. V. Burkhauser (Eds.), *The decline in employment of people with disabilities: A policy puzzle*. Kalamazoo, MI: W. E. Upjohn Institute.

Grant, G. (2005). Healthy and successful ageing. In G. Grant, P. Goward, M. Richardson, & P. Ramcharan (Eds.), *Learning disability: A life cycle approach to valuing people*. New York: Open University Press.

Greenberg, J. S., Seltzer, M. M., Orsmond, G. I., & Krauss, M.W. (1999). Siblings of adults with mental illness or mental retardation: Current involvement and expectation of future caregiving. *Psychiatric Services, 5,* 1214–1219.

Grosse, S. P., McBride, C. M., Evans, J. P., & Khoury, M. J. (2009). Personal utility and genomic information: Look before you leap. *Genetic Medicine, 11*(8), 570–574.

Ha, J., Hong, J., Seltzer, M. M., & Greenberg, J. S. (2008). Age and gender differences in the well-being of midlife and aging parents with children with mental health problems or developmental disorders: Report of a national study. *Journal of Health and Social Behavior, 49*, 301–316.

Hack, M., Taylor, H. G., Drotar, D., Schluchter, M., Cartar, L., Andreias, L., et al. (2005). Chronic conditions, functional limitations, and special health care needs of school-aged children born with extremely low birth-weight in the 1990s. *Journal of the American Medical Association, 294*, 318–325.

Hammel J., Lai, J., & Heller, T. (2002). The impact of assistive technology and environmental interventions on function and living situation status with people who are ageing with developmental disabilities. *Disability & Rehabilitation, 24*, 93–105.

Harris, S. B., Petrella, R. J., Lambert-Lanning, A., Leadbetter, W., & Cranston, L. (2004). Lifestyle management for type 2 diabetes: Are family physicians ready and willing? *Canadian Family Physician, 50*, 1235–1243.

Hartley, S. L., Barker, E. T., Seltzer, M. M., Floyd, F., Greenberg, J., Orsmond, G., et al. (2010). The relative risk and timing in divorce in families of children with an autism spectrum disorder. *Journal of Family Psychology, 24*(4), 449–457.

Hauser-Cram, P., Bronson, M. B., & Upshur, C. C. (1993). The effects of the classroom environment on the social and mastery behavior of preschool children with disabilities. *Early Childhood Research Quarterly, 8*, 479–497.

Haveman, M., Heller, T., Lee, L., Maaskant, M., Shooshtari, S., & Strydom, A. (2010). Major health risks in aging persons with intellectual disabilities: An overview of recent studies. *Journal of Policy and Practice in Intellectual Disabilities, 7*(1), 59–69.

Haveman, M., van Berkum, G., Reijnders, R., & Heller, T. (1997). Differences in service needs, time demands, and caregiving burden among parents of persons with mental retardation across the life cycle. *Family Relations, 46*(4), 417–425.

Havercamp, S. M., Scandlin, D., & Roth, M. (2004). Health disparities among adults with developmental disabilities, adults with other disabilities, and adults not reporting disability in North Carolina. *Public Health Reports, 119*, 418–426.

Health Resources and Services Administration. (2000). *Understanding Title V.* Retrieved from http://mchb.hrsa.gov/about/understandingtitlev.pdf

Heinz, W. R. (2009). Youth transitions in an age of uncertainty. In A. Furlong (Ed.), *Handbook of youth and young adulthood: New perspectives and agendas.* New York: Routledge.

Heller, T. (1999). Emerging models. In S. S. Herr & G. Weber (Eds.), *Aging, rights and quality of life: Prospects for older people with developmental disabilities.* Baltimore: Paul H. Brookes.

Heller, T., & Arnold, C. K. (2010). Siblings of adults with developmental disabilities: Psychosocial outcomes, relationships, and future planning. *Journal of Policy and Practice in Intellectual Disabilities, 7*(1), 16–25.

Heller, T., & Caldwell, J. (2005). Impact of a consumer-directed family support program on reduced out-of-home institutional placement. *Journal of Policy and Practice in Intellectual Disabilities, 2,* 63–65.

Heller, T., & Caldwell, J. (2006). Supporting aging caregivers and adults with developmental disabilities in future planning. *Mental Retardation, 44*(3), 189–202.

Heller, T., Caldwell, J., & Factor, A. (2007). Aging family caregivers: Policies and practices. *Mental Retardation and Developmental Disabilities Research Reviews, 13,* 136–142.

Heller, T., & Factor, A. (1993). Aging family caregivers: Support resources and changes in burden and placement desire. *American Journal on Mental Retardation, 98*(3), 417–426.

Heller, T., & Factor, A. (1994). Facilitating future planning and transitions out of the home. In M. M. Seltzer, M. W. Krauss, & M. P. Janicki (Eds.), *Life course perspectives on adulthood and old age* (pp. 39–52). Washington, DC: American Association on Mental Retardation.

Heller, T., Factor, A. R., Sterns, H. L., & Sutton, E. (1996). Impact of person-centered late life planning training program for older adults with mental retardation. *Journal of Rehabilitation, 16,* 77–83.

Heller, T., Kaiser, A., Meyer, D., Fish, T., Kramer, J., & Dufresne, D. (2008). *The Sibling Leadership Network: Recommendations for research, advocacy, and supports relating to siblings of people with developmental disabilities.* Chicago: Rehabilitation Research and Training Center on Aging with Developmental Disabilities: Lifespan Health and Function, University of Illinois at Chicago.

Heller, T., & Marks, B. (2006). Aging. In G. L. Albrecht (Ed.), *Encyclopedia of disability* (Vol. 1, pp. 67–78). Thousand Oaks, CA: Sage.

Heller, T., McCubbin, J. A., Drum, C., & Peterson, J. (in press). Physical activity and nutrition health promotion interventions: What is working for people with intellectual disabilities? *Intellectual and Developmental Disabilities.*

Heller, T., Miller, A. B., & Hsieh, K. (1999). Impact of a consumer-directed family support program on adults with disabilities. *Family Relations, 48,* 419–427.

Heller, T., Miller, A. B., & Hsieh, K. (2002). Eight-year follow-up of the impact of environmental characteristics on well-being of adults with developmental disabilities. *Mental Retardation, 40,* 366–378.

Heller, T., Miller, A. B., Hsieh, K., & Sterns, H. (2000). Later-life planning: Promoting knowledge of options and choice-making. *Mental Retardation, 38,* 395–406.

Heller, T., & Schindler, A. (2009). Family support interventions for families of adults with intellectual and developmental disabilities. In L. M. Glidden & M. M. Seltzer (Eds.), *International review in mental retardation: Vol. 9. Special issue on families* (pp. 300–325). New York: Academic Press.

Hintz, S. R., Kendrick, D. E., Vohr, B. E., Poole, K., & Higgins, R. D. (2008). Community supports after surviving extremely low birth-weight, extremely preterm birth: Special outpatient services in early childhood. *Archives of Pediatric and Adolescent Medicine, 162*(8), 748–755.

Hodapp, R. M., & Krasner, D. V. (1995). Families of children with disabilities: Findings from a national sample of eighth-grade students. *Exceptionality, 5*(32), 71–81.

Hogg, J., Moss, S., & Cooke, D. (1988). *Aging and mental handicap.* London: Croom Helm.

Hollins, S., & Tuffrey-Wijne, I. (2005). Promoting healthy life styles: End of life issues. In G. Grant, P. Goward, M. Richardson, & P. Ramcharan (Eds.), *Learning disability. A life cycle approach to valuing people.* New York: Open University Press.

Hooyman, N. R. (1983). Mobilizing social networks to prevent elderly abuse. *Physical and Occupational Therapy in Geriatrics, 2*(2), 21–33.

Horwitz, A. V. (1994). Predictors of adult sibling social support for the seriously mentally ill: An exploratory study. *Journal of Family Issues, 15,* 272–289.

Hudson, B. (2006). Making and missing connections: Learning disability services and the transition from adolescence to adulthood. *Disability & Society, 21*(1), 47–60.

Huws, J. C., & Jones, R. S. P. (2008). Diagnosis, disclosure, and having autism: An interpretative phenomenological analysis of the perceptions of young people with autism. *Journal of Intellectual & Developmental Disability, 33,* 99–107.

Jacobson, J. W. (2003). Prevalence of mental and behavioral disorders. In P. W. Davidson, V. P. Prasher, & M. P. Janicki (Eds.), *Mental health, intellectual disabilities and the ageing process.* Oxford, UK: Blackwell.

Janicki, M. P., McCallion, P., & Dalton, A. J. (2000). Supporting people with dementia in community settings. In M. P. Janicki & E. F. Ansello (Eds.), *Community supports for aging adults with lifelong disabilities.* Baltimore: Paul H. Brookes.

Janus, A. (2009). Disability and transition to adulthood. *Social Forces, 88*(1), 99–120.

Janvier, A., Barrington, K. J., Aziz, K., & Lantos, J. (2008). Ethics ain't easy: Do we need simple rules for complicated ethical decisions? *Acta Pædiatrica, 97*(4), 402–406.

Johnson, C. P., Kastner, T. A., & Committee on Children with Disabilities. (2005). Helping families raise children with special health care needs at home. *Pediatrics, 115*(2), 507–511.

Kane, R. L., & Kane, R. A. (2005). Ageism in healthcare and long term care. *Generations, 29*(3), 49–54.

Kapp, M. B. (1999). Health care decision making: Legal and financial considerations. In S. S. Herr & G. Weber (Eds.), *Aging, rights and quality of life: Prospects for older people with developmental disabilities.* Baltimore: Paul H. Brookes.

Kemp, B. J. (2004). Family member's perspective on aging with a disability. In B. J. Kemp & L. Mosqueda (Eds.), *Aging with a disability.* Baltimore: Johns Hopkins University Press.

Kemp, B. J., & Mosqueda, L. (2004). Introduction. In B. J. Kemp & L. Mosqueda (Eds.), *Aging with a disability: What the clinician needs to know.* Baltimore: Johns Hopkins University Press.

Kennedy, A., & Sawyer, S. (2008). Transition from pediatric to adult services: Are we getting it right? *Current Opinion in Pediatrics, 20*(4), 403–409.

Kerr, A., and Shakespeare, T. (2002). *Genetic politics: From eugenics to genome.* Cheltenham, UK: New Clarion Press.

King, D. (2001). Eugenic tendencies in modern genetics. In B. Tokar (Ed.), *Redesigning life? The worldwide challenge to genetic engineering* (pp. 171–181). New York: Zed Books.

Kingsley, E. P. (1987). Welcome to Holland. In P. Bartram, *Understanding your young child with special needs* (pp. 70–71). Philadelphia: Jessica Kingsley Publishers.

Kirshbaum, M., & Olkin, R. (2002). Parents with physical, systemic, or visual disabilities. *Sexuality and Disability, 20*(1), 65–80.

Kokkonen, J. (1995). The social effects in adult life of chronic physical illness since childhood. *European Journal of Pediatrics, 154,* 676–681.

Lachappelle, Y., Wehmeyer, M. L., Haelewyck, M. C., Courbois, Y., Keith, K. D., Schalock, R., et al. (2005). The relationship between quality of life and self-determination: An international study. *Journal of Intellectual Disability Research, 49,* 740–744.

Lavi, E., & Rosenburg, J. (2005). Disclosure of severe development disability: A survey of parents' experiences and preferences at an Israeli child development center. *Harefuah, 144*(5), 322–326, 383.

Lefly, H. P. (1987). Aging parents as caregivers of mentally ill adult children: An emerging social problem. *Hospital and Community Psychiatry, 38,* 1063–1070.

Leonard, B., Brust, J., & Sapienza, J. (1992). Financial and time costs to parents of severely disabled children. *Public Health Reports, 107*(3), 302–312.

Leonard, H., De Klerk, N., Bourke, J., & Bower, C. (2006). Maternal health in pregnancy and intellectual disability in the offspring: A population-based study. *Annals of Epidemiology, 16*(6), 448–454.

Levitz, M. (1999). Self-advocacy for a good life in our older years. In S. S. Herr & G. Weber (Eds.), *Aging, rights and quality of life: Prospects for older people with developmental disabilities.* Baltimore: Paul H. Brookes.

Lewis, A. (2009). Disability disparities: A beginning model. *Disability and Rehabilitation, 31*(14), 1136–1143.

Light, E., & Lebowitz, B. D. (Eds.). (1991). *The elderly with chronic mental illness.* New York: Springer.

Lightfoot, E. (2007). Disability. In J. A. Blackburn & C. D. Dulmus (Eds.), *Handbook of gerontology: Evidence-based approaches to theory, practice, and policy* (pp. 201–229). Hoboken, NJ: John Wiley & Sons.

Llewellyn, G., & McConnell, D. (2002). Mothers with learning difficulties and their support networks. *Journal of Intellectual Disability Research, 46*(1), 17–34.

Lloyd, V., Kalsy, S., & Gatherer, A. (2008) Impact of dementia upon residential care for individuals with Down syndrome. *Journal of Policy and Practice in Intellectual Disabilities, 5*(1), 33–38.

Lollar, D. J., & Crews, J. E. (2003). Redefining the role of public health in disability. *Annual Review of Public Health, 24,* 195–208.

Longmore, P. (2003). *Why I burned my book and other essays on disability.* Philadelphia: Temple University Press.

Ludlow, B. L. (1999). Life after loss: Legal, ethical and practical issues. In S. S. Herr & G. Weber (Eds.), *Aging, rights and quality of life: Prospects for older people with developmental disabilities.* Baltimore: Paul H. Brookes.

Lustig, D. C., & Strauser, D. R. (2007). Causal relationships between poverty and disability. *Rehabilitation Counseling Bulletin, 50*(4), 194–202.

Mansell, W., & Morris, K. (2004). A survey of parents' reactions to the diagnosis of an autistic spectrum disorder by a local service: Access to information and use of services. *Autism, 8*(4), 387–407.

McColl, M. A. (2004). Family and caregiver issues. In B. J. Kemp & L. Mosqueda (Eds.), *Aging with a disability.* Baltimore: Johns Hopkins University Press.

McNeil, J. M. (2001). *Americans with disabilities.* Household Economic Studies, Current Population Reports. Retrieved from http://www.census.gov/prod/2001pubs/p70-73.pdf

Mendes de Leon, C. F., Glass, T. A., Beckett, L. A., et al. (1999). Social networks and disability transitions across eight intervals of yearly data in the New Haven EPESE. *Journal of Gerontology Series B: Psychological Sciences and Sociological Sciences, 54,* 162–172.

Mendes de Leon, C. F., Gold, D. T., Glass, T. A., et al. (2001). Disability as a function of social networks and support in elderly African Americans and Whites: The Duke EPESE 1986–1992. *Journal of Gerontology Series B: Psychological and Sociological Sciences, 56,* 179–190.

Mirza, M., & Hammel, J. (2009). Consumer-directed goal planning in the delivery of assistive technology services for people who are ageing with intellectual disabilities. *Journal of Applied Research in Intellectual Disabilities, 22,* 445–457.

Mithaug, D., Wehmeyer, M. L., Agran, M., Martin, J., & Palmer, S. (1998). The self-determined model of instruction: Engaging students to solve their learning problems. In M. L. Wehmeyer & D. J. Sands (Eds.), *Making it happen: Student involvement in educational planning, decision-making and instruction* (pp. 299–328). Baltimore: Paul H. Brookes.

Moak, G. S. (1996). When the seriously mental ill patient grows old. In S. M. Soreff (Ed.), *Handbook for the treatment of the seriously mental ill.* Seattle, WA: Hogrefe and Huber.

Morningstar, M. E., Turnbull, A. P., & Turnbull, H. R. (1995). What do students with disabilities tell us about the family involvement in the transition from school to adult life? *Exceptional Children, 62,* 249–260.

Mosqueda, L. (2004). Psychological changes and secondary conditions. In B. J. Kemp & L. Mosqueda (Eds.), *Aging with a disability.* Baltimore: Johns Hopkins University Press.

Nadeau, L., & Tessier, R. (2006). Social adjustment of children with cerebral palsy in mainstream class: Peer perception. *Developmental Medicine and Child Neurology, 48,* 331–336.

National Council on Disability (NCD). (2005). *The Social Security Administration's efforts to promote employment for people with disabilities: New solutions for old problems.* Washington, DC: Author.

National Dissemination Center for Children with Disabilities. (2010). *Educate children (3 to 22).* Retrieved from http://www.nichcy.org/EducateChildren/Pages/Default.aspx

Nosek, M. A., Hughes, R. B., Swedlund, N., Taylor, H. B., Robinson-Whelen, S., Byrne, M., et al. (2006). Secondary conditions in a community-based sample of women with physical disabilities over a one-year period. *Archives of Physical Medicine and Rehabilitation, 87*(3), 320–327.

Nota, L., Ferrari, L., Soresi, S., & Wehmeyer, M. (2007). Self-determination, social abilities and the quality of life of people with intellectual disability. *Journal of Intellectual Disability Research, 51*(11), 850–865.

Nowak, M. (1999). International human rights standards: Aging and disabilities. In S. S. Herr & G. Weber (Eds.), *Aging, rights and quality of life: Prospects for older people with developmental disabilities* (pp. 33–43). Baltimore: Paul H. Brookes.

Nuefeld, A., Harrison, M. J., Stewart, M., & Hughes, K. (2008). Advocacy of women family caregivers: Response to nonsupportive interactions with professionals. *Qualitative Health Research, 18,* 301–310.

Offit, P. (2008). *Autism's false prophets: Bad science, risky medicine, and the search for a cure.* New York: Columbia University Press.

Öngür, D., Lin, L., & Cohen, B. M. (2009). Clinical characteristics influencing age at onset in psychotic disorders. *Comprehensive Psychiatry, 50,* 13–19.

Opel, D. J., Diekema, D. S., & Marcuse, E. K. (2008). A critique of criteria for evaluating vaccines for inclusion in mandatory school immunization programs. *Pediatrics, 122,* e504–e510.

Organisation for Economic Co-operation and Development (OECD). (2009, May). *Sickness, disability and work: Keeping on track in the economic downturn.* Paper presented at the High-Level Forum, Stockholm, Sweden. Retrieved from http://www.oecd.org/dataoecd/42/15/42699911.pdf

Orsmond, G. I., & Seltzer, M. M. (2007). Siblings of individuals with autism spectrum disorders across the life course. *Mental Retardation and Developmental Disabilities Research Reviews, 13,* 313–320.

Orsmond, G. I., Selzer, M. M., Greenberg, J. S., & Krauss, M. W. (2006). Mother-child relationship quality among adolescents and adults with autism. *American Journal on Mental Retardation, 111*(2), 121–137.

Osborne, L. A., & Reed, P. (2008). Parents' perceptions of communication with professionals during the diagnosis of autism. *Autism, 12*(3), 309–324.

Osgood, D. W., Foster, E. M., & Courtney, M. E. (2010). Vulnerable populations and the transition to adulthood. *The Future of Children, 20*(1), 209–230.

Östlie, I. L., Johansson, I., & Möller, A. (2009). Struggle and adjustment to an insecure everyday life and an unpredictable life course. *Disability and Rehabilitation, 31*(8), 666–674.

Ozawa, M. N., and Yeo, Y. H. (2006). Work status and work performance of people with disabilities: An empirical study. *Journal of Disability Policy Studies, 17*(3), 180–190.

Palmer, S., & Wehmeyer, M. L. (2003). Promoting self-determination in early elementary school: Teaching self-regulated problem-solving and goal-setting skills. *Remedial and Special Education, 24*, 115–126.

Pekkala, E. T., & Merinder, L. B. (2002). Psychoeducation for schizophrenia. *Cochrane Database of Systematic Reviews, 2*. doi: 10.1002/14651858.CD002831

Pletcher, L. C., & McBride, S. (2000). *Family-centered services: Guiding principles and practices for delivery of family-centered services.* Retrieved from http://www.nectac.org/topics/families/famctrprin.asp

Priestley, M. (2003). *Disability: A life course approach.* Cambridge, UK: Polity Press.

Pruchno, R. A., & McMullen, W. F. (2004). Patterns of service utilization by adults with a developmental disability: Type of service makes a difference. *American Journal on Mental Retardation, 109*, 362–378.

Rembis, M. A. (2009). (Re)defining disability in the "genetic age": Behavioral genetics, "new" eugenics and the future of impairment. *Disability and Society, 24*(5), 585–597.

Rimmer, J. H. (2005). The conspicuous absence of people with disabilities in public fitness and recreation facilities: Lack of interest or lack of access? *American Journal of Health Promotion, 19*, 327–329.

Rimmer, J. H. (2006). Health promotion and disability. In G. A. Albrecht (Ed.), *Encyclopedia of disability* (Vol. II, pp. 837–840). Thousand Oaks, CA: Sage.

Rimmer, J. H., Chen, M. D., McCubbin, J. A., Drum, C., & Peterson, J. (2010). Exercise intervention research on persons with disabilities: What we know and where we need to go. *American Journal of Physical Medicine and Rehabilitation, 89*, 249–263.

Rossiter, L., & Sharpe, D. (2001). The siblings of individuals with mental retardation: A quantitative integration of the literature. *Journal of Child and Family Studies, 10*, 65–84.

Ruhl, L. (1999). Liberal governance and prenatal care: Risk and regulation in pregnancy. *Economy and Society, 28*(1), 95–117.

Ryan, S., & Runswick-Cole, K. (2008). Repositioning mothers: Mothers, disabled children and disability studies. *Disability and Society, 23*(3), 199–210.

Salmon, D. A., Teret, S. P., MacIntyre, C. R., Salisbury, D., Burgess, M. A., & Halsey, N. A. (2008). Compulsory vaccination and conscientious or philosophical exemptions: Past, present, and future. *Lancet, 367*, 436–442.

Sands, R. (1995). The parenting experience of low-income single women with serious mental disorders: Families in society. *The Journal of Contemporary Human Services, 76*(2), 86–89.

Sawyer, S., & Aroni, R. (2005). Self-management in adolescents with chronic illness: What does it mean and how can it be achieved? *Medical Journal of Australia, 183*, 405–409.

Schwartz, K. D., & Lutfiyya, Z. M. (2009). "What lay ahead . . .": A media portrayal of disability and assisted suicide. *Journal of Research in Special Educational Needs, 9*(1), 27–38.

Seltzer, M. M. (1985). Informal supports for aging mentally retarded persons. *American Journal of Mental Deficiency, 90*(3), 259–265.

Seltzer, M. M., Greenberg, J. S., Floyd, F. J., Pettee, Y., & Hong, J. (2001). Life course perspectives of parenting a child with a disability. *American Journal on Mental Retardation, 106*, 265–286.

Semansky, R. M., & Koyanagi, C. (2004). The TEFRA Medicaid eligibility option for children with severe disabilities: A national study. *The Journal of Behavioral Health Services and Research, 31*(3), 334–342.

Settersten, R. A., & Ray, B. (2010). What's going on with young people today? The long and twisting path to adulthood. *The Future of Children, 20*(1), 19–41.

Shakespeare, T. (1998). Choices and rights: Eugenics, genetics and disability equality. *Disability & Society, 13*(5), 665–681.

Sharp, K., & Earle, S. (2002). Feminism, abortion, and disability: Irreconcilable differences? *Disability and Society, 17*(2), 137–145.

Shattuck, P. T., & Parish, S. L. (2008). Multilevel analysis of financial burden in families of children with special health care needs. *Pediatrics, 122*, 13–18.

She, P., & Livermore, G. A. (2007). Material hardship, poverty, and disability among working-age adults. *Social Science Quarterly, 88*, 970–989.

Sherifali, D., Ciliska, D., & O'Mara, L. (2009). Parenting children with diabetes. *The Diabetes Educator, 35*, 476–483.

Silverstein, R. (2000). Emerging disability policy framework: A guidepost for analyzing public policy. *Iowa Law Review, 85*, 1691–1796.

Simon-Rusinowitz, L., Mahoney, K. J., Shoop, D. M., Desmond, S. M., Squillace, M. R., & Sowers, J. (2000). Cash and counseling as a model to structure and finance community supports. In M. P. Janicki & E. F. Ansello (Eds.), *Community supports for aging adults with lifelong disabilities.* Baltimore: Paul H. Brookes.

Singer, G. H. S. (2006). Meta-analysis of comparative studies of depression in mothers of children with and without developmental disabilities. *American Journal on Mental Retardation, 11*(3), 155–169.

Smith, G. C., Hatfield, A. B., & Miller, D. C. (2000). Planning by older mothers for the future care of offspring with mental illness. *Psychiatric Services, 51*, 1162–1166.

Smith, J. C., Snider, D. E., Pickering, L. K., & the Advisory Committee on Immunization Practices. (2009). Immunization policy development in the United States: The role of the Advisory Committee on Immunization Practices. *Annals of Internal Medicine, 150*(1), 45–49.

Smyer, M. A., & Qualls, S. A. (1999). *Aging and mental health.* Malden, MA: Blackwell.

Stam, H., Hartman, E. E., Deurloo, J. A., Groothoff, J., & Grootenhuis, M. A. (2006). Young adult patients with a history of pediatric disease: Impact on course of life and transition into adulthood. *Journal of Adolescent Health, 39*, 4–13.

Stancliffe, R. J. (2001). Living with support in the community: Predictors of choice and self-determination. *Mental Retardation and Developmental Disabilities Research Reviews, 7*(2), 91–98.

Stapleton, D. C., Livermore, G., & Gregory, J. (2007). Beneficiary participation in Ticket to Work. *Journal of Vocational Rehabilitation, 27*(2), 95–106.

Sterns, H. L., Kennedy, E. A., Sed, C. M., & Heller, T. (2000). Later-life planning and retirement. In M. P. Janicki & E. F. Ansello (Eds.), *Community supports for aging adults with lifelong disabilities.* Baltimore: Paul H. Brookes.

Stoneman, Z. (2001). Supporting positive sibling relationships during childhood. *Mental Retardation and Developmental Disabilities Research Review, 7,* 134–142.

Stoneman, Z. (2005). Siblings of children with disabilities: Research themes. *Mental Retardation, 43*(5), 339–350.

Strydom, A., Lee, L. A., Jokinen, N., Shooshtari, S., Raykar, V., Torr, J., et al. (2009, March). *Dementia in older adults with intellectual disabilities.* IASSID Special Interest Research Group on Ageing and Intellectual Disabilities. Retrieved from https://www.iassid.org/images/documents/Aging/state%20of%20 the%20science%20dementia%202009.pdf

Swango-Wilson, A. (1995). Caregiver perceptions of sexual behaviors of individuals with intellectual disabilities. *Sexuality and Disability, 20*(3), 205–222.

Taanila, A., Syrjala, L., Kokkonen, J., & Jarvelin, M. R. (2002). Coping of parents with physically and or intellectually disabled children. *Child: Care, Health and Development, 28*(1), 73–86.

Tattersall, H., & Young, A. (2006). Deaf children identified through newborn hearing screening: Parents' experiences of the diagnostic process. *Child: Care, Health and Development, 32*(1), 33–45.

Thompson, L. (2004). Functional changes affecting people aging with disabilities. In B. J. Kemp & L. Mosqueda (Eds.), *Aging with a disability.* Baltimore: Johns Hopkins University Press.

Todd, S. (2005). Surprised endings: The dying of people with learning disabilities in residential services. *International Journal of Palliative Nursing, 11,* 80–82.

Trainor, A. A. (2010). Re-examining the promise of parent participation in special education: An analysis of cultural and social capital. *Anthropology and Education Quarterly, 41*(3), 245–263.

Tuffrey-Wijne, I., Hogg, J., & Curfs, L. (2007). End-of-life and palliative care for people with intellectual disabilities who have cancer or other life-limiting illness: A review of the literature and available resources. *Journal of Applied Research in Intellectual Disabilities, 20*(4), 331–344.

Turkel, S., & Pao, M. (2007). Late consequences of chronic pediatric illness. *Psychiatric Clinics of North America, 30,* 819–835.

Tyrell, J., & Dodd, P. (2003). Psychopathology in older age. In P. W. Davidson, V. P. Prasher, & M. Janicki (Eds.), *Mental health, intellectual disabilities and the aging process.* Oxford, UK: Blackwell.

Tyson, J. E., Younes, N., Verter, J., & Wright, L. L. (1996). Viability, morbidity, and resource use among newborns of 501–800g birth weight. *Journal of the American Medical Association, 276*(20), 1645–1651.

van Schrojenstein Lantman-de Valk, H. M. J. (2009). Healthy persons with intellectual disabilities in an inclusive society. *Journal of Policy and Practice in Intellectual Disabilities, 6*(2), 77–80.

van Schrojenstein Lantman-de Valk, H. M. J., & Walsh, P. N. (2008). Managing health problems in people with intellectual disabilities. *British Medical Journal, 337,* 1408–1412.

Verbrugge, L. M., & Yang, L. (2002). Aging with disability and disability with aging. *Journal of Disability Policy Studies, 12*(4), 253–267.

Vimarlund, V., & Olve, N. G. (2005). Economic analyses for ICT in elderly healthcare: Questions and challenges. *Health Informatics Journal, 11,* 309–321.

Wallander, J. L., & Noojin, A. B. (1995). Mothers' report of stressful experiences related to having a child with a physical disability. *Children's Health Care, 24*(4), 245–256.

Ward, K., Trigler, J., & Pfeiffer, K. (2001). Community services, issues and services gaps for individuals with developmental disabilities who exhibit inappropriate sexual behaviors. *Mental Retardation, 39*(1), 11–19.

Wehmeyer, M. L., Agran, M., & Hughes, C. (2000). A national survey of teachers' promotion of self-determination and student-directed learning. *Journal of Special Education, 34,* 58–68.

Wehmeyer, M. L., Agran, M., Hughes, C., Martin, J., Mithaug, D. E., & Palmer, S. (2007). *Promoting self-determination in students with intellectual and developmental disabilities.* New York: Guilford Press.

Wehmeyer, M. L., & Palmer, S. B. (2003). Adult outcomes for students with cognitive disabilities three years after high school: The impact of self-determination. *Education and Training in Developmental Disabilities, 38,* 131–144.

Wells, T., Sandefur, G., & Hogan, D. (2003). What happens after the high school years among young persons with disabilities? *Social Forces, 82*(2), 803–832.

White, L. (2001). Sibling relationships over the life course: A panel analysis. *Journal of Marriage and Family, 63,* 555–568.

Winn, S., & Hay, I. (2009). Transition from school for youths with a disability: Issues and challenges. *Disability and Society, 24*(1), 103–115.

Wittenburg, D., & Loprest, P. (2004). *Ability or inability to work: Challenges in moving towards a more work-focused disability definition for Social Security Administration (SSA) disability programs.* Washington, DC: Ticket to Work and Work Inventive Advisory Panel.

Wright, J. A. (2008). Prenatal and postnatal diagnosis of infant disability: Breaking the news to mothers. *Journal of Perinatal Education, 17*(3), 27–32.

Yanok, J., & Beifus, J. A. (1993). Communicating about loss and mourning: Death education for individuals with mental retardation. *Mental Retardation, 31,* 144–147.

Young, A. S., Klap, R., Sherbourne, C. D., & Wells, K. B. (2001). The quality of care for depressive and anxiety disorders in the United States. *Archives of General Psychiatry, 58,* 55–61.

Three

Chronology of Critical Events

*Robert Gould, Tamar Heller,
and Sarah Parker Harris*

1904

Sir Francis Galton, half first cousin of Charles Darwin, defines the term *eugenics* (which he first coined in 1883) in a paper he presents to the Sociological Society on May 16. He argues for planned breeding and discourages people of "sub-normal" and "feebleminded" stock from reproducing.

1905

Alfred Binet and Theodore Simon publish the first intelligence scale in France. The scale is used in both France and the United States to place children into special and segregated schools.

1911

The U.S. Congress passes a joint resolution authorizing creation of a federal commission to investigate the establishment of a system of worker's compensation. The commission focuses on the liability of employers to provide financial compensation to workers who become disabled on the job.

1912

Henry H. Goddard publishes the bestselling text *The Kallikak Family*, which includes a case study purporting to show the burden that people with disabilities place on society. The book is known for advancing the eugenics movement and increasing public support for the forced institutionalization and sterilization of people with disabilities.

1916

Congress passes the National Defense Act, which includes instructional programs to help soldiers of the "Great War" return to civilian life; the legislation is recognized as the federal government's first formal acknowledgment that it has an obligation to help persons injured in service to their country.

1918

On June 27 President Woodrow Wilson signs the Smith-Sears Veterans Vocational Rehabilitation Act, which creates a vocational rehabilitation system for disabled soldiers returning from World War I.

1920

The Fess-Smith Civilian Vocational Rehabilitation Act (Public Law 66-236) is signed by President Woodrow Wilson on June 29, creating a vocational rehabilitation program for the general population with disabilities. The Fess-Smith Act marks the start of public rehabilitation programming to provide counseling and job placement for most people with disabilities. However, people who are blind are refused service under the act.

1921

The American Foundation for the Blind is established. Initially founded to help the many blinded soldiers returning from World War I, the foundation provides a forum for people who are blind to learn and network with each other.

1922

The International Society for Crippled Children (now known as Rehabilitation International) forms in the United States. The society quickly becomes a model for other international organizations devoted to linking together people with disabilities.

Eugenicist Harry Laughlin drafts a sterilization law that becomes a model for numerous state legislatures supportive of eugenic sterilization. Laughlin's legislation labels various groups of people with disabilities and others as "defective" candidates for state-sanctioned sterilization, including "(1) feebleminded; (2) insane (including the psychopathic); (3) criminalistic (including the delinquent and wayward); (4) epileptic; (5) inebriate (including drug habitues); (6) diseased (including the tubercular, the syphilitic, the leprous, and others with chronic, infectious, and legally segregable diseases); (7) blind (including those with seriously impaired vision); (8) deaf (including those with seriously impaired hearing); (9) deformed (including the crippled); and (10) dependent (including orphans, ne'er-do-wells, the homeless, tramps, and paupers)."

1924

On March 20 the Commonwealth of Virginia becomes the first state to pass a law allowing for the forced sterilization of individuals with disabilities, including residents determined to be "feebleminded, insane, depressed, mentally handicapped, epileptic and *other*." Alcoholics, criminals, and drug addicts are also forcibly and legally sterilized under the law.

1927

On May 2 the U.S. Supreme Court rules in *Buck v. Bell* that the forced sterilization of people with disabilities is not a violation of their constitutional rights. The ruling sparks a fresh wave of state-level legislation sanctioning forced sterilization of people with disabilities. The court decision also legalizes other positions advocated by the eugenics movement, such as measures to prohibit people with disabilities from having children.

1930

On July 21 President Herbert Hoover signs Executive Order 4398, creating the Veterans Administration. This federal agency serves military veterans by providing benefits, employment assistance, and vocational rehabilitation services. The Veterans Administration takes over as the central provider of benefits for the estimated 4.7 million living veterans in the United States at the time and is a key player in providing services for returning soldiers with disabilities.

1935

By this time more than 30 states have passed laws permitting compulsory sterilization of people with disabilities and others deemed genetically unfit. The laws pertain to people in both state and federal institutions. More than 60,000 people are legally sterilized by 1970.

Bill Wilson and Dr. Bob Smith found the group Alcoholics Anonymous on May 12 in Akron, Ohio. Years later, people with disabilities in the independent living movement adopt the model of peer support used in Alcoholics Anonymous.

A group of people with disabilities, most of whom had contracted polio, holds a sit-in on May 29 at the office of New York City's Emergency Relief Bureau to demand non-segregated jobs with the Works Progress Administration and other Depression-era work-relief agencies. The group goes on to form the League of the Physically Handicapped, one of the first groups to publicly identify and protest social and employment discrimination against people with disabilities.

On August 14 Congress passes and President Roosevelt signs the Social Security Act (Public Law 74-271), creating a system of benefits for the elderly and grants to states to provide assistance to blind individuals and children with disabilities. The law extends funding for the existing vocational rehabilitation programs established by earlier legislation, and Title V of the act allows for new grants to individual states for a wide range of maternal and child health services.

1936

The League of the Physically Handicapped organizes a series of demonstrations to protest discriminatory practices in federal agencies. Actions include written papers, sit-ins, picket lines, and a trip to Washington, D.C., where the league joins with advocates from the League for the Advancement of the Deaf to meet with Roosevelt administration officials and protest discrimination in New Deal programs against people with disabilities.

1938

The Fair Labor Standards Act is signed into law by Franklin D. Roosevelt on June 25, increasing the availability of sheltered workshop programs for blind workers. Advocates for the blind and fair-employment activists herald the bill at the time, but it leads to the exploitation of workers with varying disabilities; many receive sub-minimum wages and are forced to submit to poor working conditions and long hours in sheltered workshop programs.

1940

The American Psychiatric Association develops a position statement in favor of the euthanasia of children classified as "idiots" and "imbeciles."

Paul Strachan founds the American Federation of the Physically Handicapped, the nation's first cross-disability national political organization. Devoted to ending discrimination against people with disabilities in the workplace, the organization lobbies successfully for passage of legislation establishing National Employ the Physically Handicapped Week (in 1945) and other employment-related policies and programs for people with disabilities.

Jacobus tenBroek and other activists for the blind community gather on July 1 in Wilkes-Barre, Pennsylvania, to charter the National Federation of the Blind. In 1957 the federation begins publication of the *Braille Monitor,* a leading advocacy magazine for the blind community.

1943

Congressional passage of the Barden-LaFollette Vocational Rehabilitation Act on July 6 brings physical rehabilitation initiatives and funding for certain health care services to federally funded vocational rehabilitation programs. The act leads to the creation of the first rehabilitation and job training programs for people with mental illness and cognitive disabilities in the United States.

1944

Howard Rusk begins a rehabilitation program at the U.S. Army Air Force Convalescent Center in Pawling, New York, for a group of airmen with acquired disabilities. Originally dismissed as "Rusk's Folly" by the medical establishment, the program becomes integral to Rusk's development of rehabilitative medicine. Many of Rusk's techniques for treating physical injuries and emotional, psychological, and social issues become standard medical practice.

1945

On August 11 Congress passes Joint Resolution 23, establishing the first week in October as the annual National Employ the Handicap Week, and in 1947 President Harry Truman signs the resolution into law. The law urges private sector support for the inclusion of people with disabilities in paid employment opportunities, and it also establishes the President's Committee on National Employ the Physically Handicapped Week, a permanent group that reports to Congress on employment opportunities for people with disabilities. The committee is today known as the President's Disability Employment Partnership Board.

1946

The first chapter of what will become the United Cerebral Palsy Associations, Inc., is established in New York City by parents of children with cerebral palsy. The association, together with the Association for Retarded Children, becomes a major force in the so-called parent movement of the 1950s. These parent activists successfully lobby for increased education and community supports for children with disabilities.

1949

The National Foundation for Cerebral Palsy is chartered by representatives of various groups of parents of children with cerebral palsy for the purpose of increasing accessibility nationally. The organization seeks the full social and institutional inclusion of youths with cerebral palsy and works to strengthen the rights of parents to obtain resources and information to best support their children.

Under the guidance of Tim Nugent, director of the Rehabilitation Education Center, University of Illinois students with physical disabilities hold the first National Wheelchair Basketball Tournament in Galesburg, Illinois. Wheelchair basketball and other adapted sports quickly become an integral part of lifestyle, culture, and social activity for youth and adults with disabilities over the next several decades.

1950

The National Association for Mental Health is formed by a coalition of national mental health groups with the mission of "spreading tolerance and awareness, improving mental health services, preventing mental illness, and promoting mental health." The mission statement echoes renowned advocate Clifford W. Beers's goals to support mental health treatment and improve the long-term inclusion of people with mental illness in the community.

The Association for Retarded Children of the United States (later renamed the Association for Retarded Citizens and then The Arc) is founded in Minneapolis by a cohort of concerned individuals and parents of children with intellectual disabilities from across the United States. The association is a response to the virtual absence of programs and community activities for children and adults with intellectual disabilities.

1951

Talcott Parson introduces a prominent sociological approach to disability called the "sick role," theorizing that illness and disability relieve unhealthy individuals from complying with social behavioral norms, but also obligate them to be both compliant to and appreciative of medical intervention. This influential model is critiqued from the disability studies perspective, particularly for people with disabilities who vary in their need for health care throughout the life course, and for individuals with lifelong disabilities who cannot or do not want to be cured.

A group of international advocates for deaf rights representing more than 25 different countries gathers in Rome in September and establishes the World Federation of the Deaf, an organization dedicated to connecting members of the deaf community around the world.

1952

On August 15 the President's Committee on National Employ the Physically Handicapped Week becomes the President's Committee on Employment of the Physically Handicapped (now known as the President's Disability Employment Partnership Board).

1954

On August 3 Congress passes and President Dwight D. Eisenhower signs the Vocational Rehabilitation Amendments, authorizing federal grants to expand programs available to people with physical disabilities. The amendments are the first major revisions to the national rehabilitation program since World War II–era services that were designed to support returning soldiers.

1956

On August 1 President Eisenhower signs the Social Security Amendments of 1956 into law, creating the Social Security Disability Insurance (SSDI) program for disabled workers aged 50 to 64. The amendments provide significant increases in benefits for aging individuals with disabilities who require financial assistance to secure their basic needs.

1960

On September 13 Congress passes the Social Security Amendments of 1960, which loosen benefit eligibility requirements for disabled workers and their dependents. Most notably, the law eliminates the age restriction for disabled workers receiving Social Security Disability Insurance benefits (previously, beneficiaries had to be aged 50 or older). The amendments increase financial support for aging populations as well.

1962

The clinical diagnosis of battered child syndrome is first recognized and defined, bringing attention to the physical and psychological implications of child abuse. Recently researchers estimated that the incidence of maltreatment of children with disabilities is between 1.7 and 3.4 times greater than of children without disabilities.

1963

President John F. Kennedy signs into law the Social Security Act Amendments of 1963 (Public Law 88-156) on October 24. Provisions of the law include a new grant program to improve prenatal care for women from low-income families for whom the risk of mental retardation and other "birth defects" are known to be higher than the general population. States receive financial assistance to establish programs to prevent "mental retardation and other defects."

The Developmental Disabilities Assistance and Bill of Rights Act (DD Act; Public Law 106-402) establishes programs that promote the participation of people with developmental disabilities in their communities. It also results in the development of a national network of state and territorial Developmental Disabilities Councils; University Centers for Excellence in Developmental Disabilities Education, Research, and Service; and Protection and Advocacy Systems. The federal Administration on Developmental Disabilities is established to administer this act (which was reauthorized in 2000).

The Community Mental Health Centers Act (Public Law 88-164) sets up community mental health centers throughout the country in response to the growing deinstitutionalization of people with mental illness. These centers become primary providers of social services and mental health treatment to people with mental illness in the community.

1964

The Civil Rights Act is passed on July 2 to protect the rights of African Americans and women across the United States. The legal framework of the act becomes the model for future legislation to promote the rights of people with disabilities.

1965

On April 11 Congress enacts Title I of the Elementary and Secondary Education Act of 1965 (Public Law 89-10), requiring that states and local school districts provide compensatory education to educationally disadvantaged children residing in low-income areas. Amendments to the act passed later in the year authorize aid to agencies and schools that provide specific assistance to children with disabilities.

On May 18 Lyndon B. Johnson unveils Head Start, a program administered by the Office of Economic Opportunity to provide comprehensive
education and support for low-income students and their families. The
program, which stipulates that at least 10% of program openings must be
reserved for disabled children, is the first national early intervention program for children with disabilities and is one of the longest-running federal programs designed to reduce systemic poverty in America.

On July 14 Congress passes the Older Americans Act (OAA) in response
to concerns raised by policymakers about a lack of community social services for older persons. The original legislation established grants to
states for community planning and social services, research and development projects, and personnel training in the field of aging. The law also
establishes the Administration on Aging (AoA) to administer the newly
created grant programs and to serve as the federal focal point on policy
matters concerning older persons.

On July 30 Congress passes the Social Security Acts Amendments of 1965,
authorizing health insurance benefits for the elderly and people with
qualifying disabilities.

On November 8 Congress passes the Vocational Rehabilitation Amendments of 1965. The legislation authorizes federal funding for the construction of rehabilitation centers, expands existing vocational rehabilitation
programs, and creates the National Commission on Architectural Barriers
to Rehabilitation of the Handicapped. These amendments are significant
not only for their attention to people with disabilities, but also for their
expansion of services that were previously only offered to people with
high economic needs to the entire disability community.

1967

On December 15 Congress passes the Social Security Act Amendments of
1967, which make it mandatory for states to offer early and periodic
screening for disability, as well as diagnosis and treatment services to all
children eligible for Medicaid. The legislation is formally signed by President Johnson on January 2, 1968. Early intervention screening subsequently becomes a central topic of future education legislation pertaining
to children with disabilities.

1971

The Javits-Wagner-O'Day Act (now known as the AbilityOne program) passes Congress on June 23, amending the Fair Labor Standard Act of 1938 to include people with disabilities other than blindness into the sheltered workshop system. This amendment expands the U.S. system of sheltered workshops into the principal source of employment training programs and post-secondary school service for people with cognitive and developmental disabilities.

1972

In separate cases, the U.S. District Court for the Eastern District of Pennsylvania (in *PARC v. Pennsylvania)* and the U.S. District Court for the District of Columbia (in *Mills v. Board of Education*) rule that children with disabilities cannot be excluded from public schools. These two decisions are monumental victories for disability advocates, who promptly intensify their lobbying and legal actions in pursuit of inclusive education.

A group of people with disabilities known as the Rolling Quads (including Ed Roberts, John Hessler, and Hale Zukas) formally incorporates the first U.S. center for independent living in Berkeley, California. The establishment of this independent living center sparks new legislation, such as the Rehabilitation Act of 1974, and programs to promote the creation of similar centers across the country.

1973

The term *mainstreaming* first emerges in U.S. educational policy jargon. The concept of mainstreaming, which refers to placing people with disabilities in general classrooms, becomes a popular trend in education policymaking during this period.

On September 26 President Richard M. Nixon signs the landmark Rehabilitation Act of 1973 into law. Title V and Section 504 of the bill prohibit federal programs from discriminating against "otherwise qualified handicapped" individuals. Regarded as the greatest achievement of the disability rights movement in the 1970s, the act is the first legal document that confronts discrimination against people with disabilities. In addition, disability activists unite nationally to enforce the implementation of Section 504.

1974

The first official women's wheelchair basketball game is held on February 24 between the University of Illinois and Southern Illinois University. The National Wheelchair Basketball Association introduces a new policy allowing women to play and lobbies for the inclusion of women in sporting events that had previously been organized only for men with disabilities.

1975

The American Coalition of Citizens with Disabilities is created and quickly becomes the paramount national cross-disability rights organization of the 1970s. Renowned for centralizing the disability community, it includes disability rights groups representing people who are blind, deaf, physically disabled, and developmentally disabled.

The Association of Persons with Severe Handicaps (TASH) is founded by special education professionals in response to the influx of successful right-to-education protests in the 1970s. The association is instrumental in the eventual closing of residential institutions and actively supports the goal of community living for people with disabilities.

Twenty-four-year-old Bob Hall becomes the first person in a wheelchair to complete the famed Boston Marathon in under three hours. The race organizers' decision to formally recognize Hall's accomplishment legitimizes the use of wheelchairs in marathons, paves the way for the Boston Marathon to establish formal wheelchair divisions, and opens the door for disabled athletes to be recognized at the elite level.

On November 29 Congress passes the Education for All Handicapped Children Act (Public Law 94-142). The act, which President Gerald Ford formally signs into law on December 2, 1975, requires all public schools that receive federal aid to provide a free and appropriate public education in an integrated environment to children with disabilities. Subsequently codified as the Individuals with Disabilities Education Act (IDEA), it serves as the foundation of federal disability rights legislation in education.

1976

The first Parent Training and Information Centers are founded across the United States to help parents of disabled children exercise their recently granted educational rights under the Education for All Handicapped Children Act of 1975. The information centers provide assistance and training to help parents navigate the educational system and gain needed resources for children with disabilities.

Congress amends the Higher Education Act of 1965, which provides grant support for services that support low-income and first-generation college students, to specifically include individuals with disabilities. The amendment is the first major legislation to provide support to people with disabilities in higher education.

1978

On April 24 Congress begins a legislation initiative to protect children against abuse by enacting the Child Abuse Prevention and Treatment and Adoption Reform Act of 1978, then follows up two years later with the Adoption Assistance and Child Welfare Act of 1980. These laws contain specific initiatives to adopt and protect children with special needs, including children with disabilities.

1979

The National Alliance for the Mentally Ill (NAMI) is founded. NAMI is a national advocacy and education organization that also provides resources for mental health support groups.

1980

Harilyn Rousso starts the Networking Project on Disabled Women and Girls at the YWCA in New York City to support peer networking and social inclusion for young women with disabilities. She goes on to produce a book and film titled *Disabled, Female and Proud*, which addresses discrimination against women with disabilities in such areas as sexuality and education.

1981

The Reagan administration begins carrying out a series of legislative and administrative actions to revoke disability benefits for hundreds of thousands of citizens.

Disabled Peoples' International (DPI) is officially founded in Singapore on December 4. The establishment of this organization, along with other international organizations, signifies the growing global social connection between people with disabilities.

1982

The National Council on Independent Living (NCIL) forms in the United States to represent thousands of organizations and individuals with disabilities and advocate for the rights of people with disabilities. The council is a cornerstone influence in the disability rights movement and exemplifies the growing leadership roles of people with disabilities in disabled peoples' organizations.

Doctors in Bloomington, Indiana, advise the parents of a child with Down syndrome nicknamed "Baby Doe" to opt out of surgery to unblock their newborn's esophagus because of the child's disability. Disability rights activists protest and try to intervene after initial media coverage, but "Baby Doe" dies before legal action to force the surgical procedure can take place.

1983

An infant with spina bifida, "Baby Jane Doe," is born on October 11 in Stony Brook, New York. When her parents decide against recommended surgical treatment in favor of "custodial care," a major legal battle ensues. The case eventually is brought to the U.S. Supreme Court as part of the litigation in *Bowen v. American Hospital Association,* and it spurs Congress to pass the Child Abuse Prevention and Treatment Act Amendments of 1984, which prohibit the withholding of "medically indicated" treatment from any newborn with disabilities.

On November 13 Sharon Kowalski is disabled by a drunk driver in Minnesota and is forced to live in a nursing home by her parents after they discover that she is a lesbian. Her lover, Karen Thompson, spends the next eight years fighting to free Kowalski. Thompson's campaign links the lesbian and disability rights movements' advocacy efforts for sexual rights.

1984

George Murray is the first athlete with a visible disability to be featured on the Wheaties™ cereal box cover. Murray, a wheelchair athlete, symbolizes the growing recognition of athletes with disabilities and their increased inclusion in adapted sports initiatives.

In its July 5 decision in *Irving Independent School District v. Tatro*, the U.S. Supreme Court rules in favor of a young girl with spina bifida who was refused catheterization and related medical services during the school day by her local school. The Court rules that school districts can no longer refuse to educate a disabled child because they might need such a service, and it confirms that various medical supports for children with disabilities are protected by the Education for All Handicapped Children Act of 1975.

1985

On April 29 the U.S. Supreme Court rules in *Burlington School Committee v. Department of Education* that public school districts must pay the expenses of disabled children enrolled in private school programs if the latter institutions were better able to provide an appropriate education in the least restrictive environment. The ruling expands schooling options for children with disabilities but also allows room for public schools to neglect inclusive services.

1986

On August 4 Congress passes the Education of the Deaf Act of 1986 (Public Law 99-371) to improve educational opportunities at the elementary through post-secondary level for all deaf individuals. The law extends the authority of the National Training Institute for the Deaf to better prepare individuals who are deaf for successful employment and participation in higher education.

On October 21 the Rehabilitation Act Amendments of 1986 add supported employment as a "legitimate rehabilitation outcome" and allow funding to cover supported employment rehabilitation services. These legal changes are instrumental in furthering the inclusion of people with disabilities in mainstream employment opportunities.

On November 10 President Ronald Reagan signs the Employment Opportunities for Disabled Americans Act, which allows recipients of federal disability funds to retain those benefits even after they obtain work. The legislation removes a substantial disincentive for people with disabilities to seek work, and it allows people with disabilities to gain additional benefits guaranteed to employed individuals.

1987

The first U.S. Supreme Court decision addressing the civil rights of people with contagious diseases is handed down on March 3 in *School Board of Nassau County, Fla. v. Arline*. The Court rules that according to Section 504 of the Rehabilitation Act of 1973, people with contagious diseases cannot be fired from their jobs due to prejudiced attitudes.

1988

The U.S. Supreme Court, in *Honig v. Doe*, confirms the validity of the Education for All Handicapped Children Act of 1975, which prevents children with disabilities from being expelled or suspended from the appropriate setting agreed upon in the child's Individualized Education Program without an official due process hearing. The January 20 ruling in *Honig v. Doe*, known as the "stay-put rule," further protects the rights to inclusive education for children with disabilities in public school settings.

The Technology-Related Assistance for Individuals with Disabilities Act, better known as the Technology Act, is passed by Congress on August 9. The law provides financial assistance to states to support technology-related assistance programs for individuals with disabilities of all ages. The act also defines the term "assistive technology" as a fundamental accommodation used by people with varying disabilities throughout the life course.

The Fair Housing Amendments Act (Public Law No. 100-430) provides individuals with disabilities with legal protection against discrimination in housing. Following its passage on September 13, this law provides both aging populations and those with disabilities the right to make reasonable modifications to rented housing (for instance, installing grab bars in a bathroom). It also strengthens the right to accommodations in housing rules and policies, and legalizes various practices that further accessibility (such as allowing a seeing-eye dog in a house where pets are otherwise banned).

1990

In a large ceremony on the White House lawn attended by thousands of disability rights activists, President George H. W. Bush signs the Americans with Disabilities Act into law on July 26. The most significant disability rights legislation in U.S. history, the law seeks to bring full legal citizenship to Americans with disabilities by protecting access to various spheres of public life.

The Individuals with Disabilities Education Act (IDEA, formerly known as the Education of All Handicapped Children Act) is enacted on October 30 to improve school disability services by guaranteeing the rights to "free and appropriate education" for children and youth with disabilities. The law emphasizes mainstreaming and facilitating educational placements in the least restrictive environment over segregated special education classrooms. The legislation also reauthorizes and improves disability programs, especially in the areas of transition and assistive technology.

Self-Advocates Becoming Empowered (SABE) is established as a national self-advocacy organization of people with developmental disabilities.

1991

The Resolution on Personal Assistance Services is passed at the International Personal Assistance Symposium on September 29. This resolution calls for the global recognition of personal assistant services as a basic human right. One critical aspect of personal assistant services is that they must be available at all times to people of all ages. Another area of emphasis is that people may require an increase of services throughout their lifespan.

1992

President George H. W. Bush signs the Rehabilitation Act Amendments of 1992 into law on October 29. The legislation increases access to state vocational rehabilitation services for those with the most significant disabilities. In addition, career advancement services are developed to focus on improving employment outcomes beyond entry-level positions.

1994

Two separate networks, one for elderly persons and the other for persons with disabilities, join together to form the U.S. National Coalition on Aging and Disability. The coalition, which expanded to include more than 50 organizations from both communities by 2010, works to inform policymakers and advocates of the benefits of merging some services for the two communities.

On January 24 a U.S. Circuit Court of Appeals affirms in *Holland v. Sacramento City Unified School District* that disabled children have the right to attend public school classes with non-disabled children. The ruling influences other legal judgments about the inclusion of children with disabilities in the wider general community, and it is considered a major victory in ongoing efforts to ensure enforcement of the IDEA.

On March 31 President Bill Clinton signs the Goals 2000: Educate America Act of 1994 (Public Law 103-227) to establish a framework to meet national education goals and carry out school reform for all children, including students with disabilities. The act establishes the National Education Standards and Improvement Council to monitor curriculums, student performances, and state assessment systems in an attempt to establish national academic standards for all students.

1996

The U.S. Centers for Disease Control estimate that there are 1.4 million fewer older persons with disabilities in the United States than would have been expected if the health status of older people had not improved since the early 1980s.

Diane Coleman forms the disability advocacy group Not Dead Yet, which publicly opposes Jack Kevorkian and other proponents of assisted suicide for people with disabilities. Not Dead Yet argues that the "mercy killing" of people with disabilities is similar to the eugenics thinking of the first half of the 20th century, which saw the forced sterilization of people with disabilities in the United States and the killing of thousands of people with disabilities in Nazi Germany.

The Personal Responsibility and Work Opportunity Reconciliation Act (PRWORA) is signed into law by President Bill Clinton on August 22. The legislation makes major reforms to the U.S. welfare system, ending the traditional provision of welfare benefits that started under Franklin D. Roosevelt's New Deal policies. A key policy under this act is the Temporary Assistance to Needy Families (TANF), which replaces the 1935 Aid to Families with Dependent Children program with a means-tested, cash-assistance program run by individual states. TANF includes a series of work requirements for people seeking eligibility for Social Security benefits.

1997

UNESCO releases a policy statement, titled the 1997 UNESCO Universal Declaration on the Human Genome and Human Rights, which frames the application of the new scientific developments raised by genetics. As a policy, it declares that future genetics research will be applied in ways that maintain human rights.

1998

President Bill Clinton signs the Workforce Investment Act (WIA; Public Law 105-220) into law on August 7. The legislation reauthorizes the Rehabilitation Act and strengthens linkages between disability-specific work training programs (such as vocational rehabilitation) and generic non-disability-specific workforce systems. The act is a principal law in changing the American welfare system into a "workfare" system, where individuals are required to work or participate in government-approved work training programs in order to receive Social Security benefits.

1999

The University of Illinois at Chicago, the Rehabilitation Institute of Chicago, and the National Center on Accessibility partner together to establish the National Center on Physical Activity and Disability (NCPAD). NCPAD provides information and resources to people with disabilities, caregivers, and professionals on sports and fitness activities that people with disabilities can pursue for both health and recreational purposes.

The U.S. Supreme Court affirms the right of individuals with disabilities to live in their community in the case *Olmstead v. L. C. and E. W.* The June 22 decision confirms Title II of the Americans with Disabilities Act (ADA) and requires states to place qualified individuals with mental disabilities in community settings—rather than in institutions—whenever treatment professionals determine that such placement is appropriate, the affected persons do not oppose such placement, and the state can reasonably accommodate the placement, taking into account the resources available to the state and the needs of others with disabilities.

On November 19 Congress passes the Ticket to Work and Work Incentives Improvement Act of 1999, which provides Social Security Disability Insurance (SSDI) and Supplementary Security Income (SSI) disability beneficiaries with a ticket they may use to obtain vocational rehabilitation (VR) services, employment services, and other support services from an employment network of their choice. The act is part of the new U.S. "workfare" system mandating that individuals work or participate in a series of approved work programs in order to receive Social Security benefits.

2000

In June, the Human Genome Project (HGP) completes an international effort to specify the 3 billion parts of genes that make up the DNA sequence of the entire human genome and produces its first draft. The project, which formally began in October 1990, sparks debates about the bioethical implications of research on the human genome.

2001

On June 18 President George W. Bush issues Executive Order Number 13217, which declares the commitment of the United States to community-based services and living arrangements for individuals with disabilities. The executive order is used to ensure that the mandate contained in the *Olmstead* (1999) decision—that adults with disabilities are able to live in the least restrictive settings—is implemented.

2002

President George W. Bush signs the No Child Left Behind Act into law on January 8. The measure provides funding to help education programs lift their standards, includes provisions to aid schools in increasing their test scores, and increases state accountability for student performance. The act also requires that all students in special education be held to the same achievement standards as their non-disabled peers, a stipulation that incites debates within the disability community regarding both the fairness and the feasibility of the legislation.

2003

The National Association of Social Workers (NASW) issues a policy statement delineating their core values with respect to working with people with disabilities, including self-determination, social justice, and dignity and worth of the person. The statement emphasizes that social workers have a responsibility to advocate for the rights of people who have disabilities to fully participate in society.

Mark Priestley publishes *Disability: A Life Course Approach.* The text is a canonical piece in the field of Disability Studies for considering disability throughout different stages in the life course.

The Administration on Aging and the Centers for Medicare and Medicaid jointly develop a system of coordinated informational centers, called Aging and Disabilities Resource Centers, to give elderly people and people with disabilities increased access to long-term care. The system includes at least 14 centers that specifically target families of individuals with developmental disabilities. Aging and Disabilities Resource Center programs provide information and assistance to individuals needing either public or private resources, as well as to professionals seeking assistance on behalf of their clients and individuals planning for their future long-term care needs.

2004

The Administration for Developmental Disabilities, under the U.S. Department of Health and Human Services, funds the development of

Youth Information Centers (YICs) across the country. Similar to Parent Training and Information Centers, YICs promote services for youth with disabilities in the community.

The first U.S. Disability Pride Parade takes place in downtown Chicago. Organized by disability rights advocates and organizations, the event attracts almost 2,000 people. Organizers describe the event as one intended to "change the way people think about and define disability, to break down and end the internalized shame among people with disabilities, and to promote the belief in society that disability is a natural and beautiful part of life."

2005

On March 18 Michael Schiavo is granted the legal right to remove the feeding tube of his wife Terri, who has lived for 15 years in a "persistent vegetative" state. The removal takes place over the objections of her parents and disability rights activists, and Terri dies soon after at the age of 41. The case gains national media attention, sparking heated debates about medical ethics, the rights of people with disabilities, and end-of-life issues. It also brings heightened attention to living wills and other forms of life/estate planning.

2006

The first bill in the United States requiring that students in public schools be taught the history of the disability rights movement, titled the Disability History Week Act, is passed by the West Virginia legislature and signed into law by Governor Joe Manchin on April 3. The bill, which formally establishes a statewide Disability History Week for K–12 education in the third week of October, passes largely due to the efforts of 20 young West Virginians with disabilities.

On October 17 the U.S. Congress reauthorizes the Older Americans Act, which supports the development of Aging and Disability Resource Center Programs (ADRC) throughout the country. The reauthorization supports the expansion of the ADRCs to cover all 50 states and four U.S. territories.

President George W. Bush signs the Combating Autism Act of 2006 (Public Law 109-416) into law on December 19. The measure authorizes roughly $1 billion in expenditures for screening, education, and early intervention services for children with autism.

2009

On July 24 President Barack Obama signs the UN Convention on the Rights of Persons with Disabilities. His signature reaffirms the U.S. commitment to defending the rights of all people with disabilities of all ages.

2010

The Patient Protection and Affordable Care Act (PPACA) is signed into law by President Barack Obama on March 23. The legislation includes several provisions that directly impact people with disabilities and their living choices, including the Community Living Assistance Services and Supports (CLASS) Act and the Community First Choice Option (CFC). The PPACA will allow people that become disabled to live and work in their community, without having to become impoverished to qualify for Medicaid benefits.

Four

Biographies of Key Contributors in the Field

Tamar Heller, Sarah Parker Harris, and Jeannie Zwick

A large number of individuals have made significant contributions to the study of disability issues through the life course. The biographical sketches in this chapter, presented in alphabetical order, profile some of those individuals and their contributions.

Adrienne Asch

American bioethicist specializing in issues of reproduction and disability

Adrienne Asch attended Swarthmore College in Pennsylvania, earning a bachelor's degree in philosophy in 1969. During her undergraduate years, she was an active participant in the antiwar and civil rights protests of the era. Asch pursued graduate study at Columbia University, earning a master's degree in social work in 1973. Afterward, she worked for the New York State Division of Human Rights, served on the New Jersey

Bioethics Commission, and maintained a private practice as a consultant, trainer, and psychotherapist. Asch returned to Columbia to earn a Ph.D. in social psychology in 1992. Her main area of academic interest is bioethics, and particularly the ethical, political, and social implications of human reproduction and family.

Asch has held a variety of teaching positions over the years. She taught a course at Barnard College called Disabled Persons in the American Society, for instance, as well as a course in reproductive technology at the University of Oregon and a course in human behavior at Boston University. From 1994 to 2005, she was the Henry R. Luce Professor in Biology, Ethics, and the Politics of Human Reproduction at Wellesley College, where she designed an innovative program of undergraduate study on reproductive issues, including such courses as Multi-disciplinary Approaches to Abortion, Ethical and Social Issues in Reproduction, and Women and Motherhood. She is currently the Edward and Robin Milstein Professor of Bioethics at Yeshiva University in New York, as well as a professor of family and social medicine and a professor of epidemiology and population health in Yeshiva's Albert Einstein College of Medicine.

A frequent focus of Asch's research involves the moral issues raised by new genetic testing technologies. Along with her colleague Erik Parens, Asch coordinated a two-year project for the Hastings Center, a health ethics research facility, in which a panel of experts sought to establish moral guidelines for the use of prenatal testing to uncover genetic disabilities. In 2000 Parens and Asch reported their conclusions in *Prenatal Testing and Disability Rights*. Asch argued that the use of genetic testing and selective abortion to prevent the births of babies with disabilities sends a clear message that devalues people with disabilities: "It is better not to exist than to have a disability. Your birth was a mistake. Your family and the world would be better off without you alive."

Asch has authored numerous journal articles and book chapters, including *After Baby M: The Legal, Ethical, and Social Dimensions of Surrogacy*, with A.R. Schiff. She is also the co-editor of *The Double-Edged Helix: Social Implications of Genetics in a Diverse Society*, published in 2002. A past board member of the Society for Disability Studies and the Ethical, Legal, and Social Implications Planning Group of the National Human Genome Research Institute, Asch currently serves on the boards of the American Society of Bioethics and Humanities, the Society of Jewish Ethics, and the Council for Responsible Genetics. She is the recipient of several honors and awards, including being named Blind Educator of the Year in 1997 by the National Federation of the Blind.

Further Reading

Center for Ethics at Yeshiva University: Director and Staff. (2006). Retrieved from
http://www.yu.edu/ethics/page.aspx?id=12616
Parens, E., and Asch, A. (Eds.). (2000). *Prenatal testing and disability rights.* Washington,
DC: Georgetown University Press.

James E. Birren (1918–)

American pioneer in the field of gerontology

James E. Birren was born in 1918 in Chicago, Illinois. After studying mechanical engineering and graduating in 1938 from Wright Junior College in Chicago, Birren earned a bachelor's degree in education from the Chicago Teachers College in 1941. He then entered Northwestern University's psychology graduate program, earning his master's degree and eventually his Ph.D. in 1947.

During his graduate studies at Northwestern, Birren's involvement in World War II included research on the use of amphetamines by troops. He also studied seasickness among soldiers, and this experience became part of his doctoral thesis. Birren attended the first meeting of the Gerontological Society in 1948 as an employee of the U.S. Public Health Service, where he worked as part of the gerontology unit. His research involved studying differences between the young and the old. In 1950 Birren took a job with the National Institute of Mental Health (NIMH). He pioneered the NIMH's Section on Aging, which conducted human and rat studies as part of a multidisciplinary exploration of aging.

In 1964 Birren became the director of the Program on Aging at the National Institute of Child Health and Human Development (NICHD). There he took responsibility for the intramural and extramural research programs on aging. In 1965 Birren joined the research faculty at the University of Southern California (USC). There he served as the founding director of the Ethel Percy Andrus Gerontology Center. He also helped create the Andrew Norman Institute for Advanced Study in Gerontology and Geriatrics at USC. Through his research, Birren reached the conclusion that aging was not in itself an explanation for anything, but rather a good index by which scientists could gather and group data.

In 1989 Birren moved to the University of California, Los Angeles (UCLA), where he assisted in the development of the Borun Center for Gerontological Research. He was the associate director of the UCLA Center on Aging when he retired from the university in 2003. Since his retirement, Birren's focus has been on Guided Autobiography, a method he has pioneered for recalling and organizing life stories in a person's later years through life review techniques. He is the series editor for the renowned *Handbooks of Aging*, all of which are in their sixth edition. Birren has contributed to over 250 academic journals and books, and he was inducted into the American Society on Aging (ASA) Hall of Fame in 2004.

Further Reading

Achenbaum, W. A., & Albert, D. M. (1995). *Profiles in gerontology: A biographical dictionary*. Westport, CT: Greenwood Press.
Bengston, V. L., & Schaie, K. W. (1998). *Handbook of theories of aging*. New York: Springer.

Jan B. Blacher

American expert in family research and intellectual disabilities

Jan B. Blacher earned her bachelor's degree in psychology from Brown University in 1975. She attended the University of North Carolina at Chapel Hill (UNC-CH) and obtained her Ph.D. in special education and developmental psychology in 1979.

As a graduate student, Blacher was a fellow at the Frank Porter Graham Child Development Center at UNC-CH. While studying typical development there, she befriended a professor who had a child with intellectual disabilities. This relationship piqued Blacher's interest in intellectual disabilities and its effect on families. She continued to focus on this area after joining the faculty at the University of California, Riverside (UCR).

In 1982 Blacher's first National Institutes of Health (NIH) grant at UCR allowed her to study the effects of severe disabilities on families. This research project spanned 22 years, over which time Blacher followed the lives of 100 families who were affected by severe disabilities. The NIH also supported Blacher's research into the connection between intellectual disabilities and other mental disorders in children.

Blacher's other primary area of interest has been autism. More than 20 years of research on families affected by autism led her to recognize a significant difference between Latino and Anglo experiences. Specifically, Blacher found that Latino families received inadequate support and assistance. She addressed this situation by founding the resource center SEARCH (Support, Education, Advocacy, Resources, Community, Hope) at UCR in 2007. SEARCH provides a variety of services to help children and families meet the challenges related to autism spectrum disorder and Asperger's syndrome. Although the center is available to everyone, it has a special focus on Latino families and low-income families.

Further Reading

Faculty Profiles: Jan Blacher. Retrieved from http://education.ucr.edu/faculty/blacherjan.html

SEARCH Family Autism Resource Center. Retrieved from http://searchcenter.ucr.edu

Diane Coleman

American proponent of disability rights and opponent of legalization of euthanasia and assisted suicide

Diane Coleman was adopted when she was ten days old. Misdiagnosed with muscular dystrophy at age 6, Coleman was given a life expectancy of just 12 years. Doctors later determined that she actually had spinal muscular atrophy. Due to this condition, Coleman has used a wheelchair since age 11.

Coleman obtained her bachelor's degree in psychology from the University of Illinois at Champaign-Urbana in 1976. She then entered the University of California's dual degree program, earning both her J.D. and M.B.A. in 1981. The following year, Coleman was invited to join the board of the Westside Center for Independent Living (WCIL), where she teamed with other activists to fight for rights for people with disabilities. Coleman also worked as an attorney for the State of California. She dealt with fraud cases in the enforcement division of the state's Department of Corrections, and she also served on the California Attorney General's Commission on Disability.

In 1989 Coleman moved to Tennessee to start a chapter of the American Disabled for Attendant Programs Today (ADAPT). ADAPT is a grassroots organization that fights for the civil and human rights of people with disabilities. Coleman also became co-director of the Technology Access Center of Middle Tennessee and policy analyst for the Tennessee Technology Access Project. Coleman served on both the Tennessee Advisory Committee to the U.S. Civil Rights Commission and the Advisory Committee to the Tennessee Human Rights Commission.

In 1996 Coleman founded Not Dead Yet, an organization based in Illinois that promotes disability rights and actively campaigns against the legalization of euthanasia and assisted suicide. Coleman has spoken on numerous news and radio shows, and she has also been invited to give testimony before the U.S. House of Representatives. She then served as the executive director of the nonprofit Progress Center for Independent Living in Forest Park, Illinois, which provides assistance to people with disabilities. Currently she is the assistant director of advocacy at the Center for Disability Rights in Rochester, New York.

Further Reading

Chapman, R. (2009). *Culture wars: An encyclopedia of issues, voices, and viewpoints.* Armonk, NY: M. E. Sharpe.
Cowan, K. (2004). *Issues of life, death, and identity: The role of disability advocacy and scholarship.* Retrieved from http://content.cdlib.org/view?docId=hb0j49n407&brand=oac

Judith Cook

American expert on mental health community services

Judith A. Cook received her Ph.D. in sociology from Ohio State University. She then moved on to the University of Illinois at Chicago (UIC), where she completed a post-doctoral training program in clinical research sponsored by the National Institute of Mental Health (NIMH). Cook served as research director of the Thresholds National Research and Training Center on Long-Term Mental Illness in Chicago. She then joined the faculty of UIC as a professor of sociology in psychiatry. She has risen to the position of director of the Center on Mental Health Service Research Program in UIC's Department of Psychiatry.

Under Cook's leadership, UIC has become one of the nation's leading research centers in the area of mental health and disability. The Department of Psychiatry includes two federally funded programs: the National Research and Training Center on Psychiatric Disability, which "promotes access to effective consumer-driven and community-based services for adults with serious mental illness"; and the Coordinating Center for the Employment Intervention Demonstration, which focuses on finding "new ways of enhancing employment opportunities and quality of life for mental health consumers." Cook also oversees UIC's Assertive Community Treatment (ACT) Training Institute. ACT is an established model for delivering mental health services to communities, and the institute seeks to enhance ACT services throughout the state of Illinois.

Cook's work at UIC has brought her national recognition as an expert in the mental health field. In 2002 she was tapped to participate in President George W. Bush's New Freedom Commission on Mental Health. She contributed a report to a commission subcommittee on the importance of employment and income supports to the process of rehabilitation or recovery from mental disorders. Cook also serves as a consultant with the U.S. Department of Labor, the Veteran's Administration, the National Institute of Mental Health, and other government agencies.

Cook has written extensively, with more than 150 published books, chapters, and peer-reviewed journal articles to her credit on a wide range of mental health topics, such as gender issues in mental health, the importance of self-determination in recovery, psychiatric rehabilitation, and women with HIV/AIDS. She has won numerous honors and awards, including the 2010 Researcher of the Year Award from UIC.

Further Reading

Judith A. Cook. Retrieved from http://www.psych.uic.edu/faculty/cook.htm
Judith A. Cook. Retrieved from http://www.socialinequities.ca/bio/judith-cook

Gunnar Dybwad (1909–2001)

German-born American scholar and advocate
for people with developmental disabilities

Gunnar Dybwad was born in Leipzig, Germany, on July 12, 1909. He earned a doctorate in law from the University of Halle in 1934 before fleeing Nazi Germany to join his wife Rosemary (an American exchange student who had returned home in 1933) in the United States. Dybwad spent the next several years working with juvenile delinquents in Indiana, New Jersey, and New York. In 1939 he graduated from the New York School of Social Work, and from 1943 to 1951, he served as director of Michigan's Child Welfare Program.

In 1951 Dybwad took the executive directorship of a parents' education organization called the Child Study Association of America. He remained in that position until 1957, when he began a six-year tenure as executive director of the National Association for Retarded Children (now known as the Arc of the United States), where he further burnished his reputation as an authority on intellectual disability, autism, cerebral palsy, and other mental disabilities.

During the 1950s and 1960s, Dybwad and his wife were also leaders of the International League of Societies for Persons with Mental Handicaps (now Inclusion International), an organization dedicated to championing the civil, economic, and societal rights of people with mental disabilities, as well as the their families. In 1964 Gunnar and Rosemary Dybwad accepted co-directorship of the Mental Retardation Project of the International Union for Child Welfare in Geneva, Switzerland. Under this three-year project, the couple traveled to 34 different countries to foster parental involvement and grassroots political advocacy among parents with mentally retarded children.

In 1967 Dybwad began teaching at Brandeis University, where he was professor of human development and founding director of the Starr Center for Mental Retardation at Brandeis's Florence Heller Graduate School. Dybwad's continuing advocacy work during this time is widely credited with advancing reformers' conviction that mental disability was a civil rights issue. He was an early proponent of using litigation as a tool to help children with mental disabilities gain equal access to public education institutions and to aid disabled persons in their quests for inclusion in the wider communities in which they lived.

The Dybwads also wrote numerous books, papers, and essays explaining their bedrock convictions about the untapped potential of people with developmental disabilities to meaningfully contribute to their communities and their own life paths, and they served as consultants on disability issues to organizations and governmental agencies in the United States and around the world throughout the 1970s. In 1978 Gunnar Dybwad assumed the presidency of Inclusion International, a position he held until 1982. Rosemary Dybwad died in 1992, and Gunnar Dybwad died in 2001.

Further Reading

Dybwad, G. (1999). *Ahead of his time: Selected speeches of Gunnar Dybwad* (M. A. Allard, Ed.). Washington, DC: American Association on Mental Retardation.

Spudich, H., & Eigner, W. (n.d.). Gunnar Dybwad, 1909–2001, Untiring Advocate of Persons with Special Needs. Retrieved from http://www.gunnardybwad.net

Maurice A. Feldman (1949–)

*Canadian expert in developmental disabilities and
parenting by persons with intellectual disabilities*

Maurice Abraham Feldman was born in 1949. He earned his Ph.D. in psychology in 1976 from McMaster University in Ontario, Canada. From 1986 until 1994, he was employed as director of the Behaviour Science Division of Surrey Place Centre, an agency in Toronto that provides clinical services to people living with developmental disabilities. From 1994 to 2003, Feldman was chief psychologist at Ongwanada Centre, a nonprofit organization based in Kingston, Ontario, which serves people with developmental disabilities and their families.

In 2003 Feldman joined the faculty at Brock University in St. Catharines, Ontario, where he serves as a professor and as director of the Centre for Applied Disability Services. Feldman's work at the Centre is geared toward the betterment of the lives of those affected by developmental disabilities. The Centre provides education to professionals, researchers, and educators. Feldman was formerly a chancellor's research chair, and he has been honored at Brock with the Award for Distinguished Research and Creative Activity. He is currently co-principal investigator of "The 3R's: A Human Rights Training Project for Persons with Intellectual Disabilities."

Feldman has worked extensively with parents who have intellectual disabilities and their children. His research has culminated in the development and scientific validation of a parenting education program that has been emulated in other countries, including the United States, to help prevent child neglect and behavior problems in these families. Some of Feldman's other research interests include autism, positive behavioral intervention for severe behavior disorders, and early identification and intervention for children with or at risk for developmental, behavioral, emotional, and psychiatric problems. Feldman has published numerous articles in professional journals, and he served as the editor of *Early Intervention: The Essential Readings* (2004).

Further Reading

ASD-CARC: Maurice Feldman. Retrieved from http://www.asdcarc.com/index
.php/publisher/articleview/frmArticleID/107/staticId/1
Faculty of Social Sciences–Child and Youth Studies: Maurice Feldman. Retrieved
from http://www.brocku.ca/social-sciences/undergraduate-programs/child-
and-youth-studies/faculty-contacts/maurice-feldman

Carol Gill (1949–)

American disability ethicist and psychologist

Carol Gill was born in Chicago, Illinois, in 1949. She has used a wheelchair for mobility since contracting polio at the age of five. Gill attended Chicago's Spalding High School, a school specifically set aside for "crippled children." Gill's awareness of mainstream society's prejudicial attitudes toward people with disabilities greatly increased during this period, as did her strong sense of community with other disabled people. In 1966 she entered Chicago's Saint Xavier College, where she earned a bachelor's degree in 1970. She then went on to the University of Illinois, Champaign, where she achieved a master's degree (in 1973) and Ph.D. (1979) in psychology.

Gill's professional career began in the late 1970s in California, where she worked as a rehabilitation psychologist and therapist to clients with disabilities. She briefly taught at the University of Southern California in the school's disability studies program. In 1990 she returned to Chicago, where she founded the Chicago Institute of Disability Research and joined the faculty of the University of Illinois at Chicago in the Department of Disability and Human Development (she currently serves as the school's director of graduate studies for the doctoral program in disabilitiy studies). In 1998 she became the executive officer of the Society for Disability Studies.

Gill has conducted wide-ranging research on disability issues in all of these professional capacities, and she is known as one of the country's foremost disability ethicists. A frequent writer on such subjects as disability culture and identity, women's disability issues, and disabilities studies curriculum development, Gill is also an outspoken critic of physician-assisted suicide who has frequently worked with Not Dead Yet, a national disability rights group that opposes the legalization of assisted suicide and euthanasia.

Further Reading

Gill, C. (1999). The false autonomy of forced choice: Rationalizing suicide for persons with disabilities. In J. L. Werth (Ed.), *Contemporary perspectives on rational suicide*. Philadelphia: Psychology Press.

Gill, C. (2002). Disability Rights and Independent Living Movement Oral History Project [interview with Kathy Cowan]. *Calisphere*. Retrieved from http://content .cdlib.org/view?docId=hb0j49n407;NAAN=13030&doc.view=frames&chunk .id=Carol%20J.%20Gill&toc.depth=1&toc.id=0&brand=calisphere

Laraine M. Glidden (1943–)

American researcher in the areas of intellectual disabilities, developmental disabilities, and adoptive families

Laraine Masters Glidden was born in 1943. She graduated magna cum laude with a bachelor's degree from Mount Holyoke College in Massachusetts in 1964. She continued her education at the University of Illinois, earning a master's degree in 1969 and a Ph.D. in 1970.

In 1970 Glidden launched her academic career as an assistant professor in social sciences at Clarkson University in New York. In 1973 she moved to Teachers College, Columbia University, where she served as adjunct assistant-associate professor and research associate in special education. Glidden's long tenure at St. Mary's College of Maryland began in 1976. She is currently associate-distinguished professor in the Human Development Division. During her time at St. Mary's, Glidden has been visiting professor at the London Hospital Medical College (1982–1983), visiting scholar at University of California, Berkeley (1990–1991), and visiting professor at Georgetown University in Washington, D.C. (2006–2008).

Glidden has conducted extensive research on raising children with developmental disabilities. The National Institutes of Health (NIH) funded her work on this subject for 20 years, and she helped define what it means to raise a child with special needs. Glidden's research has involved comparisons between families who knowingly adopt children with special needs and birth families of similar children. She was the recipient of the 2008 Distinguished Research Award from the Arc of the United States for her work. The award is presented annually to "an outstanding researcher who has contributed in significant ways to studies that enhance the well-being of people with intellectual and developmental disabilities and their families."

Glidden has spoken and consulted internationally in her areas of expertise. She has served as president of the Academy on Mental Retardation and of Division 33 of the American Psychological Association. Glidden has published extensively in her field, and she has served as editor of the *International Review of Research in Mental Retardation* monograph series since 1997.

Further Reading

Psychology Faculty & Staff: Dr. Laraine Masters Glidden. Retrieved from http://www.smcm.edu/psyc/facultypages/lmglidden/index.html

SMCM prof. awarded for developmentally disabled children research. (2008). *Southern Maryland Online*. Retrieved from http://somd.com/news/headlines/2008/8765.shtml

Dan Goodley (1972–)

British professor of psychology and disability studies specializing in learning disabilities and self-advocacy

Dan Goodley was born in 1972 in Nottingham, England. He graduated with honors from Manchester Metropolitan University with a bachelor's degree in psychology in 1993. He completed his Ph.D. at the University of Sheffield's Department of Sociological Studies in 1998. His wife, Dr. Rebecca Lawthom, is also a disability studies scholar; they have two daughters.

Goodley has taken an interdisciplinary approach to the study of disabilities, working in the departments of psychology, sociology, social policy, and education. He has taught at the University of Sheffield, the University of Leeds, and is currently a member of the faculty of the Research Institute for Health and Social Change at Manchester Metropolitan University.

In his research, Goodley explores the issues of exclusion and self-advocacy in the disabled population, particularly in the area of children and education. Of particular interest to him is the effect of labeling people as having "learning difficulties," which he feels marginalizes them and excludes them from society. He investigates learning disabilities in light of several theoretical approaches, including critical and community psychology and postmodernism. His research is qualitative in nature, incorporating methods from ethnography, narrative, the performing arts, and participatory research.

In works such as *Self-Advocacy in the Lives of People with Learning Difficulties: The Politics of Resilience* (2000), Goodley explores the ways in which individuals with learning disabilities are excluded from mainstream society and the impact of societal attitudes on the disabled. Goodley investigates the concept of acknowledging resilience in people with disabilities as a means to self-empowerment and self-advocacy. He also promotes the concept of enabling people with disabilities to make decisions about their lives, including those related to the services they receive from agencies and caregivers.

Goodley is a frequent collaborator with Dr. Janice McLaughlin. As recipients of funding provided by the Economic and Social Research Council (ESRC), they published *Families Raising Disabled Children: Enabling Care and Social Justice* (2008), which examines the research into the lives of children with disabilities and the roles of their parents and caregivers in outcomes. He is currently involved in a study titled "Does Every Child Matter, Post Blair? The Interconnections of Disabled Childhoods." This study, also funded by the ESRC, takes a social, political, and psychological approach to the governmental initiatives under former Prime Minister Tony Blair as they affected children with disabilities.

In addition to his academic publishing, Goodley has served as coordinator of the *Disability Studies Association Monthly*, as director of the Centre of Applied Disability Studies at the University of Sheffield, and as director of inclusive education and equality research at the Cluster School of Education, also at the University of Sheffield. Goodley is currently working on a book titled *Introducing Disability Studies: Psyche, Culture and Society* to be published by Sage.

Further Reading

Goodley, D. & Lawthom, R. (2005). *Disability and psychology: Critical introductions and reflections.* London: Palgrave.

Michael J. Guralnick

American academic specializing in early childhood development

Michael J. Guralnick is the director of the Center on Human Development and Disability (CHDD) at the University of Washington. The focus of his research is early childhood development and intervention. He began his career in the field in the 1970s, when he was the director of research and the experimental preschool for the National Children's Center in Washington, D.C. During the 1980s, he served as director of the Nisonger Center at the Ohio State University, one of the first university centers noted as a Center for Excellence in Developmental Disabilities.

Next Guralnick joined the faculty of the University of Washington, where, in addition to his responsibilities as director of the CHDD, he is also a professor of psychology and pediatrics. The CHDD—a University Center for Excellence in Developmental Disabilities and a Eunice Kennedy Shriver Intellectual and Developmental Disabilities Research Center—is one of the largest interdisciplinary centers in the country devoted to research and training in developmental disabilities. Under Guralnick's direction, more than 600 faculty, staff, and students provide clinical services and training and conduct basic and applied research.

Guralnick has published over 140 articles and book chapters in the area of early childhood development, focusing in particular on early intervention programs, inclusion, and peer-related social competence in children ages 3 to 5 with developmental delays. A grant from the National Institute of Child Health and Human Development (NICHD) funded a recent research project that investigated the effectiveness of early intervention programs on developmentally delayed preschoolers. Through the analysis of peer interaction in this subject group, Guralnick studied problems in peer relations, the development of friendships, and social competence. He developed a tool for clinicians, the Assessment of Peer Relations, that outlines the methodology to assess and improve peer-related skills.

In addition to his other publications, Guralnick was the editor of *Infants and Young Children* from 2003 to 2009. He is also the founder and chair of the International Society on Early Intervention. Guralnick has received the American Association on Intellectual and Developmental Disabilities Research Award and the American Psychological Association's Edgar A. Doll Award for outstanding scientific contributions to the field of intellectual and developmental disabilities. He has served as president of the Council for Exceptional Children's Early Childhood Division and the Association of University Centers on Disabilities. His current research efforts include investigating peer relationships in children with Down syndrome.

Further Reading

Guralnick, M. J. (2010). Early intervention approaches to enhance the peer-related social competence of young children with developmental delays: A historical perspective. *Infants and Young Children, 23,* 73–83.

Guralnick, M. J., Neville, B., Hammond, M. A., & Connor, R. T. (2008). Continuity and change from full inclusion early childhood programs through the early elementary period. *Journal of Early Intervention, 30,* 237–250.

Debra Hart

American advocate for educational opportunities
for people with intellectual disabilities

Debra Hart received a bachelor of science degree from Boston University and her master of science degree from Simmons College. She went on to pursue doctoral studies at Brandeis University, then began work in the field of education.

Hart has devoted her career to working in support of educational opportunities for children, youth, and adults with disabilities. As the director of more than 20 federal and state projects over two decades, she has helped develop curricula for K–12 systems nationwide, focusing in particular on helping students with intellectual disabilities. She has developed training programs for teachers and administrators for technology, media, and materials that encourage access, participation, and achievement among students with intellectual disabilities, particularly in the area of transitions of youth to college, adult life, and employment. She also has teaching certification for general education and for students with disabilities.

Hart is the educational coordinator at the Institute for Community Inclusion at the University of Massachusetts, Boston. Hart has directed federal grants that focus on research into access to post-secondary education for young adults with developmental disabilities. She has also served as principal investigator for the National Institute on Disability and Rehabilitation Research for the U.S. Department of Education.

In her research, Hart has demonstrated the benefits of post-secondary education for young adults with intellectual disabilities in the areas of employment and academic achievement, as well as in independence, self-advocacy, and self-esteem. She continues to advocate for young adults with developmental disabilities in her role at the institute, and she is also a member of the staff of Think College: College Options for People with Disabilities, a research and advocacy organization that is run out of the Institute for Community Inclusion.

Further Reading

Hart, D., & Grigal, M. (2004). *Individual support to increase access to an inclusive college experience for students with intellectual disabilities* [online module]. College Park: University of Maryland, Department of Special Education. Retrieved from http://www.education.umd.edu/oco

Hart, D., Mele-McCarthy, J., Pasternack, R. H., Zimbich, K., & Parker, D. R. (2004). Community college: A pathway to success for youth with learning, cognitive, and intellectual disabilities in secondary settings. *Education and Training in Developmental Disabilities, 1*(1), 54–66.

Tamar Heller

American academic specializing in lifespan transitions for people with disabilities

Tamar Heller was born in Israel and moved to the United States at the age of 5. She received a bachelor's degree in history and psychology from the

University of Wisconsin, Madison, a master's degree in psychology from Roosevelt University, and a Ph.D. in psychology from the University of Illinois at Chicago.

Heller is currently a professor and head of the Department of Disability and Human Development at the University of Illinois at Chicago, and director of the University Center for Excellence in Developmental Disabilities for Illinois. She also directs the Rehabilitation Research and Training Center on Aging with Developmental Disabilities and the Special Olympics Collaborating Research Center.

The focus of Heller's research is lifespan transitions for people with disabilities, as well as family support for people with disabilities as they age. She has also led community outreach programs, including a Family Studies and Services Program in Chicago that integrated an interdisciplinary clinic offering family services for people with disabilities. She has written over 160 publications and presented more than 300 papers in her area of expertise, on such issues as family support for caregivers of people with disabilities, health promotion and self-determination for people with disabilities, and relationship and caregiving issues involving siblings with disabilities. She has edited special issues of several periodicals in the area of disabilities, including *Technology and Disability, American Journal on Mental Retardation, Journal of Policy and Practice in Intellectual Disabilities*, and *Family Relations*. She has also co-authored and co-edited four books, including the recent volumes *Health Matters for People with Developmental Disabilities: Creating a Sustainable Health Promotion Program* and *Health Matters: The Exercise and Nutrition Health Education Curriculum for People with Developmental Disabilities*.

Heller was one of the founders of the national Sibling Leadership Network, an organization dedicated to advocacy for and with siblings with disabilities. In 2005 she was then Senator Barack Obama's delegate to the White House Conference on Aging. She is a board member and the past president of the Association of University Centers on Disability, and she serves on the boards of the International Association for the Scientific Study of Intellectual Disabilities and Keshet. Previously she served on the boards of the American Association on Intellectual and Developmental Disabilities and the European Course on Mental Retardation.

Heller has received numerous honors and awards, including the 2008 Lifetime Research Achievement Award from the International Association for the Scientific Study of Intellectual Disabilities, the 2009 Autism Ally for Public Policy Award of The Arc/The Autism Program of Illinois, and the 2009 Community Partner Award of Community Support Services.

Further Reading

Heller, T., & Caldwell, J. (2006, June). Supporting aging caregivers and adults with developmental disabilities in future planning. *Mental Retardation, 44*(3), 189–202.

Heller, T., Caldwell, J., & Factor, A. (2007). Aging family caregivers: Policies and practices. *Mental Retardation and Developmental Disabilities Research Reviews, 13*(2), 136–142.

Heller, T., Hsieh, K., & Rimmer, J. (2004). Attitudinal and psychological outcomes of a fitness and health education program on adults with Down syndrome. *American Journal on Mental Retardation, 109*(2), 175–185.

Judith E. Heumann (1947–)

American public policy official and advocate for people with disabilities

Judith Ellen Heumann was born in 1947 in Philadelphia, Pennsylvania. She was raised in Brooklyn, New York, and contracted polio at 18 months of age. Throughout her youth, she and her parents fought for and won the right for her to attend mainstream classes with non-disabled students. Heumann graduated from Long Island University in 1969 with a bachelor's degree in theater and speech, with a specialty in pathology. In 1970 the New York City public schools refused to hire her as a teacher, solely because she used a wheelchair. She sued the city and won. That same year, Heumann co-founded Disabled in Action, an advocacy organization that sought legal protection for people with disabilities.

Heumann went to graduate school at the University of California at Berkeley, earning her master's degree in public health in 1975. While in Berkeley, she co-founded the World Institute on Disability, the first public policy research think tank for disability issues. She also helped found the Center for Independent Living, the first independent living center for people with disabilities in the country. She served as its deputy director until 1982, when she became assistant to the director of the California Department of Rehabilitation. For the next 30 years, she used her expertise to help develop legislation and policies in the area of human rights for children and adults with disabilities.

In 1993 Heumann was named assistant secretary for the Office of Special Education and Rehabilitative Services for the U.S. Department of Education. She helped implement legislation for programs in special education and rehabilitation, and she also oversaw the National Institute on Disability and Rehabilitation Research. As assistant secretary, she represented the

Department of Education at the International Congress on Disability in Mexico City in 1995. She also represented the United States at the Fourth United Nations World Conference on Women in China. She served in the Department of Education until 2001, when she was named the first advisor on disability and development for the World Bank. In that role, she led the bank's efforts to develop and support policies and programs for people with disabilities around the world, promoting access to employment within the economic mainstream of their communities.

In 2007 Heumann was named director of the Department of Disability Services for Washington, D.C. In that position, she headed the Developmental Disability Administration and the Rehabilitative Services Administration. In 2010 Heumann was appointed to the U.S. Department of State, where she is special advisor for International Disability Rights. In that role, she continues to advocate for people with disabilities worldwide.

Further Reading

Heumann, J. *The Disability Rights and Independent Living Movement.* University of California, Berkeley. Retrieved from http://bancroft.berkeley.edu/collections/drilm/collection/items/heumann.html

Shaw, L. R. (2000). Judy Heumann. In B. T. McMahon & L. R. Shaw (Eds.), *Enabling lives: Biographies of six prominent Americans with disabilities.* Boca Raton, FL: CRC Press.

Matthew Janicki (1943–)

American academic and researcher specializing in aging adults with intellectual disabilities

Matthew P. Janicki is the research associate professor of human development at the Institute of Disability and Human Development at the University of Illinois at Chicago, where he also serves as director for technical assistance for the Rehabilitation Research and Training Center in Aging with Developmental Disabilities. The primary focus of his research concerns adults with intellectual disabilities, aging adults with intellectual disabilities, and community support for adults with Alzheimer's disease and their families. He is currently the principal investigator for a federally funded project examining how community agencies aid families to support adults with intellectual disabilities affected by Alzheimer's.

Janicki began his career in the field of disabilities as the director for Aging and Special Populations for the Office of Mental Retardation and Developmental Disabilities in New York State. He was also a Public Policy Leadership Fellow at the Joseph P. Kennedy Jr. Foundation, a program that brings professionals and family advocates to Washington, D.C., for one-year fellowships, allowing them to learn about policy and legislation in the area of intellectual disabilities. As a Kennedy Fellow, Janicki worked on a Senate committee and at the National Institute on Aging.

The author of many books and articles in the area of aging, dementia, public policy, and rehabilitation for people with intellectual and developmental disabilities, Janicki has also lectured and provided training for practitioners all over the world. He is a member of the Executive Committee of the International Association on the Scientific Study of Intellectual Disabilities. He also serves as editor of the *Journal of Policy and Practice in Intellectual Disabilities,* and is co-author of several books, including *Aging and Developmental Disabilities: Issues and Approaches,* a seminal book that bridged the gerontological and developmental disability literature.

Further Reading

Janicki, M. P., & Ansello, E. F. (2000). *Community support for aging adults with lifelong disabilities.* Baltimore: Paul H. Brookes.

Janicki, M. P., & Dalton, A. J. (1999*). Dementia, aging, and intellectual disabilities.* New York: Brunner/Mazel.

Alan Jette

American academic and public health official
specializing in assessment of function and disability

Alan M. Jette received his bachelor of science degree in physical therapy from the State University of New York at Buffalo in 1973. He went on to attend the University of Michigan, earning his master's in public health in 1975 and his Ph.D. in public health in 1979.

Jette is the director of the Health and Disabilities Research Institute at Boston University, where he is also a professor of Health Policy and Management. He concurrently serves as research director for the New England Regional Spinal Cord Injury Center at Boston University Hospital. Prior to his current position, he was dean of the Sargent College of Health and Rehabilitation Sciences at Boston University, where he oversaw the master's and doctoral programs in Communication Disorders, Health Sciences, Occupational Therapy, and Physical Therapy.

An internationally recognized expert in the measurement of function and disability, Jette has developed many instruments that assess a broad spectrum of disabilities. He is the current director of the Boston Contemporary Rehabilitation Outcomes Measurement Network, which is funded by the National Institutes of Health National Center for Rehabilitation Research. The author of many articles on the measurement of function and disability, he has also written extensively in the areas of rehabilitation, geriatrics, and public health, especially demographic studies regarding disability trends as they affect post-acute care. Jette was also the chair of "The Future of Disability in America," a project of the Institute of Medicine released in 2007. He is the recipient of many awards, including the Darrel J. Mase Leadership Award from the University of Florida College of Public Health and Health Professions, which is given to individuals who have made major contributions to the nation's health care.

Further Reading

Jette, A. (2006, May). Toward a common language for function, disability, and health. *Physical Therapy, 86*(5), 726–735.

Jette, A., & Haley, S. M. (2003, Spring). Comparison of functional status tools used in post-acute care. *Health Care Financing Review, 24*(3)13–25.

Bryan Kemp

American disability specialist focusing on issues involving elder abuse, geriatric mental health, and aging with disability

Bryan Kemp received his Ph.D. in clinical psychology and aging from the University of Southern California. He has since spent more than 30 years working in geriatrics, geriatric mental health, and rehabilitation. He taught for several years at the University of Southern California, where he was a professor of family medicine, psychiatry, and gerontology and headed the Rehabilitation and Training Center on Aging with Spinal Cord Injury. At USC, he was also director of the aging-related research centers at the Rancho Los Amigos National Rehabilitation Center, a major center for rehabilitation care in California.

Kemp later became a professor of medicine and psychology at the University of California–Irvine School of Medicine, whose program in gerontology is a Center for Excellence on Elder Abuse and Neglect. He has served as a medical psychologist for the university in its collaborative effort with the Orange County Elder Abuse Forensic Center. Kemp has published over 100 articles and is also an esteemed lecturer and trainer in several areas. He has developed assessment tools that measure autonomy, capacity, vulnerability, and undue influence in victims of elder abuse.

Another major area of Kemp's research is the growing population of aging people with disabilities, focusing in particular on the needs of patients, families, and caregivers in dealing with late-life complications in the health of people with disabilities. He notes that for the first time in history, there is a large population of people with disabilities who are living into middle and late life. He studies this population, now numbering more than 12 million, to discern the problems they and their families face in such areas as rehabilitation, mental health care, and quality of life.

Kemp has directed the Gerontology Outpatient Programs at Los Amigos National Rehabilitation Center, as well as the federally funded Rehabilitation Research and Training Center on Aging with a Disability. His research sponsors have included the National Institute on Disability and Rehabilitation Research, the U.S. Department of Education Office of Special Education, and the Centers for Disease Control.

Further Reading

Kemp, B., & Mosqueda, L. (Eds.). (2004). *Aging with a disability: What a clinician needs to know.* Baltimore: Johns Hopkins University Press.

Mosqueda, L., Burnight, K., Liao, S., & Kemp, B. (2004, February). Advancing the field of elder mistreatment: A new model for integration of social and medical services. *The Gerontologist, 44*(5), 703–708.

M. Powell Lawton (1923–2001)

American research scientist and pioneer in the study of gerontology

Mortimer Powell Lawton, one of the leading figures in the study of aging, was born in 1923 in Atlanta, Georgia. He received his bachelor's degree from Haverford College in 1947, and his doctorate in clinical psychology from Columbia University's Teachers College in 1952. He and his wife, Fay Gardner Lawton, had three children.

A pioneer in the field of gerontology, Lawton began his career at the Veterans Administration Hospital in Providence, Rhode Island. After several years in that position, he began working as a research psychologist at the Norristown State Hospital in Norristown, Pennsylvania. In 1963, he joined the staff of the Polisher Research Institute of the Philadelphia Geriatric Center as its first director, where he established a number of "firsts" in the care of older people. Under Lawton, the institute became the first research center to focus exclusively on aging. Just a year after joining the institute, Lawton hosted the first conference on Alzheimer's disease in the United States.

Lawton became nationally known for his research into the psychological and social aspects of aging and for his interest in creating housing and environments that met the needs of older people, especially those with Alzheimer's disease. At the Philadelphia Geriatric Center, he helped design both the services and the facilities for the aging, including the first nursing center created especially for Alzheimer's patients in the nation.

Lawton was also among the first research scientists to develop assessment tools to determine the functional abilities and needs of older patients. These included the Multilevel Assessment Instrument, which measures health, social interactions, time use, environment, and psychological well-being; the Morale Scale and the Affect Scale, which also measure well-being; and the Observed Emotion Rating Scale, which was the first assessment tool of its kind to measure the non-verbal communication of emotions in dementia patients.

Lawton was a widely published author of articles and books, including a major text in the field of gerontology, *Environment and Aging*, published in 1980. He was also the founding editor of the American Psychological Association's periodical *Psychology and Aging*, editor-in-chief of the *Annual Review of Gerontology and Geriatrics*, associate editor of *Contemporary Gerontology*, and consulting editor of the *Journal of Aging and Social Policy*.

Lawton was a member of the leading organizations in his field, including the Gerontological Society of America and the American Psychological Association, where he was president of the Division of Adult Development and Aging. In 1971, Lawton served as a delegate to the White House Conference on Aging; he later served on several national committees, including the National Technical Committee on Housing.

Lawton also lectured as a visiting professor at many colleges and universities in the nation, including the University of Pennsylvania, Syracuse University, Portland State University, and the University of Southern

California. He was also an adjunct professor of human development at Pennsylvania State University, and a professor of psychiatry at the Temple University School of Medicine. In those roles, he helped to educate and mentor a generation of doctors, nurses, social workers, and clinicians in the growing field of gerontology.

Among the many awards Lawton received were the Novartis Prize from the International Association of Gerontology, and the Distinguished Contribution Award and Distinguished Research Award, both from the American Psychological Association. His own contributions to the field of gerontology are remembered in the annual M. Powell Lawton Award, created by Polisher Research Institute and presented each year to an individual who makes strides in gerontological research that benefit older people and improve their care.

Further Reading

Dr. M. Powell Lawton, 77; elder statesman of gerontology. Retrieved from http://www.abramsoncenter.org/pri/staff/MPLawton-obit.htm

Saxon, W. (2001, February 5). Obituary of M. Powell Lawton. *New York Times*.

Gwynnyth Llewellyn

Australian academic and leading authority
on parents who have intellectual disabilities

Gwynnyth Llewellyn is professor and dean of the faculty of health sciences at the University of Sydney and director of the Australian Family and Disability Studies Research Collaboration. The main focus of her research is disability within the family. She has published widely in her field, in both Australian and international journals, concentrating especially in the areas of parents with disabilities or children with disabilities. She is the consulting editor for the *Scandinavian Journal of Disability Research* and serves on the board of the *Journal of Applied Research in Intellectual Disabilities*. She also co-edited a major work in her field, *Parents With Intellectual Disabilities: Past, Present and Futures*, published in 2010, which provides an international overview of the leading issues in research on the topic.

Llewellyn's research is funded by federal and state departments in Australia, and by the Australian Research Council and the National Health and Medical Research Council. Her ongoing research projects include "Health and Well-Being Indicators for Disabled Children and

Youth," which is funded by an international collaboration of schools affiliated with the World University Network; "The Transition from Secondary School to Adulthood: Experiences and Life Outcomes for Youth with an Intellectual Disability and Their Families," funded by the Australian Research Council; "Healthy Start: A National Strategy for Children and Parents with Intellectual Disability," which is being prepared in collaboration with the Parenting Research Centre; and "Improving Life Chances for Young Disabled Australians," which is funded by the Australian Research Council Discovery. Llewellyn is also the ministerial appointee to Community Services, Research Advisory Council, and director of the Royal Rehabilitation Centre in Sydney.

Llewellyn's academic responsibilities include supervising doctoral candidates in the health sciences at the University of Sydney, where she earned her Ph.D. She also serves as guest lecturer in family and disability studies in the graduate occupational therapy program and the undergraduate health science curriculum. As director of the Australian Family and Disabilities Studies Research Collaboration, she heads up a team of professionals from several disciplines in the health sciences—including occupational therapy, psychology, and social work—who collaborate to identify, promote, and address the issues faced by families where a parent or child has a disability.

Further Reading

Grace, R., Llewellyn, G., Wedgewood, N., Fenech, M., & McConnell, D. (2008). Far from ideal: Everyday experiences of parents and teachers negotiating an inclusive early childhood experience in the Australian context. *Topics in Early Childhood Special Education, 28*(1), 18–30.

Llewellyn, G., Mayes, R., & McConnell, D. (2008). Towards acceptance and inclusion of people with intellectual disability as parents. *Journal of Applied Research in Intellectual Disability, 21*(4), 293–295.

Jenny Morris (1950–)

*British researcher and advocate specializing in
disability issues involving women, youth, and parents*

Jenny Morris was born in 1950 in Bedford, England. She received her bachelor's degree in sociology and her doctoral degree in social policy from the London School of Economics.

In 1983, Morris sustained a spinal cord injury and became disabled. This experience galvanized her interest in the field, and she became one of the top researchers in several areas of disability studies, especially as they impact women, parents, and young people with disabilities. She has examined the experiences of people with physical, visual, mental health, and learning difficulties, and she has also researched the experiences of minority individuals with disabilities.

In her research, Morris explores the ways in which people with disabilities are marginalized in education, housing, transportation, employment, and other areas of life. She has questioned the viability of "mainstreaming" children with disabilities into non-disabled classroom environments, as well as the educational establishment's treatment of parents with disabilities in determining their own children's educational choices. Morris has also been an advocate for allowing people with disabilities to determine the care they receive, focusing in particular on areas involving choice and control.

Morris is the author of several groundbreaking studies, including *Pride Against Prejudice: Transforming Attitudes to Disability*, in which she questions existing cultural and societal attitudes toward people with disabilities, touching upon such issues as abortion, mercy killings, and sexuality. Among her other publications are *Able Lives: Women's Experience of Paralysis,* as well as special reports on disabled teenagers and social exclusion.

Morris has served as a policy consultant and advocate for disability legislation in Great Britain. She was a special advisor on the Disability Discrimination Bill and served as the executive director of the Independent Living Review for the Office for Disability Issues. Morris has also worked on independent living issues for the British government's "Improving the Life Chances of Disabled People" report and took part in a national working group examining child protection and disability. She has also been a researcher and has written for the Joseph Rowntree Foundation. For all of her work on behalf of people with disabilities, Morris was awarded the Order of the British Empire (OBE) in 2010.

Further Reading

Morris, J. (2002). *Moving into adulthood: Young disabled people moving into adulthood.* Retrieved from http://www.jrf.org.uk/publications/moving-adulthood-young-disabled-people-moving-adulthood

Morris, J. (2003). *Supporting disabled adults in their parenting role.* Retrieved from http://www.jrf.org.uk/publications/supporting-disabled-adults-their-parenting-role-0

Mark Priestley (1963–)

British academic and author specializing in disability issues

Mark Priestley was born in 1963 in Kabwe, Zambia. He did his undergraduate and graduate work at the University of Leeds, receiving his bachelor's degree in philosophy and politics in 1984, his master's degree in social and public policy in 1993, and his Ph.D. in social policy (disability studies) in 1997.

After receiving his doctorate, Priestley worked as a research fellow at the University of Leeds on several projects funded by the Economic and Social Research Council (ESRC). These included "Life as a Disabled Child" from 1991 to 1997 and "Disability, Social Policy, and the Life Course" from 1999 to 2002, reflecting his early research interests in disability policies in Britain and the life course approach to disability studies.

Priestley is currently professor of disability policy and director of the Centre for Disability Studies at the University of Leeds. His current research interests include the study of disability policies from a European as well as a global perspective. He is particularly interested in exploring the ways in which economic, political, and social inequalities affect disabled people in different cultures. His recent publications include *Disability: A Life Course Approach* and *Disability and the Life Course: Global Perspectives.*

Priestley is also the scientific director of the European Commissions' Academic Network of European Disability Experts, and is the administrator of the international discussion forum disability-research@jisc.mail.ac.uk. He has also served on the editorial board of a number of publications in the disability field, including *Disability and Society, Scandinavian Journal of Disability Research,* and *Disability Studies Quarterly,* and was a founding member of *ALTER: European Journal of Disability Research.*

Priestley has been a visiting scholar at the University of Sheffield and held a number of advisory positions on many governmental boards, including the British government's Civil Protection Office, the European Union's Social Policy Analysis Network, the National Disability Authority of Ireland, and the International Labour Organisation. He has also served in a research advisory role for several studies sponsored by the Joseph Rowntree Foundation, including "Ethnicity, Disability, and Young People" and "Housing and Disabled Children."

Further Reading

Priestley, M. (2003). *Disability: A life course approach.* Cambridge, UK: Polity Press.
Priestley, M. (2007). In search of European disability policy: Between national and global. *ALTER: European Journal of Disability Research,* 1(1), 61–74.

Ed Roberts (1939–1995)

American activist and founder of the disability rights movement

Edward Verne Roberts was born in 1939 in San Mateo, California. His parents were Verne and Zona Roberts. At the age of 14, Ed contracted polio. His life as an activist began soon thereafter. When he started college at the University of California at Berkeley in the 1960s, he was the first student with severe disabilities to attend the school. However, he faced discrimination from his first day on campus. Roberts brought the iron lung he needed with him to Berkeley, but he could not find campus housing that would accommodate him. He was offered a room in the hospital that housed the student health center, and soon he and several other severely disabled students were living there.

Calling themselves the Rolling Quads, Roberts and his fellow students began to work for change on the Berkeley campus, demanding accommodation and support services for disabled students, including barrier removal and personal attendant services, so that students with disabilities could live independently. Their efforts resulted in the Physically Disabled Student Program, the first organization of its kind in the nation.

Roberts received his bachelor's degree in political science from Berkeley in 1964, and his master's degree in 1966. He was a member of the faculty at the university for several years, while continuing to work on such key issues as accessibility, inclusion, and equality for people with disabilities. He founded the Center for Independent Living in 1972, and it became a model for similar programs for people with disabilities worldwide. In 1975 Governor Jerry Brown made Roberts director of the Department of Rehabilitation for California. In 1983 Roberts co-founded the World Institute on Disability, which became a forum for research and the dissemination of programs in education, transportation, housing, health, independent living, and other key areas for people with disabilities.

In all his work as an activist, Roberts stressed that it was important for people with disabilities to lead self-directed lives. He encouraged disabled people to challenge the perceptions held by the able-bodied community, and to see themselves not as passive objects of pity, but as self-actualizing people able to articulate their goals and to demand civil rights.

Ed Roberts died after a stroke on March 14, 1995. In August 2010, his life and work on behalf of people with disabilities was commemorated by Governor Arnold Schwarzenegger, who signed a bill declaring that January 23 (Roberts's birthday) would now be celebrated as "Ed Roberts Day" in California. The bill encourages educational programs to promote awareness of disability issues. At the University of California at Berkeley, an Ed Roberts Campus is being built that will include several organizations offering services and programs to people with disabilities.

Further Reading

Burris, M. (2010, August 2). Day to honor local disability rights activist. *The Daily Californian.*

Ed Roberts. Retrieved from http://www.ilusa.com/links/022301ed_roberts.htm

John S. Rolland (1948–)

American academic and author focusing on family-centered treatment and services

John S. Rolland was born in 1948 in Perth Amboy, New Jersey. He received his undergraduate degree in biology from the University of Pennsylvania in 1969 and his medical degree from the University of Michigan in 1973. He received a master's degree in public health from Harvard University in 1974 and completed his residency in psychiatry at Yale University's School of Medicine in 1977. At Yale, he founded the Center for Illness in Families and was a National Institute of Mental Health Fellow at the Institute for Social and Policy Studies.

Rolland is currently a clinical professor in the Department of Psychiatry and Behavioral Neuroscience at the University of Chicago's Pritzker School of Medicine, where he is the course director for the program Family Therapy and Consultation: Systemic Approaches to Clinical Practice. He is also co-founder and co-director of the Chicago Center for Family Health, where he is responsible for training staff of the Families, Illness, and Collaborative Healthcare Program. Rolland is an internationally recognized specialist for his Family Systems-Illness model, which examines the interaction of psychosocial demands and family support systems in patients coping with serious illnesses, as well as for his work with families who face serious illness, disability, and loss.

Rolland's publications include *Families, Illness, and Disability: An Integrative Treatment Model*, published in 1994, and *Individuals, Families, and the New Era of Genetics: A Biopsychosocial Perspective*, published in 2005. He has also given over 250 presentations on topics relating to families dealing with illness and disability. He is on the boards of several journals in his field, including *American Journal of Orthopsychiatry; Family Process; Journal of Marital and Family Therapy; Families, Systems, and Health;* and *AIDS Education and Prevention.*

Rolland is also a Distinguished Fellow of the American Psychiatric Association and the American Orthopsychiatric Association. He is the current president of the American Family Therapy Academy and the former chair of its Human Rights and Family Policy Committees. As president of the Chicago chapter of Physicians for Social Responsibility, Rolland led an international project in Kosovo following the war in that region, called the Kosovar Family Professional Education Collaborative, which trained staff to help families affected by trauma and loss.

Further Reading

Rolland, J. S. (2003). Mastering family challenges in illness and disability. In F. Walsh (Ed.), *Normal family processes* (3rd ed.). New York: Guilford Press.

Rolland, J. S. (2009). Chronic illness and the family life cycle. In E. Carter & M. McGoldrick (Eds.), *The expanded family life cycle: Individual, family, and social perspectives* (4th ed.). Boston: Allyn & Bacon.

K. Warner Schaie (1928–)

German-born American academic and author focusing on cognitive development through the life course

Klaus Warner Schaie was born in 1928 in Stettin, Germany. His parents were Sal and Lottie Schaie. Schaie received his bachelor's degree from the University of California, Berkeley, in 1952, and his master's and doctoral degrees in psychology from the University of Washington in 1953 and 1956, respectively. He began his academic career at Washington University in St. Louis in 1956 as a post-doctoral fellow. He taught at the University of Nebraska from 1957 to 1964, at West Virginia University from 1964 to 1973, and at the University of Southern California from 1973 to 1981, where he was executive director and dean of the Ethel Percy Andrus Gerontology

Center. In 1981 Schaie joined the faculty of Pennsylvania State University, where he has served as the Evan Pugh Professor of Human Development and Psychology since 1986.

Schaie is also the founder of the Seattle Longitudinal Study, one of the most extensive research studies into how people develop and change cognitively throughout adulthood. He began the study in 1956, in cooperation with the Group Health Cooperative of Puget Sound. That initial study included 500 people, ranging in age from the early 20s to the late 60s. The group has been evaluated every seven years since then, and new groups have also been added to the study. Its main goals include investigating the impact of health, demographic, personality, and environmental factors on cognitive abilities in aging, and also exploring if intelligence changes uniformly throughout adulthood, why there are individual differences in age-related changes, and whether intellectual decline in old age can be reversed by educational intervention.

As of 2010, more than 6,000 individuals have taken part in the Seattle Longitudinal Study. Current participants range in age from 22 to 101 years old and include more than 20 people who have been involved in the study since its inception. Siblings, children, and grandchildren of the original participants have also been included, making it the first study of cognitive development to span three generations in the nation.

Schaie has written extensively about the study, and he is also the author of several seminal textbooks in gerontology, including *Handbook of the Psychology of Aging* and *Adult Development and Aging*. His findings on aging and cognitive decline have been of increasing interest to the general public as well, and he has written and given interviews regarding how people can make lifestyle changes, including health behaviors and cognitive training, to maintain intellectual abilities into old age. He has also been involved in collecting data relating to the early detection and risk for dementia. In addition, Schaie's studies have been used in legal cases involving age discrimination and public policy practices regarding retirement. He is the recipient of the Kleemeier Award for Distinguished Research Contributions from the Gerontological Society of America and the Distinguished Scientific Contributions Award from the American Psychological Association.

Further Reading

Schaie, K. W. (2005, January 28). Observations from the Seattle Longitudinal Study of Adult Intelligence. *John Hopkins Memory Bulletin*, 23–30.

Schaie, K. W. (2008). Historical processes and patterns of cognitive aging. In S. M. Hofer & D. F. Alwin (Eds.), *Handbook on cognitive aging: Interdisciplinary perspective.* Thousand Oaks, CA: Sage.

Milton Seligman (1937–)

American academic and author focusing on children with disabilities and their families

Milton Seligman was born in 1937 in Altenkirchen, Germany. He received his master's degree in psychology from San Francisco State University in 1964 and his doctoral degree in counseling psychology from the University of Oregon in 1968.

Seligman taught at the University of Pittsburgh's School of Education for 35 years, retiring in 2005. He is now a professor emeritus in the school's Department of Psychology as well as a therapist in private practice. The focus of his research and writing is children with disabilities and the effect of those disabilities on members of their families. He has written books and journal articles about various aspects of the topic, including *Ordinary Families, Special Children: A Systems Approach to Childhood Disability.*

As the parent of a daughter with disabilities, Seligman has also focused on the father-daughter dynamic in families with a disabled child, including the essay "Reflections on a Special Father-Daughter Relationship," which he contributed to the volume *Father Voices: Reflections on Raising a Child With a Disability.* In addition, Seligman has researched and written about siblings and grandparents of children with disabilities and is completing a volume on the topic. He has also written a guide for teachers in creating effective communication practices in dealing with parents of children with disabilities.

A member of the American Psychological Association, Seligman is also an elected member of the National Register of Health Service Providers in Psychology.

Further Reading

Marshak, L. M., Seligman, M., & Prezant, F. (1999). *Disability and the family life-cycle.* New York: Basic Books.

Seligman, M., Goodwin, G., Pascal, K., Applegate, A., & Lehman, L. (1997). Mothers of children with disabilities: Perceptions of their parents' and their spouse's parents' level of support. *Education and Training in Mental Retardation and Developmental Disabilities, 32,* 293–303.

Marsha Seltzer

American academic whose research focuses
on the impact of disability on the family

Marsha Mailick Seltzer received her bachelor's degree in psychology and sociology from the University of Wisconsin in 1972, and her Ph.D. in social welfare from Brandeis University in 1978. She taught at Boston University for 10 years before joining the faculty of the University of Wisconsin in 1988.

Seltzer is a Vaughan Bascom and Elizabeth M. Boggs Professor at the University of Wisconsin and has been the director of the school's Waisman Center since 2002. The Waisman Center is a research facility focusing on human development, developmental disabilities, and neurodegenerative diseases. Seltzer's own research focuses on the effects of disability on family members. She is especially interested in how lifelong caregiving by parents and siblings of family members with disabilities—including autism, Down syndrome, and schizophrenia—impacts the well-being of those caregivers.

Funded by the National Institute on Aging, Seltzer has conducted research in three main areas. First, she has headed a 12-year study of aging families with an adult child with disabilities, researching the challenges and choices faced by aging parents as they plan the continued care for their disabled child. Her second area of research involves a comparison study of parents of children with developmental disabilities, including autism and fragile X syndrome, with parents of adult children with schizophrenia. In her third area of research, Seltzer examines the effects of raising a child with a disability based on two long-term studies. One of these studies, the Wisconsin Longitudinal Study, analyzes 50 years of data drawn from families with children with autism, fragile X syndrome, or schizophrenia. The second, based on the Midlife in the United States Study, focuses on parents of children with disabilities and includes psychosocial and biomarker data.

In addition to her research responsibilities at the Waisman Center, Seltzer is affiliated with the university's Institute on Aging, the Center for Demography of Health and Aging, and she also co-directs the center's postdoctoral training program in intellectual disabilities research. In 2006 she was chosen as the interim director for the university's Wisconsin Institutes for Discovery, which brings together scientists from across several disciplines and supports interdisciplinary research encompassing nanotechnology, biotechnology, and information technology.

Seltzer is also a prolific author, with more than 130 publications in her area of expertise. She received the Distinguished Research Award from The Arc and the Christian Pueschel Memorial Research Award from the Down Syndrome Congress.

Further Reading

Seltzer, M. M., Almeida, D. M., Greenberg, J. S., Savla, J., Stawski, R. S., Hong, J., et al. (2009). Psychosocial and biological markers of daily lives of midlife parents of children with disabilities. *Journal of Health and Social Behavior, 50,* 1–15.

Seltzer, M. M., Greenberg, J. S., Floyd, F. J., Pettee, Y., & Hong, J. (2001). Life course perspectives of parenting a child with a disability. *American Journal on Mental Retardation, 106,* 265–286.

Tom Shakespeare (1966–)

British academic, writer, and disability advocate who focuses on bioethics and the cultural and social issues of disability

Thomas William Shakespeare was born in 1966 in Norwich, England. Shakespeare has achondroplasia (dwarfism), and it has become central to his study of disability and society. Shakespeare received his master's degree in sociology from Pembroke College, Cambridge, and his doctoral degree in sociology from King's College, Cambridge.

Shakespeare became involved with the disability movement in 1986, when he co-founded Disability Action North East and the Northern Disability Arts Forum. He was a lecturer in sociology at the University of Sunderland from 1993 to 1999, a research fellow in sociology at the University of Leeds from 1996 to 1999, and director of outreach for the Policy, Ethics, and Life Sciences Research Centre at the University of Newcastle from 1999 to 2005. Always fascinated by the intersection of science and the arts, Shakespeare has also served as a fellow for NESTA (the National Endowment for Science, Technology and the Arts), working on writing and performance art in the area of disability and genetics. He has been a member of the Arts Council of England since 2004.

Shakespeare has published several books on issues in disability, including *The Sexual Politics of Disability, Exploring Disability,* and *Genetic Politics: From Eugenics to Genome.* In his book *Disability Rights and Wrongs,* he takes issue with the "social model" of disability, which says that "disability" is a construct of non-disabled society and that people with disabilities are oppressed by societal barriers. Shakespeare argues instead that individuals with disabilities, as well as those who care for them and write about them, must deal directly and realistically with the range of impairments they face.

Shakespeare is a consultant to the World Health Organization on disability and rehabilitation, and he is a regular contributor to Ouch! a Web site run by the BBC on disability issues. In addition to his prolific writings on disability, he is also a speaker and broadcaster on the topic. In 2003, RADAR awarded him the UK People of the Year Award for his work on human rights for disabled people.

In 2008, Shakespeare lost the use of his legs and became a paraplegic. He is now writing about his experiences with the rehabilitation aspects of disability.

Further Reading

Koch, T. (2008). Is Tom Shakespeare disabled? *Journal of Medical Ethics, 34*, 18–20.
Tom Shakespeare. Retrieved from http://www.bbc.co.uk/ouch/writers/tom shakespeare.shtml

Eunice Kennedy Shriver (1921–2009)

American activist and founder of the Special Olympics

Eunice Mary Kennedy Shriver was born in 1921 in Brookline, Massachusetts, to Joseph and Rose Kennedy. She was part of a power political family that included a brother, John, who became president of the United States, and two brothers, Robert and Edward, who became U.S. senators. Another sibling, Rosemary, was born with mild mental retardation that worsened after she underwent brain surgery. It was the inspiration of Rosemary that led Shriver to later found the Special Olympics.

Shriver attended Stanford University, where she was active in sports and received her bachelor's degree in sociology in 1942. After graduation, she worked for the U.S. State Department's Special War Problems Division. In 1950 she spent a year working in a women's prison in West Virginia, then moved to Chicago, where she worked for a Catholic social services organization. In 1953 Eunice Kennedy married Sargent Shriver, a career public servant, who served over the years as the first director of the Peace Corps and helped inaugurate Head Start, Vista, and many other government programs. They had five children.

In 1957 Eunice Kennedy Shriver helped establish the Joseph P. Kennedy Jr. Foundation, created to honor the memory of her eldest brother, Joseph, who died during World War II. Its mission was to prevent intellectual disabilities by finding its causes, and to improve the lives and opportunities of those born with intellectual disabilities. When John F. Kennedy became president in 1961, Shriver worked with him to develop the Presidential Committee on Mental Retardation and establish the National Institute for Child Health and Human Development.

In 1968 Shriver established the organization for which she is best known, the Special Olympics. Inspired in part by her brother's Presidential Fitness Award, Shriver developed a similar training program and Olympic competition for disabled people. The first Special Olympics took place in Chicago in 1968, with 1,000 athletes from 26 states, who competed in swimming, track and field, and hockey. Shriver inspired the athletes with the Special Olympian's oath: "Let me win. But if I cannot win, let me be brave in the attempt." The participants, in turn, inspired Shriver. "Special Olympians and their families are challenging the common wisdom that says that only intellectual achievement is the measure of human life," she declared. "They have proved that the common wisdom is wrong. Special Olympians and their families are proof that the value of human life should be measured in many ways."

Today, more than three million athletes in 175 countries take part in the Special Olympics. With Shriver as their champion, these Special Olympians and their achievements have helped to change the attitudes of millions of people around the world about what people with intellectual and physical disabilities can do.

Shriver received many honorary degrees for her work on the Special Olympics, as well as the Presidential Medal of Freedom, the highest civilian honor in the country. *Sports Illustrated* named her its first Sportsman of the Year Legacy Award recipient in 2008, recognizing her as the founder of the Special Olympics and calling her "the single most important person to have advanced the rights and enriched the lives of people with intellectual disabilities." Eunice Kennedy Shriver died on August 11, 2009, in Hyannis Port, Massachusetts.

Further Reading

Eunice Kennedy Shriver. Retrieved from http://www.eunicekennedyshriver.org/bios/eks

Sandomir, R. (2009, August 12). The mother of the Special Olympics. *New York Times, 158,* B9.

Rune Simeonsson (1940–)

American academic and early childhood specialist
focusing on developmental disabilities

Rune J. Simeonsson was born in 1940 in Beijing, China, to parents who were Christian missionaries from Sweden. The family returned to their native country in 1946, then moved to Japan in 1950, where Rune completed high school. In 1959 he moved to the United States to attend college, receiving his bachelor's degree in psychology from Tennessee Temple College in 1963, his master's degree in education and psychology from the University of Chattanooga in 1966, his master's degree in special education from George Peabody College in 1968, his doctoral degree in psychology from Peabody in 1971, and his master's degree in public health from the University of North Carolina in 1992.

Simeonsson began his academic career at the University of Nebraska Medical School, then moved to the University of Rochester Medical School. In 1976 he began teaching at the University of North Carolina, where he is a research professor of psychology and a fellow at Duke University's Frank Porter Graham Child Development Institute. Simeonsson's research focuses on child development, special education, and public health, specifically the development of tools for assessing child functioning and development, the importance of early intervention, and the role of the school and community in child health, education, and well-being.

Simeonsson has participated in the analysis of the National Early Intervention Longitudinal Study and has served as a consultant on both national and international studies of child development. He has worked with the World Health Organization to develop assessment tools similar to the International Classification of Functioning, Disability and Health for Children and Youth, and he has been coordinator of the Trans-Atlantic Consortium on early childhood intervention, which is a collaboration of three American and five European universities.

It is the goal of Simeonsson's research to develop tools that will properly assess and promote functional skill development, performance, and participation in children with disabilities. He is involved in the training of professionals from across several disciplines, including special education, psychology, and public health, to offer integrated care and services to children with disabilities.

Simeonsson is also a member of the faculty of Jonkoping University in Sweden, where he is a professor of special needs education. He is also the author of several books and many articles in his field and is a member of the American Public Health Association and the Association on Disability and Health.

Further Reading

Adolfsson, M., Simeonsson, R. J., Sauer-Lee, A., & Ellingsen, K. (2010). Major life areas. In A. Majnemer (Ed.), *Clinical and research measures for children with developmental disability: Framed by the ICF-CY.* London: MacKeith Press.

Castro, S., Lewis, S., & Simeonsson, R. J. (2010). General tasks and demands of children. In A. Majnemer (Ed.), *Clinical and research measures for children with developmental disability: Framed by the ICF-CY.* London: MacKeith Press.

Edna Szymanski (1952–)

American university president and researcher focusing on vocational and career development in people with disabilities

Edna M. Szymanski was born in 1952 in Caracas, Venezuela, and was raised in Philadelphia, Pennsylvania. She received her bachelor of science degree in biology from Rensselaer Polytechnic Institute in 1972, her master's degree in rehabilitation counseling from the University of Scranton in 1974, and her Ph.D. in special education and rehabilitation counseling from the University of Texas at Austin in 1988.

Szymanski began her career in disability studies as a vocational evaluator for a rehabilitation center, then she worked as a counselor for the Office of Vocational Rehabilitation for New York State. She joined the faculty of the University of Wisconsin in 1989, where she was associate dean of the College of Education and chair of the Department of Rehabilitation Psychology and Special Education.

Szymanski has been a prolific author and researcher since graduate school, with a focus on vocational and career development for people with disabilities. She has written more than 100 professional articles and book chapters, and she co-edited a widely used textbook in the rehabilitation field, *Work and Disability: Contexts, Issues, and Strategies for Enhancing Employment Outcomes for People With Disabilities,* now in its third edition.

Szymanski has served on committees for the National Institute on Disability and Rehabilitation Research and has won many awards for her research, including the American Rehabilitation Counseling Association's James F. Garrett Award for a Distinguished Career in Rehabilitation Research, the American Counseling Association Research Award, the Rehabilitation Education Researcher of the Year Award from the National Council on Rehabilitation Education and the McKinnon Foundation, the American Association for Counselor Education and Supervision Research Award, and the American Rehabilitation Counseling Association Distinguished Professional Award.

During her time at the University of Wisconsin, Szymanski realized that she had a gift for college administration, which she likened to the work of a rehabilitation counselor. "Our goal was to get the best possible match for the person and his or her environment," she explained. In 1999 she decided to pursue academic administration and moved to the University of Maryland, where she was dean and professor in the College of Education through 2006. In 2006 she was named senior vice president of academic affairs and provost at the University of Maine, Orono. In 2008 Szymanski was named president of Minnesota State University, Moorhood, where she serves as the school's first female president.

Further Reading

Szymanski, E. M. (1999). Disability, job stress, the changing nature of careers, and the career resilience portfolio. *Rehabilitation Counseling Bulletin, 42,* 279–289.

Szymanski, E. M., Mizelle, N. D., Tansey, T. N., Tschopp, M. K., & Willmering, P. P. (2000). The paradox of undergraduate rehabilitation education. *Rehabilitation Education, 14,* 27–31.

Fernando Torres-Gil

American expert on long-term care and the politics of aging

Fernando M. Torres-Gil was born to migrant farm workers in Salinas, California. After contracting polio at the age of 6 months, he spent many of his formative years at Shriner's Hospital in San Francisco, undergoing rehabilitation and surgeries to improve function in his legs. Torres-Gil attended Hartnell Community College in Salinas and graduated with an associate's degree in political science in 1968. He continued his education at San Jose State University, where he earned his bachelor's degree in political science with honors in 1970. Torres-Gil pursued graduate studies at the Heller Graduate School in Social Policy and Management at

Brandeis University, earning a master'degree in social work in 1972 and a Ph.D. in social policy, planning, and research in 1976.

Torres-Gil started his career in government service in 1978, when President Jimmy Carter appointed him to serve on the Federal Council on Aging. He worked as White House fellow and special assistant to the Secretary of Health, Education, and Welfare (1978–1979), and as special assistant to the Secretary of Health and Human Services (1979–1980). Torres-Gil also served as an administrator with the House of Representatives Select Committee on Aging—the largest committee in Congress—holding the position of staff director from 1985 to 1987.

Shortly after taking office, President Bill Clinton named Torres-Gil as the first Assistant Secretary for Aging in the U.S. Department of Health and Human Services. In this role, he consolidated federal programs for the elderly and promoted the importance of such issues as aging, long-term care, and disability. Torres-Gil also managed the Administration on Aging, coordinated the White House Conference on Aging in 1995, and participated as a member of Clinton's Welfare Reform Working Group.

Torres-Gil is currently a professor of social welfare and public policy at the University of California, Los Angeles (UCLA), where he also serves as associate dean of academic affairs at the university's School of Public Affairs. He is the director of UCLA's Center for Policy Research on Aging. Before going to UCLA, Torres-Gil taught gerontology and public administration at the University of Southern California (USC). He continues to teach at USC as an adjunct professor of gerontology. He is the author of six books, including *The New Aging: Politics and Change in America* (1992), and more than 80 articles for professional journals on issues of social policy and aging.

In recognition of his academic accomplishments, Torres-Gil was elected a fellow of the Gerontological Society of America in 1985 and of the National Academy of Public Administration in 1995. A past president of the American Society on Aging, he is currently a member of the National Academy of Social Insurance and the San Francisco Bay Area Polio Survivors. He serves on the board of directors of several organizations, including the National Committee to Preserve Social Security and Medicare, the AARP Foundation, and the California Endowment. In 2005 California Governor Arnold Schwarzenegger named Torres-Gil a delegate to the White House Conference on Aging, and in 2009 President Barack Obama appointed him as one of eight board members of the National Council on Disability (NCD).

Further Reading

AARP. (2010). *AARP leadership profile: Fernando Torres-Gil.* Retrieved from http://www.aarp.org/about-aarp/leadership/info-2010/fernando_torres-gil.html

UCLA School of Public Affairs. (n.d.). *Fernando Torres-Gil.* Retrieved from http://publicaffairs.ucla.edu/fernando-torres-gil

Ann P. Turnbull (1947–)

American academic focusing on issues of family and disability

Ann Patterson Turnbull was born in 1947 in Tuscaloosa, Alabama. She received her bachelor's degree in special education and mental retardation from the University of Georgia in 1968, her master's degree in special education and mental retardation from Auburn University in 1971, and her doctoral degree in special education and mental retardation from the University of Alabama in 1972. She is co-director with Rud Turnbull of the Beach Center on Disability at the University of Kansas. They had three children, Amy, Kate, and Jesse, called Jay. Jay, who died in 2009, was born with multiple disabilities and was the inspiration for the Beach Center.

Ann Turnbull has worked in the field of disability studies as a researcher, teacher, professor, and advocate for almost 40 years. She began her career as an assistant professor in the School of Education at the University of North Carolina at Chapel Hill, where she worked from 1973 to 1980. In 1980 she joined the faculty of the University of Kansas, where she is currently Distinguished Professor in the Department of Special Education, senior scientist at the Schiefelbusch Institute for Life Span Studies, and co-director of the Beach Center on Disability.

The focus of Turnbull's research is the family and disability, including family involvement and advocacy, school and community inclusion, and education policy. She has been principal investigator on over 20 research grants from the federal government and a Public Policy Fellow in Mental Retardation for the Joseph P. Kennedy Jr. Foundation. The author of 14 books, including several key textbooks in the area of special education, Turnbull has also written or contributed more than 200 professional articles and book chapters. She serves on the editorial boards and contributes to several key journals in her field, including *Exceptional Children, Mental Retardation,* and the *Journal of the Association for Persons With Severe Handicaps.*

The Beach Center, founded by the Turnbulls in 1988, is devoted to research, training teachers and graduate students, and providing assistance and information to families and individuals with disabilities. The center includes six subcenters that focus on families, public policy, school-wide reform, self-determination (including access to curriculum and technology), legal implications of the human genome project, and the education of students with significant support needs, including deaf-blindness.

Turnbull is the recipient of many awards for her research and service, including the Century Award in Mental Retardation, which was presented in 1999 by a consortium of organizations to 36 individuals who made the most significant impact in the fields of developmental disabilities and mental retardation in the 20th century. In addition, Ann and Rud Turnbull share the Ross and Marianna Beach Distinguished Professorship at the University of Kansas.

Further Reading

Dr. Ann Turnbull. Retrieved from http://www.beachcenter.org/staff/staffdetail
    .aspx?id=24

Turnbull, A. (2009, August 11). Attitudes toward the intellectually disabled
    [Interview]. NPR, *Talk of the Nation*. Retrieved from http://www.npr.org/
    templates/story/story.php?storyId=111781649

Turnbull, H. R., Turnbull, A., & Wehmeyer, M. (2010). *Exceptional lives: Special educa-
    tion in today's schools* (6th ed.). Upper Saddle River, NJ: Merrill/Prentice Hall.

Rud Turnbull (1937–)

American academic and lawyer focusing on disability law and policy

H. Rutherford Turnbull III, known as Rud, was born in 1937 in New York City. He received his bachelor's degree from Johns Hopkins University in 1959, his law degree from the University of Maryland Law School in 1964, and his master of law degree from Harvard Law School in 1969. He is the co-director with Ann Turnbull of the Beach Center on Disability at the University of Kansas. They had three children, Amy, Kate, and Jesse, called Jay. Jay, who died in 2009, was born with multiple disabilities and was the inspiration for the Beach Center.

Although he is now a non-practicing attorney, Turnbull began his professional career as a lawyer, and he worked in private practice from 1968 to 1969. In 1969 he joined the Institute of Government at the University of

North Carolina at Chapel Hill as a professor of public law and government, and he was also a faculty member at the Bush Institute on Policy for Families and Children.

In 1980 Turnbull joined the faculty of the University of Kansas, where he is the co-director of the Beach Center on Disability, the Marianna and Ross Beach Distinguished Professor, and senior research scientist at the Life Span Institute. The focus of his research is law and policy in several key areas of disability studies, including special education, mental disability, the ethics of intervention with people with disabilities, and issues regarding families of people with disabilities.

Turnbull has authored or co-authored 28 books, more than 50 monographs, more than 150 professional articles, and more than 75 book chapters. He writes on a wide range of disability policy issues, including the nature of core concepts in disability, the effects of policy on people with disabilities and their families, the development and implementation of disability policy, disability and criminal justice, abuse and neglect of people with disabilities, and long-term care and end-of-life decisions for people with disabilities.

The Beach Center, founded by the Turnbulls in 1988, is devoted to research, training teachers and graduate students, and providing assistance and information to individuals with disabilities and their families. The center includes six subcenters that focus on families, public policy, schoolwide reform, self-determination (including access to curriculum and technology), legal implications of the human genome project, and the education of students with significant support needs, including deaf-blindness.

Turnbull has served as president of the American Association on Mental Retardation and as chairman of the American Bar Association Commission on Disability Law, and he has testified before the U.S. Congress on disability law and the rights of people with disabilities. He is the recipient of many awards, including the Century Award in Mental Retardation, given by a consortium of organizations to 36 individuals who made the most significant impact in the fields of developmental disabilities and mental retardation in the 20th century.

Further Reading

Rud Turnbull. Retrieved from http://www.beachcenter.org/staff/staffdetail .aspx?id=15

Turnbull, H. R., Turnbull, A., & Wehmeyer, M. (2010). *Exceptional lives: Special education in today's schools* (6th ed.). Upper Saddle River, NJ: Merrill/Prentice Hall.

Lois M. Verbrugge (1945–)

American gerontologist and social demographer focusing on disabilities in older adults

Lois M. Verbrugge was born in 1945 in Boston, Massachusetts. After receiving her bachelor's degree in French and mathematics from Stanford University in 1967, she pursued graduate studies at the University of Michigan, earning her master's degree in public health in 1970 and her doctoral degree in demography and sociology in 1974.

Verbrugge began her career at Johns Hopkins University, where she was a research scientist and assistant professor. She joined the faculty of the University of Michigan in 1983, where she is currently Senior Distinguished Research Scientist Emerita and Research Professor Emerita at the Institute of Gerontology. She is also a Research Affiliate at the Population Studies Center at Michigan and the Michigan Center on the Demography of Aging.

Verbrugge's research focuses on several key areas encompassing both empirical and theoretical issues in disability as it affects older adults. She has studied health trends for American adults, disability associated with osteoarthritis and heart disease, sex differences in health and mortality, the issues of aging with disability and disability with aging, and the social and physical effects of disabling conditions in mid-life and after.

Verbrugge's research projects in the area of disability studies and aging include "Clinical Strategies to Reduce Osteoarthritis Disability," funded by the National Institute of Child Health and Human Development, and "Activities in Mid- and Late-Life: A New Lens," for the Michigan Center on Demography and Aging. She was a visiting professor at the Asia Research Institute, National University of Singapore, from 2004 to 2005, and has incorporated her research there into comparative studies of the U.S. and Singapore populations.

Verbrugge has received several awards for her work, including a Research Career Development Award from the National Institute of Child Health and Human Development, a Special Emphasis Research Career Award from the National Institute on Aging, and the American Psychological Association's Distinguished Contribution to Women's Health Award. She is also an active author, co-author, and editor, contributing to professional journals in the areas of medical sociology, public health, and gerontology.

Further Reading

Verbrugge, L. M., Mehta, K. K., & Wagenfeld-Heitz, E. (2006). Views of disability in the United States and Singapore. *Research on Aging, 28*(2), 216–239.

Verbrugge, L. M., & Yang, L. S. (2002). Aging with disability, and disability with aging. *Journal of Disability Policy Studies, 12,* 253–267.

Paul Wehman

*American academic focusing on the transition
from adolescence to adulthood and supported
employment for people with disabilities*

Paul Wehman received his bachelor's degree in business administration from Western Illinois University in 1970, his master's degree in general and experimental psychology from Illinois State University in 1972, and his Ph.D. in behavioral disabilities and rehabilitation psychology from the University of Wisconsin in 1976.

Wehman joined the faculty of Virginia Commonwealth University in 1976, and over the past 35 years he has pioneered the development of supported employment at the university. He has focused his research on expanding supported employment to people with severe disabilities, including those with mental retardation, traumatic brain injury, spinal cord injury, and autism. He has also written extensively on transition issues for young adults with disabilities, especially in the movement from school to employment.

Currently, Wehman is a professor in the Department of Physical Medicine and Rehabilitation at VCU, with a joint appointment in the Department of Teaching and Learning Rehabilitation Counseling. He is also director of the Rehabilitation Research and Training Center on Workplace Supports and Job Retention, and chair of the Division of Rehabilitation Research. Since joining VCU, he has been the principal investigator for many federally funded research grants, including the U.S. Department of Labor's Training and Technical Assistance Project on Self Employment and VCU's Diversity and Empowerment Project. He is responsible for a $6.25 million annual budget for the Research and Training Center, with fiscal and program oversight for over 20 federal grants and a staff of 65 researchers and staff.

Wehman is a prolific author, co-author, and editor, with more than 200 professional articles, 24 book chapters, and 40 books among his publications. He is also the editor-in-chief of the *Journal of Vocational Rehabilitation*. He is the recipient of many awards, including the Joseph P. Kennedy Jr. Foundation International Award in Mental Retardation, the Distinguished

Service Award from the President's Committee on Employment for Persons with Disabilities, and the Mary Switzer Fellowship for the National Rehabilitation Association. In 2000 Wehman was named one of the 50 most influential special educators of the millennium by *Remedial and Special Education*. In 2006 he was elected a Life Long Emeritus Member of APSE: The Employment Network, and in 2007 he received the VCU School of Medicine Research Recognition Award.

Further Reading

Getzel, E. E., & Wehman, P. (Eds.). (2005). *Going to college: Expanding opportunities for people with disabilities*. Baltimore: Paul H. Brookes.
Wehman, P., Smith, M. D., & Schall, C. (2009). *Autism and the transition to adulthood: Success beyond the classroom*. Baltimore: Paul H. Brookes.

Michael Wehmeyer (1957–)

American academic focusing on education and self-determination for people with intellectual disabilities

Michael Wehmeyer was born in Wichita, Kansas. He studied special education and intellectual disabilities at the University of Tulsa, receiving his bachelor's degree in 1980 and his master's degree in 1982. He also earned a master's degree in experimental psychology at the University of Sussex in 1988, and he received his doctoral degree in human development and communication sciences from the University of Texas at Dallas in 1989.

Wehmeyer began his career at the Texas Department of Mental Health and Mental Retardation in 1989. From 1990 to 1999, he worked for The Arc of the United States, serving in a number of roles, including director of its Self-Determination Program. He is currently professor of special education at the University of Kansas, where he is also director of the Center on Developmental Disabilities and associate director of the Beach Center on Disability.

The Beach Center, founded by Ann and Rud Turnbull in 1988, is devoted to research, training teachers and graduate students, and providing assistance and information to individuals with disabilities and their families. The center includes six subcenters that focus on families, public policy, school-wide reform, self-determination (including access to curriculum and technology), legal implications of the human genome project, and the education of students with significant support needs, including deaf-blindness.

The focus of Wehmeyer's research is self-determination, transition, and educational issues, including access to the general curriculum for students with significant disabilities and technology use by people with cognitive disabilities. He directs many federally funded research projects in the area of the education of students with intellectual and developmental disabilities.

Wehmeyer has published more than 180 articles or book chapters, and he has also been the author, co-author, or co-editor of 19 books on disability. He is editor-in-chief for the journal *Remedial and Special Education* and also serves as a consulting editor for a number of professional journals, including *Exceptional Children, Intellectual and Developmental Disabilities, Journal of Special Education*, and the *American Journal of Mental Retardation*.

Wehmeyer is currently president of the American Association on Intellectual and Developmental Disabilities and is a past president of the Council for Exceptional Children's Division on Career Development and Transition. He is the recipient of many awards, including the first Distinguished Early Career Research Award from the Council for Exceptional Children's Division for Research, which he received in 1999. In May 2003 he was honored with the American Association on Mental Retardation's National Education Award.

Further Reading

Sands, D. J., & Wehmeyer, M. L. (Eds.). (1996). *Self-determination across the life span: Independence and choice for people with disabilities*. Baltimore: Paul H. Brookes.

Wehmeyer, M. L. (2007). *Promoting self-determination in students with developmental disabilities*. New York: Guilford Press.

Wolf Wolfensberger (1934–)

*American academic who developed the theory of
social role valorization for people with disabilities*

Wolf Wolfensberger was born in 1934 in Mannheim, Germany, and immigrated to the United States in 1950. He earned his bachelor's degree from Siena College, his master's degree in clinical psychology from St. Louis University, and his doctoral degree in psychology, specializing in mental retardation and special education, from Peabody College.

In 1964 Wolfensberger joined the University of Nebraska Medical School's Nebraska Psychiatric Institute, where he worked as a research scientist in mental retardation for seven years. In 1971 he was a visiting scholar at the National Institute on Mental Retardation in Toronto, Canada. Two years later he joined the faculty of Syracuse University's Special Education Department, where he established the Training Institute on Human Services Planning, Leadership, and Change Agentry, which provides training to individuals who wish to be agents of change in human services. He is now a professor emeritus at Syracuse University and continues to direct the Training Institute.

Wolfensberger's research focuses on the ideologies, structures, and patterns of human service systems, particularly as they affect people with intellectual and developmental disabilities and their families. In the 1970s he became an outspoken advocate for "normalization," or the idea that people with disabilities should be given access to educational and living conditions that were as close as possible to those of persons without disabilities. In the 1990s Wolfensberger developed the theory of social role valorization, which addresses the social devaluation of impaired and other vulnerable people in society, and seeks to increase the value, respect, and dignity accorded to people with disabilities. Wolfensberger's theories have proven to be of international importance, as governments outside of the United States adopted his ideas in their development of human service systems for people with disabilities.

Wolfensberger's scholarship includes more than 40 books as author or co-author, as well as more than 250 book chapters and professional papers. Among his books are *Changing Patterns in Residential Services for the Mentally Retarded* and *The Principle of Normalization*, both of which are considered primary texts in the field. His research is considered so significant that Syracuse University received a grant from the Annie E. Casey Foundation to organize his archives and books, which will eventually become and part of the University Library's Special Collections. In 1999 Wolfensberger was honored with the Century Award in Mental Retardation, which was presented by a consortium of organizations to 36 individuals who made the most significant impact in the fields of developmental disabilities and mental retardation in the 20th century.

Further Reading

Dr. Wolf Wolfensberger. Retrieved from http://www.srvip.org/about_wolfens berger.php

Sherrill, C. (2003, Summer). Normalization or valorization: Which should be our aim? *Palaestra, 19*(3), 56–58.

Five

Annotated Data, Statistics, Tables, and Graphs

Robert Gould, Tamar Heller, and Sarah Parker Harris

T his chapter presents a wide range of data on the experiences and outlooks of Americans with disabilities at various stages of the life course. The data that follow are arranged in six major sections: (1) Birthrights, (2) Childhood, (3) Youth, (4) Adulthood, (5) Aging, and (6) Death and Dying.

Birthrights

Abortion

The legacy of eugenic sterilization of people with disabilities casts a shadow over the history of birth decisions for and of people with disabilities in the United States. There is little quantitative data available from

major statistical clearinghouses regarding the number of eugenic steriliza-
tions and coerced birth decisions of people with disabilities. The lasting
effect of the eugenics movement is reflected, however, in current perceptions of prenatal diagnosis. Figure 1 shows the result of a 1999 random
survey of 499 doctors who gave genetic screening advice to parents who
had received a neonatal diagnosis that their child would have Down syndrome. Survey results indicated that 63% of doctors sought to be unbiased
in the medical advice they provided—but "unbiased" advice from doctors has been regarded by disability advocates as focusing on negative
aspects of disability (Parens & Asch, 1999). The most expansive study of
prenatal diagnosis and its impact on birth decisions comes from the

Figure 1   Primary Care Physicians' Advice to Parents When Providing
Neonatal Diagnosis of Down Syndrome in Genetic Screening
Procedures, 1999

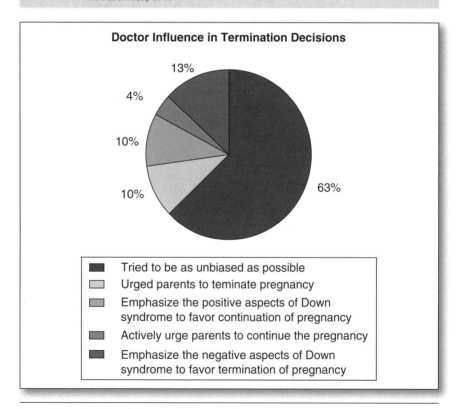

Source: Wertz, D. C. (2000). Drawing lines: Notes for policymakers. In E. Parens & A. Asch (Eds.),
Prenatal testing and disability rights (pp. 261–287). Washington, DC: Georgetown University Press.

United Kingdom. Mansfield, Hopfer, and Marteau (1999) conducted a systematic review of international medical literature. They estimated that between 92% and 96% of prenatal diagnoses of Down syndrome led to abortion during the 1980s and 1990s.

Birth Decisions

The Centers for Disease Control and Prevention (CDC) provides the most comprehensive statistical information on people born with physical disabilities in the United States. Table 1 provides the CDC's 2007 findings regarding the number of live births with varying "congenital anomalies," sorted by the age of the mother at the time of birth. Few national studies have analyzed the CDC birth rates of people with congenital disabilities except for trends in the births of people with spina bifida (Table 2 and Figure 2) and anencephalus (Table 3 and Figure 3). Figure 2 and Figure 3 display the general decrease in the rate of births of children with spina bifida and anencephalus, respectively, along with the "confidence interval," which is a standard measure of statistical reliability.

Childhood

Early Intervention

The main services for young children with disabilities in the United States are provided through Individuals with Disabilities Act (IDEA) Early Intervention Services. Table 4 includes the estimated U.S. population of children with disabilities according to specific conditions (including confidence intervals for the estimates). Figure 4 displays the upward trend in the number of yearly recipients of Early Intervention Services under the IDEA. Table 5 presents data on the age breakdown of recipients of Early Intervention Services; Figure 5 details the primary setting for outlay of those services.

Youth

Education

The Individuals with Disabilities Education Act (IDEA) is the major educational law that ensures access to educational services for youth with

Table 1 Number and Rate of Live Births With "Congenital Anomalies" in the United States, 2007

Risk Factor, Characteristic, Procedure, and Anomaly	All Births	Factor Reported	All Ages	Under 20 Years	20–24 Years	25–29 Years	30–34 Years	35–39 Years	40–54 Years	Not Stated
Congenital Anomalies										
Anencephaly	4,285,617	524	12.3	14.7	12.8	13.2	9.8	11.2	*	35,388
Meningomyelocele or spina bifida	4,285,617	731	17.2	18.7	16.8	18.3	17.2	14.2	*	35,388
Omphalocele or gastroschisis	4,285,617	1,630	38.4	110.6	55.9	24.9	16.9	14.0	*	35,388
Cleft lip or palate	4,285,617	3,225	75.9	87.2	78.7	74.8	72.3	67.1	83.9	35,388
Down syndrome	4,285,617	2,040	48.0	26.4	27.2	25.2	40.8	110.8	361.0	35,388
Non-Hispanic White										
Risk Factors in This Pregnancy										
Diabetes	2,310,333	97,324	42.3	16.6	26.9	39.0	50.7	66.3	84.7	9,773
Hypertension, pregnancy associated	2,310,333	100,347	43.6	46.9	45.2	44.2	40.6	41.8	51.0	9,773
Hypertension, chronic	2,310,333	25,665	11.2	4.5	6.8	10.2	12.9	18.1	26.6	9,773

Risk Factor, Characteristic, Procedure, and Anomaly	All Births	Factor Reported	All Ages	Under 20 Years	20–24 Years	25–29 Years	30–34 Years	35–39 Years	40–54 Years	Not Stated
Obstetric Procedures and Characteristics of Labor or Delivery										
Induction of labor	2,310,333	624,256	271.2	309.3	293.7	281.6	252.9	232.2	219.5	8,289
Tocolysis	2,310,333	38,122	16.6	20.3	18.3	16.5	15.4	14.3	14.3	12,243
Meconium, moderate or heavy	2,310,333	86,962	37.8	41.9	38.9	37.3	36.6	36.9	37.2	8,525
Breech or malpresentation	2,310,333	129,348	56.9	44.8	47.0	54.0	62.5	71.4	81.6	35,445
Precipitous labor	2,310,333	51,136	22.3	14.0	19.2	22.2	24.8	26.7	26.2	12,253
Congenital Anomalies										
Anencephaly	2,301,568	275	12.0	15.1	11.5	13.8	9.8	10.7	*	17,442
Meningomyelocele or spina bifida	2,301,568	457	20.0	26.1	18.8	20.3	21.3	15.1	*	17,442
Omphalocele or gastroschisis	2,301,568	958	41.9	148.1	71.1	27.5	16.8	15.1	*	17,442
Cleft lip or palate	2,301,568	2,102	92.0	138.2	100.7	86.6	85.3	74.5	94.1	17,442
Down syndrome	2,301,568	1,287	56.3	37.7	29.8	30.7	48.5	115.8	373.2	17,442

Source: Martin, J. A., Hamilton, B. E., Sutton, P. D., Ventura, S. J., Mathews, T. J., Kirmeyer, S., & Osterman, M. J. K. (2010). Births: Final data for 2007. National Vital Statistics Reports, 58, 24. Hyattsville, MD: National Center for Health Statistics. Retrieved from http://www.cdc.gov/nchs/data/nvsr/nvsr58/nvsr58_24.pdf

** Figure does not meet standards of reliability or precision; based on fewer than 20 births in the numerator.

Note: Rates are number of live births with specified risk factors, procedures, or anomaly per 1,000 live births in specified group; congenital anomalies are per 100,000 live births.

Table 2   Birth Rates of Children With Spina Bifida in the United States, 1991–2006

	Spina Bifida Cases	Total Live Births	Rate	95% Confidence Intervals for Rate	
2006	700	3,890,949	17.99	16.66	19.32
2005	698	3,887,109	17.96	16.62	19.29
2004	755	3,860,720	19.56	18.16	20.95
2003	702	3,715,577	18.89	17.50	20.29
2002	734	3,645,770	20.13	18.68	21.59
2001	730	3,640,555	20.05	18.60	21.51
2000	759	3,640,376	20.85	19.37	22.33
1999	732	3,533,565	20.72	19.22	22.22
1998	790	3,519,240	22.45	20.88	24.01
1997	857	3,469,667	24.70	23.05	26.35
1996	917	3,478,723	26.36	24.65	28.07
1995	975	3,484,539	27.98	26.22	29.74
1994	900	3,527,482	25.51	23.85	27.18
1993	896	3,562,723	25.15	23.50	26.80
1992	816	3,572,890	22.84	21.27	24.41
1991	887	3,564,453	24.88	23.25	26.52

Source: Mathews, T. J., & Hamilton, B. E. (2009). *Trends in spina bifida and anencephalus in the United States, 1991–2006.* Hyattsville, MD: National Center for Health Statistics. Retrieved from http://www.cdc.gov/nchs/data/hestat/spine_anen/spine_anen.pdf

disabilities in the United States. It was passed in 1990 as a revision (and renaming) of the Education for All Handicapped Children Act (EAHCA), which was originally signed into law in 1975. Children and youth (ages 3 to 21) with disabilities are eligible to receive special education and related services under IDEA.

Table 3   Birth Rates of Children With Anencephalus in the United States, 1991–2006

	Anencephalus Cases	Total Live Births	Rate	95% Confidence Intervals for Rate	
2006	436	3,890,949	11.21	10.15	12.26
2005	432	3,887,109	11.11	10.07	12.16
2004	401	3,860,720	10.39	9.37	11.40
2003	441	3,715,577	11.14	10.07	12.22
2002	348	3,645,770	9.55	8.54	10.55
2001	343	3,640,555	9.42	8.42	10.42
2000	376	3,640,376	10.33	9.28	11.37
1999	382	3,533,565	10.81	9.73	11.89
1998	349	3,519,240	9.92	8.88	10.96
1997	434	3,469,667	12.51	11.33	13.69
1996	416	3,478,723	11.96	10.81	13.11
1995	408	3,484,539	11.71	10.57	12.84
1994	387	3,527,482	10.97	9.88	12.06
1993	481	3,562,723	13.50	12.29	14.71
1992	457	3,572,890	12.79	11.62	13.96
1991	655	3,564,453	18.38	16.97	19.78

Source: Mathews, T. J., & Hamilton, B. E. (2009). *Trends in spina bifida and anencephalus in the United States, 1991–2006.* Hyattsville, MD: National Center for Health Statistics. Retrieved from http://www.cdc.gov/nchs/data/hestat/spine_anen/spine_anen.pdf

Collection of EAHCA data began in 1976. Initially, data were collected for preschool children ages 3 to 5 by disability type, as well as for children and youth ages 6 to 21. Beginning in 1986, collection of data for children under the age of 5 was suspended by law. In 2000, however, states were again mandated to collect data by disability for preschool-aged children.

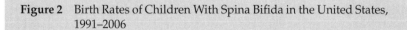

Figure 2   Birth Rates of Children With Spina Bifida in the United States, 1991–2006

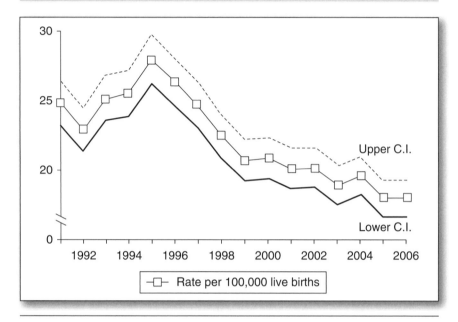

Source: Mathews, T. J., & Hamilton, B. E. (2009). *Trends in spina bifida and anencephalus in the United States, 1991–2006.* Hyattsville, MD: National Center for Health Statistics. Retrieved from http://www.cdc.gov/nchs/data/hestat/spine_anen/spine_anen.pdf

Table 6 tracks the percentage of children from the kindergarten class of 1998–1999 who received special education services over the course of five years, concluding with the 2003–2004 school year. Table 7 displays the number and percentage of students with different disabilities that received services from IDEA/EAHCA during selected years, beginning with the 1976–1977 school year and concluding with the 2007-2008 school year. Table 8 tracks the environments in which students received IDEA services from fall 1989 to fall 2007. The most noticeable trend is the increase in the amount of time students served under IDEA programs spent in general classrooms. Figure 6 provides a visual representation of the shift toward increased general classroom attendance. The data in Figure 7 indicate that people with disabilities are less likely to attend four-year institutions of higher learning than people without disabilities.

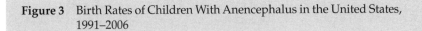

Figure 3   Birth Rates of Children With Anencephalus in the United States, 1991–2006

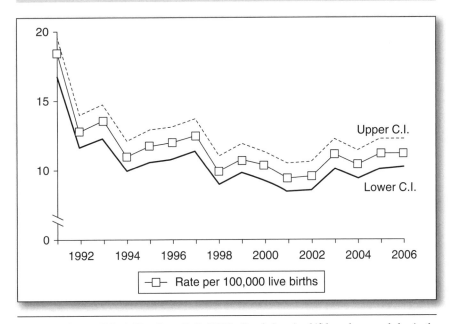

Source: Mathews, T. J., & Hamilton, B. E. (2009). *Trends in spina bifida and anencephalus in the United States, 1991–2006.* Hyattsville, MD: National Center for Health Statistics. Retrieved from http://www.cdc.gov/nchs/data/hestat/spine_anen/spine_anen.pdf

Table 4   Prevalence of Disability Among Children Under 15 Years Old by Specific Measures of Disability, 2005 (numbers in thousands)

Characteristic	Number	90% C.I. (±)[1]	Percent	90% C.I. (±)[1]
Under 3 years	12,008	476	100.0	(X)
With a disability	228	67	1.9	0.6
With a developmental delay	206	63	1.7	0.5
Difficulty moving arms or legs	‡60	34	0.5	0.3
No disability	11,779	471	98.1	0.6

(Continued)

Table 4 (Continued)

Characteristic	Number	90% C.I. (±)[1]	Percent	90% C.I. (±)[1]
3 to 5 years	12,339	482	100.0	(X)
With a disability	475	96	3.8	0.8
With a developmental delay	387	87	3.1	0.7
Difficulty walking, running, or playing	227	67	1.8	0.5
No disability	11,864	473	96.2	0.8
6 to 14 years	36,361	792	100.0	(X)
With a disability	4,654	300	12.8	0.8
Severe	1,584	176	4.4	0.5
Not severe	069	244	8.4	0.6
With no disability	31,708	746	87.2	0.8
Difficulty doing regular schoolwork	2,528	222	7.0	0.6
Difficulty getting along with others	672	115	1.8	0.3
With one or more selected conditions	2,116	203	5.8	0.5
A learning disability	1,024	141	2.8	0.4
Mental retardation	‡195	62	0.5	0.2
Other developmental disability[2]	347	82	1.0	0.2
Other developmental condition[2]	1,066	144	2.9	0.4
With a developmental disability or condition	1,325	161	3.6	0.4
Difficulty seeing words or letters	278	74	0.8	0.2
Severe	‡44	29	0.1	0.1
Not severe	234	68	0.6	0.2
Difficulty hearing conversation	244	69	0.7	0.2

Characteristic	Number	90% C.I. (±)[1]	Percent	90% C.I. (±)[1]
Severe	‡16	18	–	–
Not severe	228	67	0.6	0.2
Difficulty with speech	719	119	2.0	0.3
Severe	‡138	52	0.4	0.1
Not severe	581	107	1.6	0.3
Difficulty walking or running	748	121	2.1	0.3
Used a wheelchair or similar device	‡83	40	0.2	0.1
Use a cane, crutches, or walker	‡60	34	0.2	0.1
Had used for 6 months or more	‡49	31	0.1	0.1
With an ADL limitation	263	72	0.7	0.2
Needed personal assistance	236	68	0.6	0.2
Did not need personal assistance	‡27	23	0.1	0.1

Source: Brault, M. (2008). *Americans with disabilities: 2005* (Current Populations Reports, P70–117). Washington, DC: U.S. Census Bureau. Retrieved from http://www.census.gov/prod/2008 pubs/p70-117.pdf

(X) Not applicable.

– Represents or rounds to zero.

‡Since this estimate is less than 200,000 or based upon a population less than 200,000 (implying questionably small sample size), the estimate, its confidence interval estimate, and any other estimate associated with it are unlikely to be accurate enough to reveal useful information.

[1]A 90% confidence interval is a measure of an estimate's variability. The larger the confidence interval in relation to the size of the estimate, the less reliable the estimate. For further information on the source of the data and accuracy of the estimates, including standard errors and confidence intervals, go to www.census.gov/sipp/sourceac/S&A04W1toW7(S&A-7).pdf

[2]A child was considered to have a developmental disability if a "yes'" response was received to a question about the presence of mental retardation or to a question about the presence of some other developmental disability, such as autism or cerebral palsy. A child was considered to have a developmental condition if a "yes'" response was received to a question about the presence of a developmental condition for which the child had received therapy or diagnostic services.

Figure 4   Total Number of Infants and Toddlers Receiving Individuals with
Disabilities Education Act (IDEA) Early Intervention Services, 1994–2008

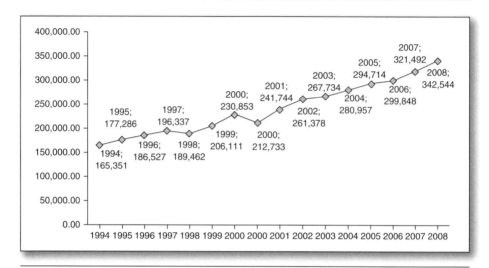

Sources: Compiled from U.S. Department of Education. (2006). *28th annual report to Congress on the implementation of the Individuals with Disabilities Education Act.* Washington, DC: Author. Retrieved from http://www2.ed.gov/about/reports/annual/osep/2006/parts-b-c/28th-vol-1.pdf; U.S. Department of Education. (2002). *24th annual report to Congress on the implementation of the Individuals with Disabilities Education Act.* Washington, DC: Author. Retrieved from http://www2.ed.gov/about/reports/annual/osep/2002/section-ii.pdf; U.S. Department of Education, Office of Special Education Programs, Data Analysis System. (2008). *OMB #1820-0557: Infants and toddlers receiving early intervention services in accordance with part C.* Washington, DC: Author. Retrieved from https://www.ideadata.org/PopulationData.asp

Peer Networks and Integration

Youth with disabilities frequently face barriers to social integration with peers who do not have disabilities, both during and after the school day. For example, many youth with disabilities across the country are legally exempted from physical education activities. Figure 8 breaks down the legislation for people with different types of disability by the state, middle, and high school level. The data indicate that exemptions are most commonly approved by individual schools.

Outside of the classroom, little reliable data exists on the physical and leisure time activities of youth with disabilities. The lack of statistical inquiry or research on culture and leisure for youth with disabilities coincides with the barriers to participation in social activities for youth

Table 5 Number and Percentage of Infants and Toddlers Receiving Early Intervention Services (under IDEA, Part C) by Age and State: Fall 2009

State	Birth to 12 Months	1 Year	2 Years	Birth Through 2 Years Total	3 to 4 Years	4 to 5 Years	5 or older	Percentage of Population[1]	Birth Through 2 Years (cumulative count)
Alabama	334	1,021	1,743	3,098	—	—	—	1.63	5,975
Alaska	164	236	275	675	—	—	—	2.00	1,458
Arizona	544	1,705	3,123	5,372	—	—	—	1.72	10,429
Arkansas	247	982	1,491	2,720	—	—	—	2.19	—
California	5,410	14,333	18,595	38,338	—	—	—	2.29	—
Colorado	699	1,579	2,878	5,156	—	—	—	2.35	—
Connecticut	516	1,479	2,748	4,743	—	—	—	3.78	9,287
Delaware	103	263	474	840	—	—	—	2.33	1,402
District of Columbia	45	73	213	331	—	—	—	1.42	—
Florida	1,489	4,127	8,861	14,477	—	—	—	2.06	—
Georgia	631	1,757	3,244	5,632	—	—	—	1.24	11,432
Hawaii	238	643	1,199	2,080	—	—	—	3.78	6,085

(Continued)

Table 5 (Continued)

State	Birth to 12 Months	1 Year	2 Years	Birth Through 2 Years Total	3 to 4 Years	4 to 5 Years	5 or older	Percentage of Population[1]	Birth Through 2 Years (cumulative count)
Idaho	394	584	938	1,916	—	—	—	2.52	3,663
Illinois	1,950	5,597	10,719	18,266	—	—	—	3.38	36,142
Indiana	1,156	3,312	5,596	10,064	—	—	—	3.74	19,798
Iowa	710	1,215	1,847	3,772	—	—	—	3.05	—
Kansas	562	1,019	1,982	3,563	—	—	—	2.84	7,200
Kentucky	382	1,554	3,141	5,077	—	—	—	2.92	—
Louisiana	997	2,142	1,409	4,548	—	—	—	2.27	—
Maine	90	290	619	999	—	—	—	2.37	—
Maryland	1,126	2,282	3,770	7,178	—	—	—	3.11	14,301
Massachusetts	1,890	4,702	8,540	15,132	—	—	—	6.51	31,173
Michigan	1,538	3,311	5,814	10,663	—	—	—	2.88	19,916
Minnesota	543	1,478	2,728	4,749	—	—	—	2.15	—
Mississippi	325	789	1,149	2,263	—	—	—	1.66	—

State	Birth to 12 Months	1 Year	2 Years	Birth Through 2 Years Total	3 to 4 Years	4 to 5 Years	5 or older	Percentage of Population[1]	Birth Through 2 Years (cumulative count)
Missouri	676	1,339	2,185	4,200	—	—	—	1.72	—
Montana	109	212	328	649	—	—	—	1.69	1,635
Nebraska	188	456	890	1,534	98	—	—	1.86	—
Nevada	253	570	1,069	1,892	—	—	—	1.54	3,814
New Hampshire	212	507	1,025	1,744	—	—	—	4.04	3,598
New Jersey	739	3,060	6,706	10,505	—	—	—	3.14	20,074
New Mexico	789	1,686	2,194	4,669	734	18	0	5.08	5,684
New York	2,906	9,884	20,086	32,876	—	—	—	4.41	—
North Carolina	1,382	3,077	5,512	9,971	—	—	—	2.48	17,606
North Dakota	178	302	429	909	—	—	—	3.39	1,542
Ohio	2,587	4,719	7,030	14,336	—	—	—	3.21	—
Oklahoma	571	1,061	1,448	3,080	—	—	—	1.86	—

(Continued)

189

Table 5 (Continued)

State	Birth to 12 Months	1 Year	2 Years	Birth Through 2 Years Total	3 to 4 Years	4 to 5 Years	5 or older	Percentage of Population[1]	Birth Through 2 Years (cumulative count)
Oregon	303	886	1,573	2,762	—	—	—	1.84	—
Pennsylvania	2,389	5,374	9,397	17,160	—	—	—	3.82	31,805
Puerto Rico	256	1,319	3,365	4,940	—	—	—	3.61	—
Rhode Island	291	584	996	1,871	—	—	—	5.12	3,730
South Carolina	488	1,480	2,632	4,600	—	—	—	2.44	—
South Dakota	109	299	621	1,029	—	—	—	2.81	1,029
Tennessee	586	1,487	2,184	4,257	—	—	—	1.65	—
Texas	4,405	9,000	15,169	28,574	—	—	—	2.29	57,110
Utah	339	995	1,950	3,284	—	—	—	1.96	—
Vermont	73	247	456	776	—	—	—	3.93	—
Virginia	626	1,882	3,780	6,288	—	—	—	1.95	12,017
Washington	454	1,542	3,010	5,006	—	—	—	1.83	9,593
West Virginia	376	783	1,313	2,472	—	—	—	3.87	5,146

State	Birth to 12 Months	1 Year	2 Years	Birth Through 2 Years Total	3 to 4 Years	4 to 5 Years	5 or older	Percentage of Population[1]	Birth Through 2 Years (cumulative count)
Wisconsin	716	1,706	3,578	6,000	—	—	—	2.72	—
Wyoming	150	361	596	1,107	—	—	—	4.46	—
50 states, D.C., and P.R.	44,234	111,291	192,618	348,143	832	18	0	2.67	352,644
American Samoa	25	33	42	100	—	—	—	2.06	139
Guam	33	67	60	160	—	—	—	1.57	245
Northern Marianas	10	7	33	50	—	—	—	1.39	—
Virgin Islands	39	63	49	151	—	—	—	2.97	—
U.S. and outlying areas	44,341	111,461	192,802	348,604	832	18	0	2.67	353,028

Source: U.S. Department of Education, Office of Special Education Programs. (2009). *Number and percentage of infants and toddlers receiving early intervention services (under IDEA, Part C) by age and state: Fall 2009.* Retrieved from https://www.ideadata.org/tables33rd%5CAR_C-13.xls

[1]Percentage of population = Number of children birth through 2 served under IDEA Part C, divided by population birth through 2, multiplied by 100.

— Data not available.

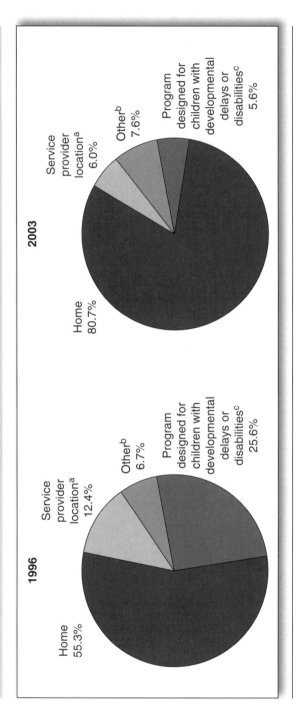

Figure 5 Locations Where Early Intervention Services Are Provided, 1996 and 2003

1996

Home
55.3%

Service
provider
location[a]
12.4%

Other[b]
6.7%

Program
designed for
children with
developmental
delays or
disabilities[c]
25.6%

2003

Home
80.7%

Service
provider
location[a]
6.0%

Other[b]
7.6%

Program
designed for
children with
developmental
delays or
disabilities[c]
5.6%

Source: U.S. Department of Education. (2006). *28th annual report to Congress on the implementation of the Individuals with Disabilities Education Act.* Washington, DC: Author. Retrieved from http://www2.ed.gov/about/reports/annual/osep/2006/parts-b-c/28th-vol-1.pdf

[a]*Service provider location* includes an office, clinic, or hospital where the infant or toddler comes for short periods of time (e.g., 45 minutes) to receive early intervention services. These services may be delivered individually or to a small group of children.

[b]In 1996, *other* included the settings *program designed for typically developing children* (2.4%), *residential facility* (0.7%), *family child care* (0.6%) and *other nonspecified* (2.9%). In 2003, *other* included the settings *program designed for typically developing children* (4.2%), *residential facility* (<0.1%), *hospital* (0.1%) and *other nonspecified* (3.3%). Family child care was not a service setting category in 2003 and therefore does not appear in the 2003 chart.

[c]*Program designed for children with developmental delay or disabilities* refers to an organized program of at least one hour in duration provided on a regular basis. The program is usually directed toward the facilitation of one or more developmental areas. Examples include early intervention classrooms/centers and developmental child care programs.

Table 6 Percentage of the Kindergarten Class of 1998–1999 Receiving Special Education in Various Grades, by Primary Disability and Student and School Characteristics, 1998–1999 Through 2003–2004

Student or School Characteristic	Kindergarten			Grade 1			Grade 3			Grade 5		
	All Disabilities	SLI[1]	LD[2]	All Disabilities	SLI[1]	LD[2]	All Disabilities	SLI[1]	LD[2]	All Disabilities	SLI[1]	LD[2]
All students	4.14	2.27	0.48	5.36	1.80	1.22	9.36	1.42	3.26	11.89	1.35	6.49
Student Characteristics												
Sex												
Male	5.29	2.90	0.59	6.60	2.18	1.47	12.62	1.83	4.43	14.82	1.65	8.53
Female	2.90	1.61	0.36	4.05	1.40	0.95	5.88	0.97	2.01	8.75	1.04	4.31
Race/ethnicity												
White, non-Hispanic	4.60	2.62	0.45	5.83	2.02	1.36	9.64	1.62	3.40	12.45	1.32	6.66
Black, non-Hispanic	4.21	1.81	0.58	5.46	1.52	0.70	9.31	1.00	2.69	11.94	1.64!	5.47
Hispanic	3.26	1.95	0.54	3.98	1.45	1.19!	8.66	0.86	3.36	11.35	1.35!	7.22
Other/more than one race, non-Hispanic	2.79	1.56	0.32	4.72	1.64	1.30!	9.19	2.25	3.17	9.35	0.99	5.92

(Continued)

Table 6 (Continued)

Student or School Characteristic	Kindergarten			Grade 1			Grade 3			Grade 5		
	All Disabilities	SLI[1]	LD[2]	All Disabilities	SLI[1]	LD[2]	All Disabilities	SLI[1]	LD[2]	All Disabilities	SLI[1]	LD[2]
Poverty[3]												
Poor	5.82	2.77	1.02	6.96	1.89	1.91	13.14	1.38	4.27	18.26	2.90	8.39
Nonpoor	3.71	2.18	0.32	4.85	1.90	0.83	8.01	1.37	2.95	9.60	0.94	5.72
School Characteristics												
School control												
Public	4.62	2.54	0.54	5.94	1.95	1.38	10.21	1.54	3.58	12.89	1.52	7.00
Private	1.35	0.75	0.11	1.38	0.75!	0.12!	2.53	0.44!	0.58	4.65!	0.11!	2.87!
Urbanicity												
Central city	2.97	1.36	0.38	3.12	0.74	0.53	8.25	1.04	2.52	10.47	1.42	6.54
Urban fringe/large town	4.77	3.02	0.44	5.52	2.26	0.99	9.77	1.54	3.49	11.07	1.13	5.77
Small town/rural	5.01	2.45	0.74	8.83	2.74	2.85	10.75	1.83	4.24	14.65	1.97	7.02

Student or School Characteristic	Kindergarten			Grade 1			Grade 3			Grade 5		
	All Disabilities	SLI[1]	LD[2]	All Disabilities	SLI[1]	LD[2]	All Disabilities	SLI[1]	LD[2]	All Disabilities	SLI[1]	LD[2]
Region												
Northeast	6.19	3.24	0.72	5.56	1.38	1.29	11.15	0.92	4.13	12.68	1.45!	7.13
Midwest	2.62	1.20	0.47	4.61	0.81	0.92	8.82	1.51	3.72	12.74	1.12!	8.03
South	5.34	3.08	0.58	7.51	2.96	1.71	10.69	1.87	3.26	11.90	1.53	5.21
West	1.97	1.21!	0.10	2.24	1.18	0.62!	6.26	0.92	2.08	10.81	1.25!	6.85
Poverty concentration[4]												
Higher poverty	5.62	2.94	0.79	7.00	2.35	2.15	10.23	1.43	3.68	12.21	1.46	6.24
Lower poverty	3.86	2.16	0.35	5.91	2.14	1.08	8.36	1.66	3.52	12.77	1.49	7.24

Source: U.S. Department of Education, National Center for Education Statistics. (2007, July). *Demographic and school characteristics of students receiving special education in the elementary grades*, Table 2. Retrieved from http://nces.ed.gov/pubs2007/2007005.pdf

! Interpret data with caution. Standard error is more than one-third as large as the estimate.

[1]Speech or language impairment.

[2]Specific learning disability.

[3]Children in families whose incomes are at or below the poverty threshold are classified as poor; those in families with incomes above the poverty threshold are classified as nonpoor.

[4]Higher poverty schools are those with 50% or more students eligible for the National School Lunch Program; lower poverty schools are those with fewer than 50% of students eligible.

Table 7 Number and Percentage Distribution of 3- to 21-Year-Olds Served Under the IDEA, and Number Served as a Percentage of Total Public School Enrollment, by Type of Disability: Selected School Years, 1976–1977 Through 2007–2008

Type of Disability	1976–77	1980–81	1990–91	1995–96	2000–01	2003–04	2004–05	2005–06	2006–07	2007–08
				Number Served (in thousands)						
All disabilities	**3,694**	**4,144**	**4,710**	**5,572**	**6,296**	**6,634**	**6,719**	**6,713**	**6,686**	**6,606**
Specific learning disabilities	796	1,462	2,129	2,578	2,868	2,831	2,798	2,735	2,665	2,573
Speech or language impairments	1,302	1,168	985	1,022	1,409	1,441	1,463	1,468	1,475	1,456
Mental retardation	961	830	534	571	624	593	578	556	534	500
Emotional disturbance	283	347	389	437	481	489	489	477	464	442
Hearing impairments	88	79	58	67	78	79	79	79	80	79
Orthopedic impairments	87	58	49	63	83	77	73	71	69	67

Type of Disability	1976–77	1980–81	1990–91	1995–96	2000–01	2003–04	2004–05	2005–06	2006–07	2007–08
Other health impairments	141	98	55	133	303	464	521	570	611	641
Visual impairments	38	31	23	25	29	28	29	29	29	29
Multiple disabilities	—	68	96	93	133	140	140	141	142	138
Deaf-blindness	—	3	1	1	1	2	2	2	2	2
Autism	—	—	—	28	94	163	191	223	258	296
Traumatic brain injury	—	—	—	9	16	23	24	24	25	25
Developmental delay	—	—	—	—	178	305	332	339	333	358
Preschool disabled[1]	+	+	390	544	+	+	+	+	+	+
Number Served as a Percentage of Total Public School Enrollment[2]										
All disabilities	**8.3**	**10.1**	**11.4**	**12.4**	**13.3**	**13.7**	**13.8**	**13.7**	**13.6**	**13.4**

(Continued)

Table 7 (Continued)

Type of Disability	1976–77	1980–81	1990–91	1995–96	2000–01	2003–04	2004–05	2005–06	2006–07	2007–08
Specific learning disabilities	1.8	3.6	5.2	5.8	6.1	5.8	5.7	5.6	5.4	5.2
Speech or language impairments	2.9	2.9	2.4	2.3	3.0	3.0	3.0	3.0	3.0	3.0
Mental retardation	2.2	2.0	1.3	1.3	1.3	1.2	1.2	1.1	1.1	1.0
Emotional disturbance	0.6	0.8	0.9	1.0	1.0	1.0	1.0	1.0	0.9	0.9
Hearing impairments	0.2	0.2	0.1	0.1	0.2	0.2	0.2	0.2	0.2	0.2
Orthopedic impairments	0.2	0.1	0.1	0.1	0.2	0.2	0.2	0.1	0.1	0.1
Other health impairments	0.3	0.2	0.1	0.3	0.6	1.0	1.1	1.2	1.2	1.3
Visual impairments	0.1	0.1	0.1	0.1	0.1	0.1	0.1	0.1	0.1	0.1

Type of Disability	1976–77	1980–81	1990–91	1995–96	2000–01	2003–04	2004–05	2005–06	2006–07	2007–08
Multiple disabilities	—	0.2	0.2	0.2	0.3	0.3	0.3	0.3	0.3	0.3
Deaf-blindness	—	#	#	#	#	#	#	#	#	#
Autism	—	—	—	0.1	0.2	0.3	0.4	0.5	0.5	0.6
Traumatic brain injury	—	—	—	#	#	#	#	#	0.1	0.1
Developmental delay	—	—	—	—	0.4	0.6	0.7	0.7	0.7	0.7
Preschool disabled[1]	†	†	0.9	1.2	†	†	†	†	†	†

Source: U.S. Department of Education, National Center for Education Statistics. (2008). *Number and percentage distribution of 3- to 21-year-olds served under the Individuals with Disabilities Education Act (IDEA), Part B, and number served as a percentage of total public school enrollment, by type of disability: Selected school years, 1976–77 through 2007–08,* Table A-6-1. Retrieved from http://nces.ed.gov/programs/coe/2010/section1/table-cwd-1.asp

—Not available.

†Not applicable.

#Rounds to zero.

[1]Beginning in 1976, data were collected for preschool age children ages 3–5 by disability type; those data are combined above with data for children and youth ages 6–21. However, the 1986 Amendments to the Education of the Handicapped Act (now known as IDEA) mandated that data not be collected by disability for students ages 3–5. For this reason, data from the 1990s on preschoolers with disabilities are reported in a separate row. Beginning in 2000–2001, states were again required to report data on preschool children by disability.

[2]Based on the total prekindergarten through 12th-grade enrollment in public schools.

Table 8 Percentage of Students 6 to 21 Years Old Served in Varying Educational Environments Under IDEA, Selected Years, Fall 1989 Through Fall 2007

Years	Regular School, Time Outside General Class			Separate School for Students With Disabilities		Separate Residential Facility		Home-Bound/ Hospital Placement
	Less Than 21 Percent	21–60 Percent	More Than 60 Percent	Private	Public	Private	Public	
1989	31.7	37.5	24.9	3.2	1.3	0.7	0.3	0.6
1990	33.1	36.4	25.0	2.9	1.3	0.6	0.3	0.5
1994	44.8	28.5	22.4	2.0	1.0	0.5	0.3	0.6
1995	45.7	28.5	21.5	2.1	1.0	0.4	0.3	0.5
1996	46.1	28.3	21.4	2.0	1.0	0.4	0.3	0.5
1997	46.8	28.8	20.4	1.8	1.0	0.4	0.3	0.5
1998	46.0	29.9	20.0	1.8	1.1	0.4	0.3	0.5
1999	45.9	29.8	20.3	1.9	1.0	0.4	0.3	0.5

Years	Regular School, Time Outside General Class			Separate School for Students With Disabilities		Separate Residential Facility		Home-Bound/ Hospital Placement
	Less Than 21 Percent	21–60 Percent	More Than 60 Percent	Private	Public	Private	Public	
2000	46.5	29.8	19.5	1.9	1.1	0.4	0.3	0.5
2001	48.2	28.5	19.2	1.7	1.2	0.4	0.4	0.4
2002	48.2	28.7	19.0	1.7	1.2	0.3	0.4	0.5
2003	49.9	27.7	18.5	1.7	1.1	0.3	0.4	0.5
2004	51.9	26.5	17.6	1.8	1.2	0.3	0.3	0.4
2005	54.2	25.1	16.7	1.8	1.2	0.3	0.3	0.5
2006	53.7	23.7	17.6	2.94*	—	0.41*	—	0.4
2007	56.8	22.4	15.4	3.01*	—	0.41*	—	0.4

Source: U.S. Department of Education, Office of Special Education Programs. (2009). *Percentage distribution of students 6 to 21 years old served under Individuals with Disabilities Education Act, Part B, by educational environment and type of disability: Selected years, fall 1989 through fall 2007, Table 51.* Retrieved from http://nces.ed.gov/programs/digest/d09/tables/dt09_051.asp

*Data for 2006 and 2007 combine public and private schools and combine public and private residential facilities.

Figure 6   Comparison of the Percentage of Individuals Served Under IDEA by
Environment Type, 1989 Versus 2007

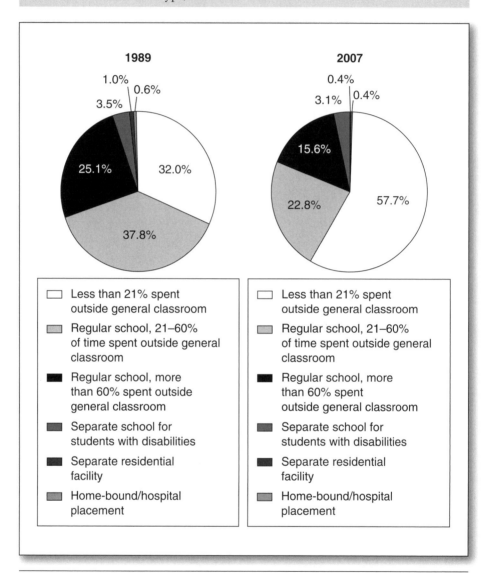

Source: U.S. Department of Education, Office of Special Education Programs. (2009). *Percentage
distribution of students 6 to 21 years old served under Individuals with Disabilities Education Act,
Part B, by educational environment and type of disability: Selected years, fall 1989 through fall 2007,*
Table 51. Retrieved from http://nces.ed.gov/programs/digest/d09/tables/dt09_051.asp

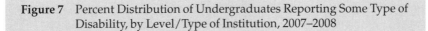

Figure 7   Percent Distribution of Undergraduates Reporting Some Type of
Disability, by Level/Type of Institution, 2007–2008

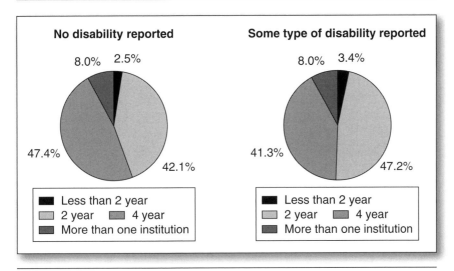

Source: U.S. Department of Education, National Center for Education Statistics (2010, September). *Profile of undergraduate students 2007–2008,* Table 1.1. Washington, DC: NCES Data Analysis System. Retrieved from http://nces.ed.gov/pubs2010/2010205.pdf

with disabilities. For example, youth with disabilities are more than twice as likely to live in households with an annual income under $25,000 as youth in the general population (see Table 9). The reported percentage of people with disabilities who socialize with friends, neighbors, and relatives is lower than those without disabilities (see Figure 9).

Table 9   Average Annual Household Incomes of Youth Ages 12–17 With
Disability Versus General Population, 1999

Annual Household Income	Youth Ages 12–17 With Disabilities	General Youth Population Ages 12–17
Less than $12,500	35% of households	18% of households
Less than $25,000	68% of households	18% of households

Source: National Council on Disability. (2000). *Transition and post-school outcomes for youth with disabilities: Closing the gaps to post-secondary education and employment.* Washington, DC: Author. Retrieved from http://www.ncd.gov/newsroom/publications/2000/transition_11-01-00.htm

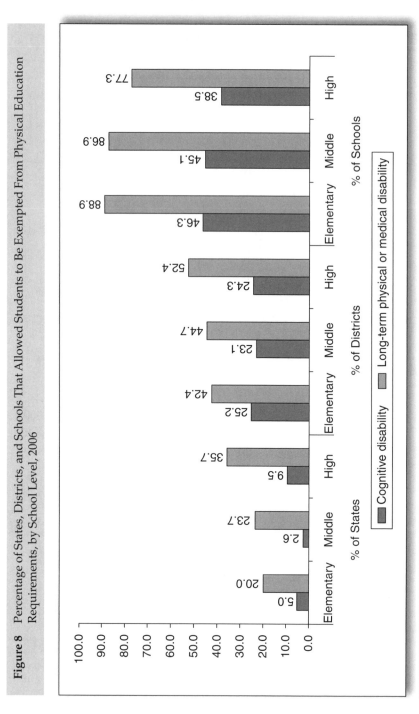

Figure 8 Percentage of States, Districts, and Schools That Allowed Students to Be Exempted From Physical Education Requirements, by School Level, 2006

Source: Lee, S. M., Burgeson, C. R., Fulton, J. E., & Spain, C. G. (2007, October 1). Physical education and physical activity: Results from the school health policies and programs study 2006, Table 2. *Journal of School Health, 77*(8), 435–463. Retrieved from http://www.ashaweb.org/files/public/JOSH_1007/josh_77_8.log_p_435.pdf

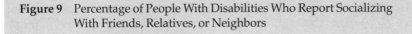

Figure 9   Percentage of People With Disabilities Who Report Socializing
With Friends, Relatives, or Neighbors

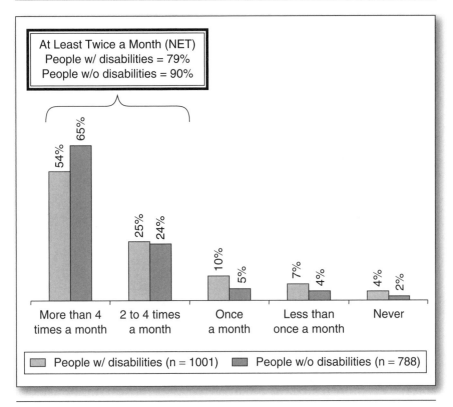

Source: Kessler Foundation and National Organization on Disability. (2010). *The ADA, 20 years later: Survey of Americans with disabilities,* Table 7A. New York: Harris Interactive. Retrieved from http://www.2010disabilitysurveys.org/pdfs/surveyresults.pdf

Sexuality

People with disabilities face additional barriers to inclusion in regard to sexuality. Studies indicate that people with disabilities are less likely than those without disabilities to receive the social and emotional support they need (Figure 10). Additionally, people with disabilities are more frequently the victims of sexual abuse (Westat, 1993). Data collected from 22 states by the U.S. Department of Health and Human Services' Administration for Children and Families (2010) showed a total of 218,165 children were the reported victims of sexual abuse in 2008.

Figure 10   Percentage of Individuals Who Report That They Always or
Usually Get the Social and Emotional Support They Need, 2006

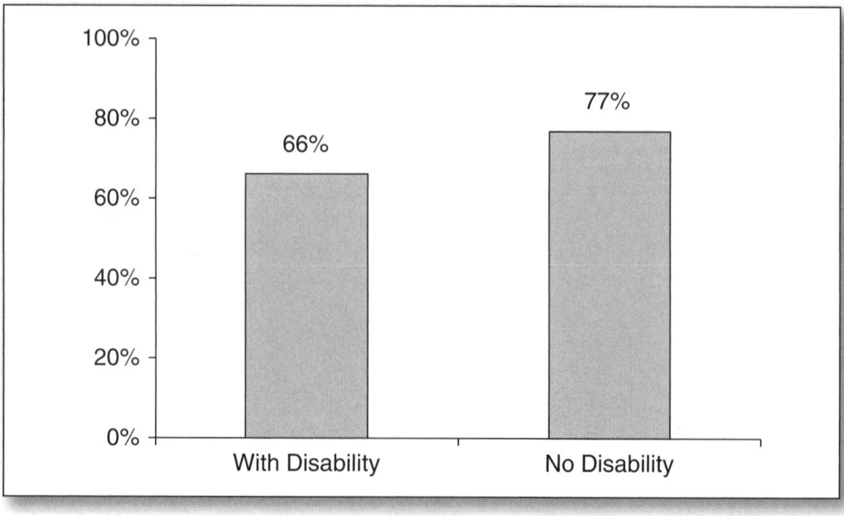

Source: National Council on Disability. (2008). *Keeping track: National disability status and program performance indicators.* Washington, DC: Author. Retrieved from http://www.ncd.gov/newsroom/publications/2008/Indicators_Report.html

Of these children, 32,712 or 15% had some form of disability. The most frequently reported types of impairments among the victims of sexual abuse were "other medical condition" (6.2%), "behavioral problems" (5.3%), and "emotionally disturbed" (3.7%).

Adulthood

Employment

People with disabilities face varying barriers to inclusion in the employment sector. Table 10 breaks down the average monthly earnings of people according to their specific impairment and presents the percentage of the working population according to impairment type. Table 10 also presents estimates of monthly income and the total percentage of individuals with disability status in the workforce. These U.S. Census

Bureau statistics indicate that people with any disability status (1) are less likely to be employed than people without a disability, and (2) have a lower median monthly income than people without a disability. Data from the Department of Health and Human Services in Figure 11 show increased reporting of disability with age. Approximately 10.9% of the working-age population reports having a disability as compared to 7.6% of children. Broken down by race, non-Hispanic Black individuals are the most likely racial group to report disability.

Counts of disability vary according to definition and surveillance method. When looking at disability as it relates specifically to employment, 8.4% of the population has a work disability as compared to 10.9% of individuals who experience any sort of functional limitation in activity (Centers for Disease Control, 2007). People with disabilities face further barriers to employment when compared to people without disabilities. Table 11 presents the trend data of people with disabilities who report experiencing different risk factors that impede full inclusion in the employment sector. The two most dramatic reported differences are that people with disability are more than twice as likely as people without disability to report experiencing poverty and inadequate transportation. Studies also indicate that, in general, people with disabilities are less likely to be employed than peers without disabilities that have the same level of educational attainment (Figure 12).

Parenting

Studies of the experiences of people with disabilities in significant social events have historically been lacking, even though people with disabilities experience the same life course events as people without disabilities. For example, very little statistical analysis or quantitative data exists on the family experience of people with disabilities (LaPlante, 1996). The best estimates to date of households led by a family member with a disability use data from the 1990 U.S. Census, which found that an estimated 28.5% of all American families had a member with a disability (Table 12). Data compiled more recently by the National Council on Disability and presented in Figure 13 indicates that 49% of partnered families have at least one partner with a disability. Rates of disability for single-person households were 18.4% for males and 21.7% for females. Additionally, 49% of people with disabilities report having been married as compared to 61% of people without disabilities.

Table 10 Disability Status, Employment, Monthly Earnings, and Monthly Family Income Among Individuals 21 to 64 Years Old by Specific Measures of Disability: 2005 (numbers in thousands, earnings and income in dollars)

Characteristic	Total	90% C.I. (±)	Employed						Median Monthly Family Income	90% C.I. (±)
			Number	90% C.I. (±)	Percent	90% C.I. (±)	Median Monthly Earnings	90% C.I. (±)		
Total	**170,349**	**1,212**	**131,538**	**1,210**	**77.2**	**0.4**	**2,500**	**23**	**4,333**	**37**
Disability status										
With a disability	28,145	708	12,836	491	45.6	1.3	1,917	68	2,700	68
Severe	18,710	587	5,737	332	30.7	1.5	1,458	96	2,182	69
Covered by Medicare or received social security or supplemental security income	8,600	405	798	125	9.3	1.4	375	82	1,782	71
Covered by Medicare	4,432	293	384	87	8.7	1.9	422	111	1,921	99
Received social security	6,083	342	573	106	9.4	1.7	400	97	2,105	97

Characteristic	Total	90% C.I. (±)	Employed							
			Number	90% C.I. (±)	Percent	90% C.I. (±)	Median Monthly Earnings	90% C.I. (±)	Median Monthly Family Income	90% C.I. (±)
Received supplemental security income	3,756	270	343	82	9.1	2.1	302	107	1,339	76
Not covered by Medicare and not receiving social security or supplemental security income	10,110	438	4,939	309	48.9	2.2	1,732	110	2,600	124
Not severe	9,435	423	7,099	369	75.2	2.0	2,250	89	3,801	139
No disability	142,204	1,219	118,702	1,191	83.5	0.4	2,539	24	4,669	42
Seeing/hearing/speaking										
Difficulty seeing words/letters	4,103	282	1,673	181	40.8	3.4	1,932	182	2,188	142
Severe	779	123	204	63	26.2	7.0	1,957	670	1,743	259

(Continued)

Table 10 (Continued)

Characteristic	Total	90% C.I. (±)	Employed							
			Number	90% C.I. (±)	Percent	90% C.I. (±)	Median Monthly Earnings	90% C.I. (±)	Median Monthly Family Income	90% C.I. (±)
Not severe	3,323	254	1,469	169	44.2	3.8	1,925	188	2,253	162
Difficulty hearing conversation	3,756	270	2,219	208	59.1	3.6	2,252	178	3,162	208
Severe	449	94	257	71	57.2	10.3	1,920	506	2,514	400
Not severe	3,307	253	1,962	195	59.3	3.8	2,369	186	3,240	227
Difficulty with speech	1,521	172	560	105	36.8	5.5	1,575	321	2,260	236
Severe	230	67	64	35	27.7	13.1	1,168	866	2,377	532
Not severe	1,291	159	496	99	38.4	6.0	1,645	365	2,252	258
Walking/using stairs/ambulatory aids										
Difficulty walking	11,219	460	3,295	253	29.4	1.9	1,810	136	2,290	91

Characteristic	Total	90% C.I. (±)	Employed						Median Monthly Family Income	90% C.I. (±)
			Number	90% C.I. (±)	Percent	90% C.I. (±)	Median Monthly Earnings	90% C.I. (±)		
Severe	5,539	327	1,082	145	19.5	2.4	1,600	230	1,950	106
Not severe	5,679	331	2,213	208	39.0	2.9	2,000	167	2,739	150
Difficulty using stairs	10,969	455	3,259	251	29.7	1.9	1,768	132	2,258	91
Severe	3,154	247	575	106	18.2	3.0	1,315	265	1,777	128
Not severe	7,815	386	2,684	228	34.3	2.4	1,836	143	2,494	118
Used a wheelchair or similar device	1,393	165	237	68	17.0	4.5	1,833	679	2,135	243
Used a cane, crutches, or walker	3,907	275	828	127	21.2	2.9	2,000	342	2,175	147

Source: Brault, M. (December 2008). *Americans with disabilities: 2005.* Current Populations Reports P70–117. Table B-3. Washington, DC: U.S. Census Bureau. Retrieved from http://www.census.gov/prod/2008pubs/p70-117.pdf

211

Figure 11   Percentage of the Working-Age Population (18–65) Versus Children (0–17) Reporting an Activity Limitation, 2006

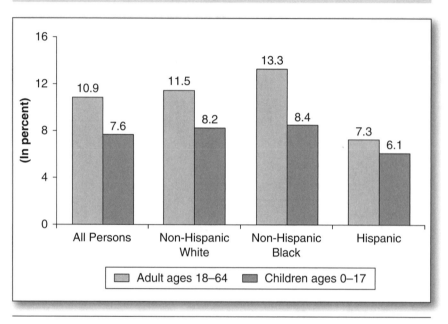

Source: U.S. Department of Health and Human Services. (2008). *Indicators of welfare dependence: Annual report to Congress,* Figure WORK 7. Washington, DC: Author. Retrieved from http://www.aspe.hhs.gov/hsp/indicators08/ch3.shtml#work7

Table 11   Comparison of People With and Without Disabilities on Key Indicator Measures Related to Social Inclusion, 2010

	People With Disabilities	*People Without Disabilities*	*Gap in Percentage Points*
Base:	**1,001**	**788**	
	Percentage		
Employment			
Works either full or part-time (18–64)	21	59	38

	People With Disabilities	People Without Disabilities	Gap in Percentage Points
Poverty*			
Annual household income $15,000 or less	34	15	19
Education*			
Has not graduated from high school	17	11	6
Health care*			
Did not get needed care on at least one occasion in past year	19	10	9
Transportation*			
Inadequate transportation considered a problem	34	16	18
Socializing			
Socializes with close friends, relatives, or neighbors at least twice a month	79	90	11
Going to restaurants			
Goes to a restaurant at least twice a month	48	75	27
Attendance at religious services			
Goes to church, synagogue, or any other place of worship at least once a month	50	57	7
Political participation**			
Voter turnout in the presidential election	59 (2008)	59	0
Satisfaction with life			
Very satisfied with life in general	34	61	27

(Continued)

Table 11 (Continued)

	People With Disabilities	People Without Disabilities	Gap in Percentage Points
Access to mental health services[*]			
Did not get help from mental health professional on at least one occasion in past year	7	3	4
Technology			
Uses a computer/electronic device to access the Internet	85	54	31
Financial situation[*]			
Struggling to get by or living paycheck to paycheck	58	34	24

Source: Harris Interactive. (2010). *The ADA, 20 years later: Kessler Foundation/National Organization on Disability survey of Americans with disabilities,* Exhibit 2. New York: Author. Retrieved from http://www.2010disabilitysurveys.org/pdfs/surveyresults.pdf

[*]These variables are "negative" in that a higher score indicates more of a disadvantage.

[**]*Source:* 2008 Harris Poll.

Aging

Retirement

The prevalence of disability becomes higher in populations as they age. Table 13 presents the estimated total number of people with disabilities over the age of 65 years according to disability status. The need for assistance also increases for people with disabilities as they get older (Figure 14). The acquisition of disability is a contributing factor to retirement for some people. Figure 15 presents the ten most common acquired disabilities in the United States among adults. Without support, the acquisition of disability can have negative effects on the aging population. The acquisition of disability right before retirement age (between the ages of 55 and 65 years) directly correlates with a higher chance of experiencing poverty. Figure 16 shows the rate at which people who acquire disability between the ages of 51 and 64 years are affected by poverty in the general population.

Figure 12   Estimated Employment Rate by Educational Attainment, People With Disabilities Versus People With No Disabilities, 2005

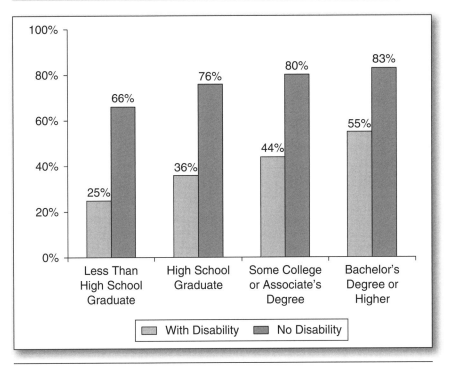

Source: National Council on Disability. (2008). *Keeping track: National disability status and program performance indicators*, Exhibit 5.3. Washington, DC: Author. Retrieved from http://www.ncd.gov/newsroom/publications/2008/Indicators_Report.html

Table 12   Distribution of Families With Disabilities by Race and Composition (in percent)

	All	*White*	*Black*	*Hispanic*
Partnered families				
Families with members with disability	28.5	28.5	30.6	21.5
One partner with disability	19.0	19.0	20.3	13.7
Both partners with disability	6.1	6.1	6.8	4.0
Children with disability	4.0	4.0	4.5	4.7
Other relative with disability	1.3	1.2	2.2	1.3

(Continued)

Table 12 (Continued)

Families headed by a single male				
With members with disability	29.6	29.5	32.9	17.8
Householder with disability	18.4	17.8	21.9	10.4
Children with Disability	5.9	6.0	6.5	2.7
Other relative with disability	11.0	11.4	11.6	6.6
Families headed by a single female				
With members with disability	32.7	32.8	33.3	30.3
Householder with disability	21.7	21.9	21.8	18.4
Children with disability	12.9	12.5	13.8	12.8
Other relative with disability	5.5	5.7	5.2	4.7

Source: LaPlante, M. P., & National Institute on Disability and Rehabilitation Research (U.S.). (1996). *Families with disabilities in the United States,* Table B. Washington, DC: U.S. Dept. of Education, Office of Special Education and Rehabilitative Services.

Figure 13   Marriage Status, People With Disabilities Versus People With No Disabilities, 2005

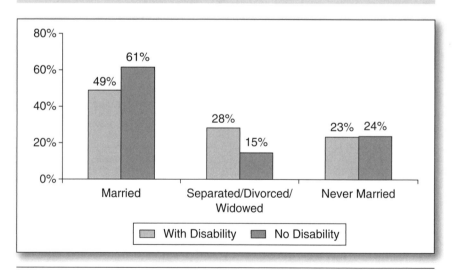

Source: National Council on Disability. (2008). *Keeping track: National disability status and program performance indicators,* Exhibit 5.17. Washington, DC: Author. Retrieved from http://www.ncd.gov/newsroom/publications/2008/Indicators_Report.html

Table 13   Prevalence of Disability Among Individuals 65 Years and Older by Specific Measures of Disability, 2005 (numbers in thousands)

Characteristic	Number	90% C.I. (±)	Percent	90% C.I. (±)
Total	**35,028**	**780**	**100.0**	**(X)**
Disability status				
With a disability	18,133	578	51.8	1.2
Severe	12,943	493	36.9	1.1
Not severe	5,190	316	14.8	0.8
No disability	16,895	559	48.2	1.2
Seeing/hearing/speaking				
With a disability	6,508	353	18.6	0.9
Severe	1,464	169	4.2	0.5
Not severe	5,045	312	14.4	0.8
Difficulty seeing	3,534	262	10.1	0.7
Severe	964	137	2.8	0.4
Not severe	2,570	224	7.3	0.6
Difficulty hearing	3,915	275	11.2	0.7
Severe	527	102	1.5	0.3
Not severe	3,387	256	9.7	0.7
Difficulty with speech	753	121	2.1	0.3
Severe	120*	48	0.3	0.1
Not severe	633	111	1.8	0.3
Walking/using stairs				
With a disability	13,346	500	38.1	1.1
Severe	7,852	387	22.4	1.0
Not severe	5,493	325	15.7	0.9

(Continued)

Table 13 (Continued)

Characteristic	Number	90% C.I. (±)	Percent	90% C.I. (±)
Difficulty walking	11,098	458	31.7	1.1
Severe	7,036	367	20.1	0.9
Not severe	4,063	280	11.6	0.8
Difficulty using stairs	10,576	447	30.2	1.1
Severe	4,134	283	11.8	0.8
Not severe	6,442	352	18.4	0.9
Used a wheelchair	1,823	188	5.2	0.5
Used a cane/crutches/walker	6,256	347	17.9	0.9
For 6 months or longer	5,308	320	15.2	0.8
Mental				
With a disability	4,006	278	11.4	0.8
With 1 or more selected conditions	1,884	192	5.4	0.5
A learning disability	226	67	0.6	0.2
Mental retardation	96*	43	0.3	0.1
Alzheimer's, senility, or dementia	1,328	161	3.8	0.5
Other mental/emotional condition	485	97	1.4	0.3
With 1 or more selected symptoms	1,761	185	5.0	0.5
Depressed or anxious	1,188	152	3.4	0.4
Trouble getting along with others	279	74	0.8	0.2

Characteristic	Number	90% C.I. (±)	Percent	90% C.I. (±)
Trouble concentrating	1,065	144	3.0	0.4
Trouble coping with stress	927	135	2.6	0.4
Difficulty managing money/bills	2,579	224	7.4	0.6

Source: Brault, M. (2008). *Americans with disabilities: 2005* (Current Populations Reports P70–117), Table B-1. Washington, DC: U.S. Census Bureau. Retrieved from http://www.census.gov/prod/2008pubs/p70-117.pdf

*Since this estimate is less than 200,000 or based upon a population of less than 200,000 (implying questionably small sample size), the estimate, its confidence interval estimate, and any other estimate associated with it are unlikely to be accurate enough to reveal useful information.

Long-Term Care and Support

Many people with disabilities receive diverse systems of support throughout their lifetimes. One essential support for aging populations is the use of assistive technology. The needs of aging populations coalesce with the needs of people with disabilities, and the likelihood of receiving support with activities of daily living (ADLs) increases with age. As Table 14 indicates, the use of assistive technology is almost eight times as common with individuals 85 years and older as it is with individuals ages 55 to 65. Table 14 presents the percentage of individuals who report receiving assistance with at least one ADL, sorted by age group and gender, and the percentage of people who use assistive technologies.

Another vital part of the support system for many people with disabilities is the support of unpaid caregivers. The 2009 report "Care Giving in the U.S." by the National Alliance for Caregiving and the AARP gives the most comprehensive overview of the population of caregivers to date. An estimated 28% of the overall population is identified as caregivers, having provided free care in the last 12 months. The U.S. caregiver population predominantly provides care for adults (Table 15). Care recipients are reported to have a wide variety of disabilities; 95% of caregivers provided care to an individual with a physical or mental condition that required caregiving support (Figure 17). The majority of care recipients are aging

Figure 14   Disability Prevalence and the Need for Assistance by Age, 2005 (in percent)

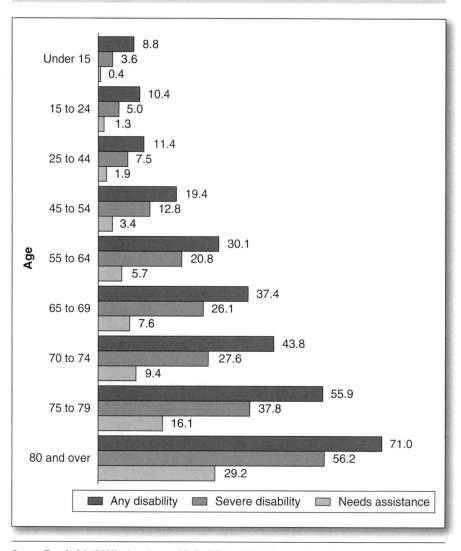

Source: Brault, M. (2008). *Americans with disabilities: 2005* (Current Populations Reports, P70–117), Figure 2. Washington, DC: U.S. Census Bureau. Retrieved from http://www.census.gov/prod/2008pubs/p70-117.pdf

Note: The need for assistance with activities of daily living was not asked of children under 6 years.

Figure 15   Top Ten Causes of Acquired Disability During Adulthood, 2004

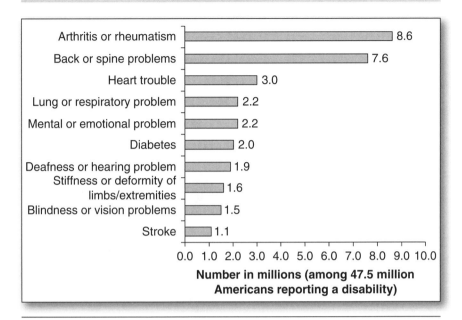

Source: Centers for Disease Control and Prevention. (2004). *Top 10 causes of disability among U.S. adults.* Retrieved from http://www.cdc.gov/arthritis/data_statistics/national_nhis.htm; Data Source: U.S. Census Bureau (2005, June-September). *2004 survey of income and program participation,* Wave 5. As reported in: Hootman, J. M., Brault, M. W., Helmick, C. G., Theis, K. A., & Armour, B. S. (2009, May 1). Prevalence and most common causes of disability among adults—United States, 2005, Table 2. *Morbidity and Mortality Weekly Report 58*(16), 421–426.

populations, with 72% of care recipients over age 50 (Figure 18). The report also indicates that women comprise the majority of caregivers (66%) and care recipients (62%) (Figure 19). Most caregivers—86% of the total—are unpaid family members (Table 16). Many of these caregivers have extra work duties in addition to providing care, as seen in Figure 20.

Death and Dying

End-of-Life Issues

The issue of end-of-life care is a highly contested matter in the disability community. One issue is that people with disabilities may

Figure 16   Poverty Rates Before and After Disability for Adults Who Become Disabled Between Age 51 and 64, 2009

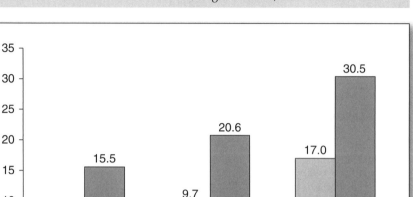

Source: Johnson, R. W., Favreault, M. M., & Mommaerts, C. (2010, January). Disability just before retirement often leads to poverty. *Older Americans' Economic Security 22*, Figure 1. Washington, DC: The Urban Institute. Retrieved from http://www.urban.org/Uploaded PDF/412009_disability_retirement.pdf

not be given the same choices as people without disabilities due to social and environmental barriers to full equality. An example of such a barrier is that people with disabilities are more likely to experience poverty later in life and are less likely to be able to afford preferred methods of care (Figure 21).

People with disabilities and rights-based Disabled Peoples Organizations (DPOs) have been critical of society's flawed linkages of disability with dying. The Centers for Disease Control reported, for instance, that "disability" did not rank among the top 15 causes of death in the United States (Table 17).

Table 14   Total Percentage of the Population Over the Age of 55 Receiving Assistance for Activities of Daily Living, 2007

Women	55–64 Years Old	65–74 Years Old	75–84 Years Old	85+ Years Old
One or more ADL limitations	13.1	15.7	25.6	49.4
Receive help with ADL(s)	4.9	5.2	10.7	27.8
Use assistive device(s)	6.8	10	21.7	50.6
Men	55–64 Years Old	65–74 Years Old	75–84 Years Old	85+ Years Old
One or more ADL limitations	9.9	12.0	19.0	31.6
Receive help with ADL(s)	3.2	4.5	8.0	16.2
Use assistive device(s)	4.4	7.5	16.2	35.0

Source: U.S. National Institutes of Health. (2007). *The health and retirement study: Growing older in America,* Figures 1-12.1 and 1-12.2. Bethesda, MD: National Institute on Aging. Retrieved from http://www.nia.nih.gov/researchinformation/extramuralprograms/behavioralandsocial research/hrsfull.htm

Table 15   Estimated Number of Caregivers as Percentage of Total Population, by Age of Primary Care Recipient, 2009

Type of Recipient	Prevalence	Estimated Number of Caregivers
Overall	**28.5%**	**65.7 million**
Only child recipients	1.7%	3.9 million
Only adult recipients	21.2%	48.9 million
Both adult and child recipients	5.6%	12.9 million

Source: National Alliance for Caregiving and AARP. (2009). *Caregiving in the U.S., 2009,* Figure 3. Bethesda, MD: Authors. Retrieved from http://www.caregiving.org/data/Caregiving_in_the_US_2009_full_report.pdf

Figure 17   Reported Conditions of Recipients of Care: Affirmative
Responses to Question "Would you say that your [relation]
needs/needed care because of any . . . ," 2009

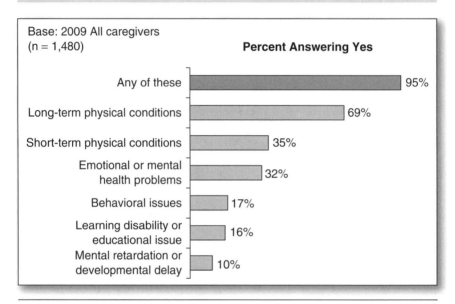

Source: National Alliance for Caregiving and AARP. (2009). *Caregiving in the U.S., 2009,*
Figure 33. Bethesda, MD: Authors. Retrieved from http://www.caregiving.org/data/
Caregiving_in_the_US_2009_full_report.pdf

Figure 18   Ages of Care Recipients: Percentage of Caregivers That Serve
Select Age Groups, 2009

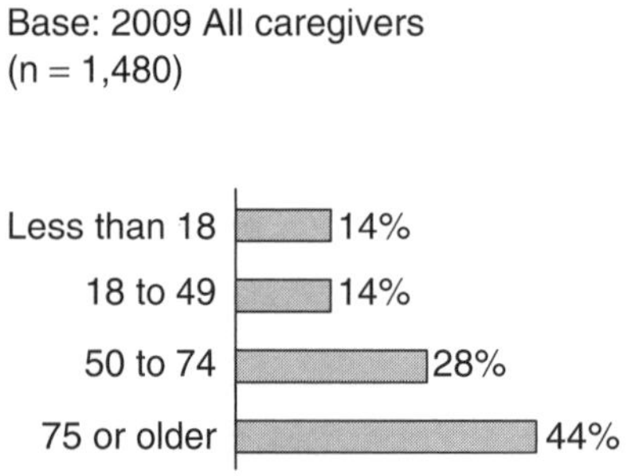

Base: 2009 All caregivers (n = 1,480)		Caregivers of Recipient Age 18+	
		2004 (n = 1,247)	2009 (n = 1,307)
Less than 18	14%	–	–
18 to 49	14%	20%	16%
50 to 74	28%	35	32
75 or older	44%	43	51

Source: National Alliance for Caregiving and AARP. (2009). *Caregiving in the U.S., 2009,*
Figure 8. Bethesda, MD: Authors. Retrieved from http://www.caregiving.org/data/
Caregiving_in_the_US_2009_full_report.pdf

Figure 19   Genders of Care Recipients and Givers: Percentage of Caregivers That Identify as Male and Female, 2009

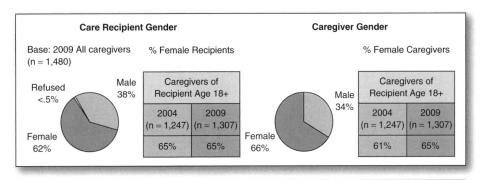

Source: National Alliance for Caregiving and AARP. (2009). *Caregiving in the U.S., 2009,* Figure 7. Bethesda, MD: Authors. Retrieved from http://www.caregiving.org/data/Caregiving_in_the_US_2009_full_report.pdf

Table 16   Relationship Between Caregivers and Care Recipients: Percent of Total Caregiving Population, 2009

	2009 Caregivers (n = 1,480)
Relative	**86%**
Parent	36
Child	14
Parent-in-law	8
Grandparent or grandparent-in-law	8
Spouse or partner	5
Sibling	5
Grandchild	3
Uncle, aunt	3
Sibling-in-law	1
Other relatives	4

(Continued)

Table 16 (Continued)

	2009 Caregivers (n = 1,480)
Non-relative	**14**
Friend	11
Neighbor	1
Foster child	<.5

Source: National Alliance for Caregiving and AARP. (2009). *Caregiving in the U.S., 2009,* Figure 12. Bethesda, MD: Authors. Retrieved from http://www.caregiving.org/data/Caregiving_in_the_US_2009_full_report.pdf

Figure 20   Additional Employment Obligations of Caregivers, 2009

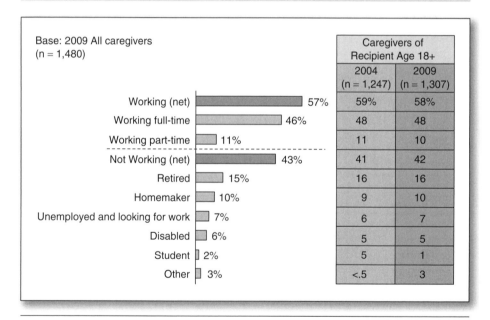

Source: National Alliance for Caregiving and AARP. (2009). *Caregiving in the U.S., 2009,* Figure 49. Bethesda, MD: Authors. Retrieved from http://www.caregiving.org/data/Caregiving_in_the_US_2009_full_report.pdf

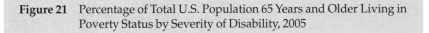

Figure 21   Percentage of Total U.S. Population 65 Years and Older Living in
Poverty Status by Severity of Disability, 2005

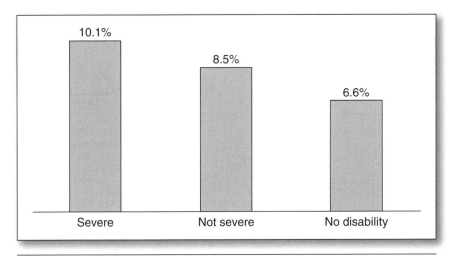

Source: Brault, M. (2008). *Americans with disabilities: 2005* (Current Populations Reports, P70–117),
Table B-2. Washington, DC: U.S. Census Bureau. Retrieved from http://www.census.gov/
prod/2008pubs/p70-117.pdf

Table 17   Top 15 Causes of Death in the United States, 2007

Rank	Cause of Death	Number	Percent of Total Deaths
	All causes	2,423,712	100.0
1	Diseases of heart	616,067	25.4
2	Malignant neoplasms	562,875	23.2
3	Cerebrovascular diseases	135,952	5.6
4	Chronic lower respiratory diseases	127,924	5.3
5	Accidents (unintentional injuries)	123,706	5.1

(Continued)

Table 17 (Continued)

Rank	Cause of Death	Number	Percent of Total Deaths
6	Alzheimer's disease	74,632	3.1
7	Diabetes mellitus	71,382	2.9
8	Influenza and pneumonia	52,717	2.2
9	Nephritis, nephrotic syndrome and nephrosis	46,448	1.9
10	Septicemia	34,828	1.4
11	Intentional self-harm (suicide)	34,598	1.4
12	Chronic liver disease and cirrhosis	29,165	1.2
13	Essential hypertension and hypertensive renal disease	23,965	1.0
14	Parkinson's disease	20,058	0.8
15	Assault (homicide)	18,361	0.8
. . .	All other causes	451,034	18.6

Source: U.S. Centers for Disease Control, Division of Vital Statistics. (2010, May). *Deaths: Final data for 2007, 58,* 19, Table B. Hyattsville, MD: Author. Retrieved from http://www.cdc.gov/NCHS/data/nvsr/nvsr58/nvsr58_19.pdf

Spirituality

People reported as having functional impairments are more likely to receive end-of-life care in nursing homes than people without impairments. It is thus important to investigate the range of end-of-life services offered in nursing homes. Religious care and general counseling are prevalent services offered in nursing homes related to spirituality in the end of the life course. Table 18 presents the distribution of varying end-of-life services offered to people inside nursing homes. In general, people with disabilities appear to attend places of worship with less frequency than people without disabilities (Figure 22).

Table 18 Total Number of Nursing Home Residents Receiving End-of-Life (EOL) Care by Type of Service Provided, 2004

Formal Service or Treatment	Nursing Home Residents Receiving EOL Care		Nursing Home Residents Who Started EOL Care on or Prior to Admission to Nursing Home		Nursing Home Residents Who Started EOL Care After Admission to Nursing Home	
	Number	Percent Distribution	Number	Percent Distribution	Number	Percent Distribution
Nursing home residents receiving EOL care	37,800	100.00	9,200	100.0	28,000	100.0
Services Received in the 7 Days Prior to Interview						
Pain management	22,000	58.3	*6,600	*72.1	15,100	53.8
Symptom management	20,800	55.1	5,400	58.9	15,400	55.1
Emotional support for family	19,600	52.0	*4,000	*43.5	15,600	55.8
Pastoral or spiritual care	15,100	39.9	*3,400	*37.0	11,400	40.8
Grief, loss, and bereavement counseling	10,500	27.7	*	*	8,500	30.3
Counseling or assistance with ethical or legal issues	10,300	27.2	*	*	*7,100	*25.2
Other services	7,800	20.6	*	*	*5,000	*17.9
Death preparation	*6,500	*17.3	*	*	*5,100	*18.1

(Continued)

Table 18 (Continued)

Formal Service or Treatment	Nursing Home Residents Receiving EOL Care		Nursing Home Residents Who Started EOL Care on or Prior to Admission to Nursing Home		Nursing Home Residents Who Started EOL Care After Admission to Nursing Home	
	Number	Percent Distribution	Number	Percent Distribution	Number	Percent Distribution
Types of Formal Care or Treatments Received in 7 Days Prior to Interview						
Aggressive pain management including radiation for pain relief	13,800	36.5	*4,100	*44.1	9,400	33.6
Oxygen-respiratory therapy	11,800	31.3	*4,000	*43.9	7,800	27.8
Bowel training regimen	10,000	26.5	*	*	7,400	26.4
Subcutaneous therapy, IV therapy, parenteral hydration, and artificial nutrition	*3,600	*9.7	*	*	*3,200	*11.6
Durable medical equipment	*3,600	*9.5	*	*	*	*

Source: Bercovitz, A., Decker, F. H., Jones, A., & Remsburg, R. E. (2008, October 8). *End-of-life care in nursing homes: 2004 national nursing home survey* (National Health Statistics Reports 9). Washington, DC: U.S. Department of Health and Human Services. Retrieved from http://www.cdc.gov/nchs/data/nhsr/nhsr009.pdf

*Figure does not meet standards of reliability or precision because the sample size is less than 30. Estimates accompanied by an asterisk (*) indicate that the sample size is between 30 and 59, or the sample size is greater than 59 but has a relative standard error of 30% or more.

Figure 22   Rates of Attendance at Religious Services, People With
Disabilities Versus People Without Disabilities

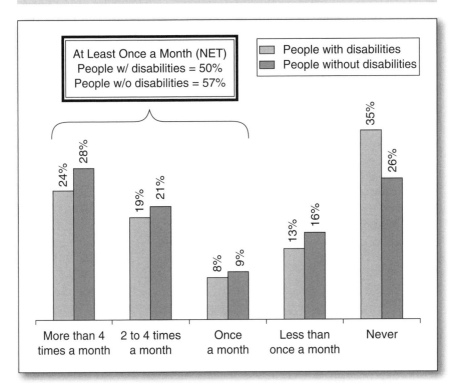

Source: Kessler Foundation and National Organization on Disability (2010). *The ADA, 20 years later: Survey of Americans with disabilities,* Table 8A. New York: Harris Interactive. Retrieved from http://www.2010disabilitysurveys.org/pdfs/surveyresults.pdf

References

Centers for Disease Control and Prevention. (2007). *National Health Interview Survey (NHIS),* 2007 data release. Hyattsville, MD: U.S. Department of Health and Human Services, National Center for Health.

LaPlante, M. P., & National Institute on Disability and Rehabilitation Research (U.S.). (1996). *Families with disabilities in the United States.* Washington, DC: U.S. Department of Education, Office of Special Education and Rehabilitative Services.

Mansfield, C., Hopfer, S., & Marteau, T. M. (1999, January 1). Termination rates after prenatal diagnosis of Down syndrome, spina bifida, anencephaly, and Turner and Klinefelter syndromes: A systematic literature review. European Concerted Action: DADA (decision-making after the diagnosis of a fetal abnormality). *Prenatal Diagnosis, 19*(9), 808–812.

National Alliance for Caregiving, & AARP. (2009). *Caregiving in the U.S., 2009*. Bethesda, MD: Authors. Retrieved from http://www.caregiving.org/data/Caregiving_in_the_US_2009_full_report.pdf

Parens, E., & Asch, A. (1999, January 1). The disability rights critique of prenatal genetic testing: Reflections and recommendations. *The Hastings Center Report, 29*(5).

U.S. Department of Health and Human Services, Administration for Children and Families, Administration on Children, Youth and Families, Children's Bureau. (2010). *Child maltreatment 2008,* Table 3-13. Retrieved from http://www.acf.hhs.gov/programs/cb/pubs/cm08/table3_13.htm

Westat, Inc. (1993). *A report on the maltreatment of children with disabilities*. Washington, DC: National Center on Child Abuse and Neglect.

Six

Annotated List of Organizations and Associations

Tamar Heller, Sarah Parker Harris,
and Jeannie Zwick

This chapter provides a list of organizations and associations involved in disability issues at all stages of life. The listings are organized into two main sections. The first section, U.S. government organizations, is arranged by agency. The second section provides a list of major non-government organizations and associations engaged in issues related to disability through the life course.

U.S. Government Organizations

Administration for Children and Families
370 L'Enfant Promenade, SW
Washington, DC 20447

Web site: http://www.acf.hhs.gov
The Administration for Children and Families is responsible for federal programs that promote the economic and social well-being of families, children, individuals, and communities.

Administration on Aging
One Massachusetts Avenue, NW
Washington, DC 20001
Telephone: (202) 619-0724
Fax: (202) 357-3555
E-mail: aoainfo@aoa.hhs.gov
Web site: http://www.aoa.gov
The mission of the Administration on Aging (AoA) is to develop a comprehensive, coordinated, and cost-effective system of home and community-based services that helps elderly individuals maintain their health and independence in their homes and communities.

Administration on Developmental Disabilities
370 L'Enfant Promenade, SW
Mail Stop HHH 405-D
Washington, DC 20447
Telephone: (202) 690-6590
Fax: (202) 690-6904
Web site: http://www.acf.hhs.gov/programs/add
The Administration on Developmental Disabilities (ADD) is responsible for implementation of the Developmental Disabilities Assistance and Bill of Rights Act of 2000, known as the DD Act. ADD's staff and programs are part of the Administration for Children and Families.

Centers for Disease Control and Prevention–Disability
1600 Clifton Road
MS E-87
Atlanta, GA 30333
Telephone: (800) 232-4636; (888) 232-6348 (TTY)
E-mail: cdcinfo@cdc.gov
Web site: http://www.cdc.gov/ncbddd/disabilityandhealth/index.html
The Centers for Disease Control and Prevention (CDC) work to "identify the causes of birth defects and developmental disabilities, help children to develop and reach their full potential, and promote health and well-being among people of all ages with disabilities. CDC also works to prevent injuries, such as traumatic brain injury, and their resulting disabilities."

Department of Education
National Institute on Disability and Rehabilitation Research
400 Maryland Avenue, SW
Mailstop PCP-6038
Washington, DC 20202
Telephone/TTY: (202) 245-7640
Fax: (202) 245-7323
Web site: http://www2.ed.gov/about/offices/list/osers/nidrr/index.html
The National Institute on Disability and Rehabilitation Research (NIDRR) provides leadership and support for a comprehensive program of research related to the rehabilitation of individuals with disabilities. All of NIDRR's efforts are aimed at improving the lives of individuals with disabilities from birth through adulthood.

Department of Health and Human Services
200 Independence Avenue, SW
Washington, DC 20201
Telephone: (877) 696-6775
Web site: http://www.hhs.gov
The Department of Health and Human Services (HHS) is the principal agency for protecting the health of all Americans and providing essential human services. HSS includes more than 300 programs, covering a wide spectrum of activities. In addition to the services they deliver, the HHS programs provide for equitable treatment of beneficiaries nationwide, and they enable the collection of national health and other data.

Department of Labor
Office of Disability Employment Policy
200 Constitution Avenue, NW
Washington, DC 20210
Telephone: (866) 633-7365; (877) 889-5627 (TTY)
Web site: http://www.dol.gov/odep/index.htm
The Department of Labor's Office of Disability Employment Policy (ODEP) provides national leadership on disability employment policy by developing and influencing the use of evidence-based disability employment policies and practices, building collaborative partnerships, and delivering authoritative and credible data on employment of people with disabilities.

Disability.gov
U.S. Department of Labor
Office of Disability Employment Policy (ODEP)
Frances Perkins Building
200 Constitution Avenue, NW

Washington, DC 20210
E-mail: disability@dol.gov
Web site: http://www.disability.gov
Disability.gov is a federal Web site that contains disability-related resources on programs, services, laws, and regulations to help people with disabilities lead full, independent lives. The mission of the Web site is "to connect people with disabilities, their family members, veterans, caregivers, employers, service providers, and others with the resources they need to ensure that people with disabilities can fully participate in the workplace and in their communities."

National Council on Disability

1331 F Street, NW, Suite 850
Washington, DC 20004
Telephone: (202) 272-2004; (202) 272-2074 (TTY)
Fax: (202) 272-2022
E-mail: ncd@ncd.gov
Web site: http://www.ncd.gov
The National Council on Disability (NCD) describes itself as "an independent federal agency, composed of 15 members appointed by the President, by and with the consent of the U.S. Senate. The purpose of NCD is to promote policies, programs, practices, and procedures that guarantee equal opportunity for all individuals with disabilities, and that empower individuals with disabilities to achieve economic self-sufficiency, independent living, and inclusion and integration into all aspects of society."

National Institute of Child Health and Human Development

P.O. Box 3006
Rockville, MD 20847
Telephone: (800) 370-2943; (888) 320-6942 (TTY)
Fax: (866) 760-5947
E-mail: NICHDInformationResourceCenter@mail.nih.gov
Web site: http://www.nichd.nih.gov
The Eunice Kennedy Shriver National Institute of Child Health and Human Development (NICHD) was established by Congress in 1962. The institute conducts and supports research on topics related to the health of children, adults, families, and populations. Central goals of the institute include reducing infant deaths; improving the health of women, men, and families; understanding reproductive health and fertility/infertility; learning about growth and development; examining, preventing, and treating problems of birth defects and intellectual and developmental disabilities; and enhancing the well-being of persons through the lifespan with optimal rehabilitation research.

National Institute on Aging

Building 31, Room 5C27
31 Center Drive, MSC 2292

Bethesda, MD 20892
Telephone: (301) 496-1752; (800) 222-4225 (TTY)
Fax: (301) 496-1072
Web site: http://www.nia.nih.gov
The institute's mission is to support and conduct genetic, biological, clinical, behavioral, social, and economic research related to the aging process, diseases and conditions associated with aging, and other special problems and needs of older Americans. To this end, the NIA fosters the development of research and clinician scientists in aging and communicates information about aging and advances in research on aging to the scientific community, health care providers, and the public.

National Institute on Deafness and Other Communication Disorders

31 Center Drive, MSC 2320
Bethesda, MD 20892-2320
Telephone: (800) 241-1044; (800) 241-1055 (TTY)
Fax: (301) 402-0018
E-mail: nidcdinfo@nidcd.nih.gov
Web site: http://www.nidcd.nih.gov
NIDCD is mandated to conduct and support biomedical and behavioral research and research training in the normal and disordered processes of hearing, balance, smell, taste, voice, speech, and language. The institute also conducts and supports research and research training related to disease prevention and health promotion; addresses special biomedical and behavioral problems associated with people who have communication impairments or disorders; and supports efforts to create devices that substitute for lost and impaired sensory and communication function.

National Institute on Mental Health

6001 Executive Boulevard
Room 8184, MSC 9663
Bethesda, MD 20892-9663
Telephone: (866) 615-6464; (866) 415-8051 (TTY)
Fax: (301) 443-4279
E-mail: nimhinfo@nih.gov
Web site: http://www.nimh.nih.gov
NIMH provides national leadership dedicated to understanding, treating, and preventing mental illnesses through basic research on the brain and behavior, and through clinical, epidemiological, and services research.

National Institutes of Health

9000 Rockville Pike
Bethesda, MD 20892

Telephone: (301) 496-4000; (301) 402-9612 (TTY)
E-mail: nihinfo@od.nih.gov
Web site: http://www.nih.gov
The National Institutes of Health (NIH), a part of the U.S. Department of Health and Human Services, is the federal agency primarily responsible for conducting and support-ing medical research. It is composed of 27 institutes and centers.

Office of Disability
200 Independence Avenue, SW
Room 637D
Washington, DC 20201
E-mail: ODInfo@hhs.gov
Web site: http://www.hhs.gov/od
The Office on Disability (OD) oversees the implementation and coordination of programs and policies that enhance the health and well-being of people with disabilities across all ages, races, and ethnicities. Efforts to fulfill OD's mission are organized around three themes: improve access to community living services and supports, integrate health services and social supports, and provide strategic support on disability matters.

Office of Special Education and Rehabilitative Services
400 Maryland Avenue, SW
Washington, DC 20202-7100
Telephone: (202) 245-7468
Web site: http://www.ed.gov
The Office of Special Education and Rehabilitative Services (OSERS) is committed to improving outcomes for people with disabilities of all ages. It provides funding and offers a variety of supports to states, school districts, parents, and individuals in the areas of spe-cial education, vocational rehabilitation, and research.

Office of Special Education Programs
400 Maryland Avenue, SW
Washington, DC 20202-7100
Telephone: (202) 245-7459
Web site: http://www2.ed.gov/about/offices/list/osers/osep/index.html
The Office of Special Education Programs (OSEP) is dedicated to improving results for infants, toddlers, children, and youth with disabilities ages birth through 21 by providing leadership and financial support to programs at the state and local levels.

Substance Abuse and Mental Health Services Administration (SAMHSA)
SAMHSA's Health Information Network
P.O. Box 2345
Rockville, MD 20847-2345

Telephone: (877) 726-4727; **(800)** 487-4889 (TTY)
Fax: **(240)** 221-4292
E-mail: SAMHSAInfo@samhsa.hhs.gov
Web site: http://www.samhsa.gov
SAMHSA's mission is to reduce the impact of substance abuse and mental illness on America's communities. The agency's programs are carried out through:

- *The Center for Mental Health Services (CMHS), which focuses on the prevention and treatment of mental disorders.*
- *The Center for Substance Abuse Prevention (CSAP), which seeks to prevent and reduce the abuse of illegal drugs, alcohol, and tobacco.*
- *The Center for Substance Abuse Treatment (CSAT), which supports the provision of effective substance abuse treatment and recovery services.*
- *The Office of Applied Studies (OAS), which has primary responsibility for the collection, analysis and dissemination of behavioral health data.*

Non-Government Organizations

Alzheimer's Association

225 N. Michigan Avenue, Floor 17
Chicago, IL 60601-7633
Telephone: (312) 335-8700; (312) 335-5886 (TDD)
Fax: (866) 699-1246
E-mail: info@alz.org
Web site: http://www.alz.org
The Alzheimer's Association provides support and information to people with Alzheimer's, as well as caregivers. Additionally, the association helps to raise funds to sponsor research aimed at eliminating the disease and improving care of Alzheimer's patients.

American Association of Health and Disability (AAHD)

110 N. Washington Street, Suite 328-J
Rockville, MD 20850
Telephone: (301) 545-6140
Fax: (301) 545-6144
E-mail: contact@aahd.us
Web site: http://www.aahd.us
The American Association of Health and Disability works across all levels of government to prevent secondary health complications in people with disabilities. AAHD works to identify effective strategies that will eliminate the health disparities between those with disabilities and the rest of the population. Beyond advocacy, the AAHD supports both research and education to further its goals.

American Association of People with Disabilities (AAPD)

1629 K Street, NW, Suite 950
Washington, DC 20006
Telephone: (202) 457-0046 (V/TTY); (800) 840-8844 (V/TTY)
Fax: (202) 457-0473
Web site: http://www.aapd-dc.org

The American Association of People with Disabilities is a membership organization that brings together individuals across different types of disabilities to provide a unified voice on issues of political, economic, and social change. The AAPD especially works toward implementing the regulations and goals of the American with Disabilities Act.

American Association of Retired Persons (AARP)

601 E Street, NW
Washington, DC 20049
Telephone: (888) 687-2277; (877) 434-7598 (TTY); (877) 627-3350 (Spanish); 1-2-2-434-3525 (International)
Web site: http://www.aarp.org

AARP is a nonprofit membership organization that helps people age 50 and over advocate and find resources to improve their lives. AARP's mission is to "enhance the quality of life for all as we age, leading positive social change and delivering value to members through information, advocacy and service."

American Association on Intellectual and Developmental Disabilities (AAIDD)

501 3rd Street, NW, Suite 200
Washington, DC 20001
Telephone: (800) 424-3688
Fax: (202) 387-2193
E-mail: anam@aaidd.org
Web site: http://www.aamr.org

The American Association on Intellectual and Developmental Disabilities advocates for full societal inclusion, self-determination, and fulfilling lives for people with intellectual and developmental disabilities. The association's advocacy focuses on progressive policies, research, and promoting effective practices. AAIDD especially works to serve professionals who work with individuals with these disabilities.

American Disabled for Attendant Programs Today (ADAPT)

ADAPT in Denver
201 South Cherokee
Denver, CO 80223
Telephone: (303) 733-9324

E-mail: adapt@Adapt.org
Web site: http://www.adapt.org

ADAPT of Texas
1640-A E. 2nd Street, Suite 100
Austin, TX 78702
Telephone: (512) 442-0252
E-mail: adapt@Adapt.org
Web site: http://www.adapt.org
ADAPT is a grassroots community organization that fights to move people with disabilities out of nursing homes and other institutions into "real homes" with community support. ADAPT advocates nonviolent direct action and civil disobedience in order to achieve its goal.

American Society on Aging (ASA)
71 Stevenson Street, Suite 1450
San Francisco, CA 94105-2938
Telephone: (415) 974-9600; (800) 537-9728
Fax: (415) 974-0300
E-mail: info@asaging.org
Web site: http://www.asaging.org
The American Society on Aging is a professional organization committed to enhancing the knowledge and skills of members working to improve the lives of older adults and their families. ASA focuses on all aspects of aging: physical, emotional, social, economic, and spiritual. The professionals represented include practitioners, educators, researchers, business people, and policymakers.

APSE, The Network on Employment
451 Hungerford Drive, Suite 700
Rockville, MD 20850
Telephone: (301) 279-0060
Fax: (301) 251-3762
Web site: http://www.apse.org
APSE is a national organization that works for integrated employment and career advancement for those with disabilities. APSE is present in 35 states and maintains an international presence as well. APSE supports an annual conference to advance its goal of integrated employment.

Arc of the United States (The Arc)
1660 L Street, NW, Suite 301
Washington, DC 20036
Telephone: (202) 534-3700; (800) 433-5255

Fax: (202) 534-3731

E-mail: info@thearc.org

Web site: http://www.thearc.org

The Arc is a community-based organization for those with either intellectual or developmental disabilities. Each local chapter of Arc shares the core values of people first, democracy, visionary leadership, community participation, diversity, and integrity and excellence. The Arc works for every individual and family to ensure they have what they need to be active citizens of their communities and the larger U.S. democracy.

Association of University Centers on Disabilities (AUCD)

1010 Wayne Ave., Suite 920

Silver Spring, MD 20910

Telephone: (301) 588-8252

Fax: (301) 588-2842

E-mail: aucdinfo@aucd.org

Web site: http://www.aucd.org/template/index.cfm

The Association of University Centers on Disabilities (AUCD) is a national network of university-based interdisciplinary programs. Network members include: 67 University Centers for Excellence in Developmental Disabilities (UCEDD); 39 Leadership Education Neurodevelopmental Disabilities (LEND) Programs; and 19 Intellectual and Developmental Disability Research Centers (IDDRC). These programs, located in every U.S. state, are affiliated with universities or medical centers and provide a vital link between university and community resources.

Association on Higher Education and Disability (AHEAD)

107 Commerce Center Drive, Suite 204

Huntersville, NC 28078

Telephone: (704) 947-7779

Fax: (704) 948-7779

Web site: http://www.ahead.org

AHEAD is a professional membership organization that helps to develop policies and provide services that benefit people with disability throughout all areas of higher education. AHEAD promotes equal participation in higher education by those with disabilities and also provides support for professionals working toward that goal.

Autism Society of America

4340 East-West Highway, Suite 350

Bethesda, MD 20814

Telephone: (301) 657.0881; (800) 328-8476

Web site: http://www.autism-society.org

The Autism Society seeks to increase public awareness of the challenges faced by individuals with all levels of autism. The society hopes that this increased awareness will improve the lives of—and expand services provided for—autistic individuals. Beyond campaigning for awareness, the society provides information about current treatments, education, and research on autism.

Autism Speaks
2 Park Avenue, 11th Floor
New York, NY 10016
Telephone: (212) 252-8584
Fax: (212) 252-8676
E-mail: contactus@autismspeaks.org
Web site: www.autismspeaks.org
Autism Speaks is an advocacy group aimed at improving the lives of those with autism. Autism Speaks' primary focus is on funding biomedical research into the causes, prevention, treatments, and cures for autism. Beyond this, Autism Speaks works to raise public awareness about autism.

Brain Injury Association of America (BIAA)
1608 Spring Hill Road, Suite 110
Vienna, VA 22182
Telephone: (703) 761-0750
Fax: (703) 761-0755
Web site: http://www.biausa.org
The Brain Injury Association of America helps families and professionals who are dealing with life-altering and devastating traumatic brain injuries. BIAA works to provide information, education, and support to millions of Americans living with traumatic brain injuries, as well as their families and caregivers.

Burton Blatt Institute
900 S. Crouse Avenue
Crouse-Hinds Hall, Suite 300
Syracuse, NY 13244-2130
Telephone: (315) 443-2863
Fax: (315) 443-9725
Web site: http://bbi.syr.edu
The Burton Blatt Institute creates a collaborative environment between the public and private sectors to advance the participation of those with disabilities in all aspects of society. Beyond creating a dialogue, the institute seeks to expand entrepreneurial innovation and best business practices to help those with disabilities.

Council on Quality and Leadership (CQL)
100 West Road, Suite 406
Towson, MD 21204
Telephone: (410) 583-0060
Fax: (410) 583-0063
E-mail: info@thecouncil.org
Web site: http://www.thecouncil.org
The Council on Quality and Leadership works with professionals and advocates who work on behalf of individuals with disabilities. The council provides these professionals with research, training, workshops, and certification programs designed to improve the quality of the services they provide to their clients.

Disability Rights Education and Defense Fund (DREDF)
2212 Sixth Street
Berkeley, CA 94710
Telephone: (800) 348-4232 (V/TTY); (510) 644-2555 (V/TTY)
Fax: (510) 841-8645
E-mail: info@dredf.org
Web site: http://www.dredf.org
The Disability Rights Education and Defense Fund fights for the civil rights of individuals with disabilities and parents of children with disabilities. The fund engages in legal advocacy, training, education, public policy, and legislative action to accomplish this goal.

Easter Seals Inc.
233 South Wacker Drive, Suite 2400
Chicago, IL 60606
Telephone: (312) 726-6200; (800) 221-6827; (312) 4258 (TTY)
Fax: (312) 726-1494
Web site: http://www.easterseals.com
Easter Seals is a network of over 550 sites throughout the United States and Australia that provide individualized services to children and adults with disabilities, including those with autism. Easter Seals provide medical rehabilitation, training and employment services, children's services, adult and senior services, and camping and recreational activities.

Family Caregiver Alliance (FCA)
180 Montgomery Street, Suite 1100
San Francisco, CA 94104
Telephone: (415) 434-3388; (800) 445-8106
Fax: (415) 434-3508

E-mail: info@caregiver.org
Web site: http://www.caregiver.org
The Family Caregiver Alliance is a community-based nonprofit organization that provides support for family members and friends who provide long-term care for disabled relatives or friends at home. The FCA sponsors health services and provides support to caregivers at the local, state, and national level.

Family Voices, Inc.

2340 Alamo, SE, Suite 102
Albuquerque, NM 87106
Telephone: (505) 872-4774; (888) 835-5669
Fax: (505) 872-4780
Web site: http://www.familyvoices.org
Family Voices works to provide family-centered care and support for children with disabilities or special health care needs. Family Voices provide the resources necessary to make informed decisions about services and care. Beyond these resources, Family Voices acts as an advocate for improving policies to support these families and children.

Gerontological Society of America

1220 L Street, NW, Suite 901
Washington, DC 20005
Telephone: (202) 842-1275
Fax: (202) 842-1150
Web site: www.geron.org
The Gerontological Society of America promotes research on aging. The society also disseminates results of the research to practitioners and individuals so that it has the greatest impact possible. In addition, the Society supports the education of new aging researchers in higher education.

Human Services Research Institute (HSRI)

2236 Massachusetts Avenue
Cambridge, MA 02140
Telephone: (617) 876-0426
Fax: (617) 492-7401
Web site: http://www.hsri.org
The Human Services Research Institute works with government agencies to improve services for those with disabilities. HSRI works to develop support systems, enhance participation among those receiving services, improve the capacity of state delivery systems, and increase the use of research to guide policy development and practice.

Institute for Community Inclusion (ICI)
University of Massachusetts, Boston
100 Morrissey Boulevard
Boston, MA 02125
Telephone: (617) 287-4300; (617) 287-4350 (TTY)
Fax: (617) 287-4352
E-mail: ici@umb.edu
Web site: http://www.communityinclusion.org
The Institute for Community Inclusion is a national and international leader for promoting community inclusion for people with all types of disabilities across the lifespan. ICI, based at the University of Massachusetts Boston and Children's Hospital Boston, offers "training, research, consultation, community outreach, and clinical and employment services."

Institute on Disability and Human Development (IDHD)
Department of Disability and Human Development
The University of Illinois at Chicago
1640 West Roosevelt Road
Chicago, IL 60608-6904
Telephone: (312) 413-8833; (312) 413-0453 (TTY)
Fax: (312) 413-4098
E-mail: idhd@uic.edu
Web site: http://www.idhd.org
The Institute on Disability and Human Development (IDHD) is a national leader in research, clinical and community service activities, and interdisciplinary pre-service training in disability studies offered through the Department of Disability and Human Development at the University of Illinois at Chicago. It conducts scholarship and community-based services across the spectrum of disability, including advocacy, culture, education, health promotion, history, policy, and technology.

Kessler Foundation
300 Executive Drive, Suite 150
West Orange, NJ 07052
Telephone: (973) 324-8362
Fax: (973) 324-8373
E-mail: info@kesslerfoundation.org
Web site: http://www.kesslerfoundation.org
The Kessler Foundation is a public charity that supports rehabilitation research and prepares individuals with disabilities for the workplace. The Kessler Foundation works with individuals with physical disabilities caused by strokes, multiple sclerosis, nervous system

injuries, and other chronic conditions. Beyond the work done at its own research and reha-
bilitation locations, the Kessler Foundation makes grants each year to other institutions
that pursue similar goals.

Kids as Self Advocates (KASA)
2340 Alamo, SE, Suite 102
Albuquerque, NM 87106
Telephone: (888) 835-5669
Fax: (505) 872-4780
E-mail: info@fvkasa.org
Web site: http://www.fvkasa.org
KASA focuses on self-advocacy as a means for improvement. KASA members speak pub-
licly on issues that affect youth living with disabilities. KASA's three key approaches to
change are informing youth about their rights, providing peer support and training, and
changing systems to include youth with disabilities.

Learning Disabilities Association of America (LDA)
4156 Library Road
Pittsburgh, PA 15234-1349
Telephone: (412) 341-1515
Fax: (412) 344-0224
Web site: http://www.ldanatl.org
The Learning Disabilities Association of America advocates for individuals with learning
disabilities to empower them and help them participate fully in society. Part of this mission
involves helping others learn about and understand the nature of learning disabilities so
they may be effectively addressed by society. LDA also works to reduce the incidence of
learning disabilities in future generations.

National Alliance for Caregiving (NAC)
4720 Montgomery Lane, 2nd Floor
Bethesda, MD 20814
E-mail: info@caregiving.org
Web site: http://www.caregiving.org
The National Alliance for Caregiving is a nonprofit coalition of national member organiza-
tions focused on issues of family caregiving. Alliance members include grassroots organi-
zations, professional associations, service organizations, disease-specific organizations,
government agencies, and corporations throughout the United States. NAC provides sup-
port to its members and advocates for policies that increase the resources devoted toward
caregiving. The organization also works to improve the quality of life and care received by
individuals with disabilities.

National Association of Councils on Developmental Disabilities (NACDD)

1660 L Street, NW, Suite 700
Washington, DC 20036
Telephone: (202) 506-5813
Fax: (202) 506-5846
E-mail: info@nacdd.org
Web site: http://www.nacdd.org
The NACDD promotes the development and sustaining of "inclusive communities and self-directed services" for individuals with developmental disabilities. This national association is formed from representatives of state-level councils throughout the United States.

National Association of Parents with Children in Special Education (NAPCSE)

1431 W. South Fork Drive
Phoenix, AZ 85045
Telephone: (800) 754-4421
Fax: (800) 424-0371
E-mail: contact@napcse.org
Web site: http://www.napcse.org
NAPCSE focuses on providing educational resources to parents of children with disabilities. The goal of providing this information is to enable parents to become effective advocates for their children in all areas of their lives.

National Association of Rehabilitation Research Training Centers (NARRTC)

Web site: www.ilr.cornell.edu/edi/narrtc/index.shtml
NARRTC promotes the full inclusion of persons with disabilities in America through research and training programs. NARRTC has a "commitment to full community work integration, participation, and access for all persons with disabilities and supports the right to self determination and choice. The association also values diversity and respects the contributions of all persons to the research and training process."

National Association of the Deaf (NAD)

8630 Fenton Street, Suite 820
Silver Spring, MD 20910
Telephone: (301) 587-1788; (301) 587-1789 (TTY)
Fax: (301) 587- 1791
Web site: http://www.nad.org
The National Association of the Deaf is a civil rights organization in the United States that promotes the rights of the deaf and hard of hearing. A core value of the association is

the use of American Sign Language. Beyond this value, NAD supports education, employment, health services, and technology that will improve the lives of its members. NAD is also active in the legislative process at the federal level.

National Center for Learning Disabilities (NCLD)
381 Park Avenue South, Suite 1401
New York, NY 10016
Telephone: (212) 545-7510; (888) 575-7373
Fax: (212) 545-9665
E-mail: ncld@ncld.org
Web site: http://www.ncld.org
The National Center for Learning Disabilities works to ensure that both children and adults with learning disabilities succeed in all aspects of life through improved learning opportunities. NCLD promotes research on effective methods of learning and communicates this information to parents, professionals, and instructors to improve actual learning environments. Beyond these direct efforts to improve learning, NCLD advocates for public policies that will improve learning opportunities.

National Center for the Study of Postsecondary Educational Supports (NCSPES)
Center on Disability Studies
University Center for Excellence on Developmental Disabilities
University of Hawaii at Manoa
1776 University Avenue, UA 4-6
Honolulu, HI 96822
Telephone: (808) 956-5011
Fax: (808) 956-7878
E-mail: ncset@hawaii.edu
Web site: http://www.rrtc.hawaii.edu
The National Center for the Study of Postsecondary Educational Supports is a partnership of six organizations involved in a wide range of efforts focused on the secondary education and transition of youth with disabilities. NCSPES coordinates national resources, offers technical assistance, and disseminates information related to secondary education and transition for youth with disabilities in order to create opportunities for youth to achieve successful futures.

National Center on Secondary Education and Transition (NCSET)
Institute on Community Integration
University of Minnesota
150 Pillsbury Drive, SE
6 Pattee Hall
Minneapolis, MN 55455

Telephone: (612) 624-2097
Fax: (612) 624-9344
E-mail: ncset@umn.edu
Web site: http://www.ncset.org
The National Center on Secondary Education and Transition has four goal areas of improvement for students with disabilities: (1) access and success in secondary education; (2) planning for post-school life; (3) post-school results including employment, post-secondary education, and independent living; and (4) collaboration between education and support systems at all levels of development. NCSET accomplishes these goals by coordinating and leading other institutions with similar goals, by providing technical assistance to other groups and researchers to help them advance, and by disseminating information to education workers, parents, and youth with disabilities.

National Council on Aging (NCOA)
1901 L Street, NW, 4th Floor
Washington, DC 20036
Telephone: (202) 479-1200
Web site: http://www.ncoa.org
The National Council on Aging is a nonprofit organization that advocates and provides services for older Americans, especially those who are vulnerable and disadvantaged. The NCOA accomplishes its mission by working with thousands of organizations across the country to help seniors find work, secure their benefits, ensure their access to quality health services, and keep them active and independent.

National Council on Independent Living (NCIL)
1710 Rhode Island Avenue, NW, Fifth Floor
Washington, DC 20036
Telephone: (202) 207-0334; (202) 207-0340 (TTY); (877) 525-3400
Fax: (202) 207-0341
Web site: http://www.ncil.org
The National Council on Independent Living (NCIL) is a membership-driven organization that seeks to ensure that people with disabilities are "valued equally and participate fully" in society by advocating for human and civil rights throughout the United States. NCIL is run by and for those with disabilities and arose out of organizations formed by the Rehabilitation Act of 1973. NCIL focuses on promoting and providing information about disability rights legislation.

National Disability Rights Network (NDRN)
900 Second Street, NE, Suite 211
Washington, DC 20002

Telephone: (202) 408-9514; (202) 408-9521 (TTY)
Fax: (202) 408-9520
E-mail: info@ndrn.org
Web site: http://www.napas.org
The National Disability Rights Network is a nonprofit legal-based advocacy organization for people with disabilities in the United States. NDRN works through training, technical assistance, legal support, and legislative advocacy. It collaborates with both individuals in general society and individuals within the juvenile and criminal justice systems.

National Federation of the Blind
200 East Wells Street at Jernigan Place
Baltimore, MD 21230
Telephone: (410) 659-9314
Fax: (410) 685-5653
Web site: http://www.nfb.org
The National Federation of the Blind advocates for its 50,000 members throughout the United States. The federation works to promote independence through education, research, and technology. Among the programs supported are the International Braille and Technology Center for the Blind, which is the largest evaluation and demonstration center for technology used by the blind, and NFB-NEWSLINE, a service that uses computer speech technology to transmit newspaper texts freely to the blind over the telephone.

National Organization on Disability (NOD)
Washington Office
888 Sixteenth Street, NW, Suite 800
Washington, DC 20006
Telephone: (202) 293-5960; (202) 293-5968 (TTY)
Fax: (202) 293-7999

New York Office
5 East 86th Street
New York, NY 10028
Telephone: (646) 505-1191
Fax: (646) 505-1184
Web site: http://www.nod.org
The National Organization on Disability works to expand the workforce participation of people with disabilities in the United States. NOD works by forming and evaluating pilot programs that place people with disabilities in the general workforce. NOD communicates and advocates for its successful programs to policymakers, other researchers, and service providers.

NISH

8401 Old Courthouse Road
Vienna, VA 22182
Telephone: (571) 226-4660
Fax: (703) 849-8916
E-mail: info@nish.org
Web site: http://www.nish.org
NISH creates employment opportunities for the blind and people with severe disabilities. It accomplishes this mission by securing federal contracts through the AbilityOne Program for its network of community-based, nonprofit agencies. According to NISH, more than 600 participating nonprofit organizations employ these individuals and provide quality goods and services to the federal government at a fair market price.

PACER Center (Parent Advocacy Coalition for Educational Rights)

8161 Normandale Boulevard
Minneapolis, MN 55437-1044
Telephone: (952) 838-9000; (800) 537-2237; (952) 838-0190
Fax: (952) 838-0199
E-mail: pacer@pacer.org
Web site: http://www.pacer.org
PACER works to expand the opportunities and quality of life of children with disabilities. It places a special emphasis on ensuring that a free and appropriate public education is made available to all children.

Rehabilitation Research Training Center on Aging with Intellectual and Developmental Disabilities (RRTCADD): Life Span Health and Function

Department of Disability and Human Development (DHD)
College of Applied Health Sciences (CAHS)
University of Illinois at Chicago (UIC)
1640 West Roosevelt Road, M/C 626
Chicago, IL 60608-6904
Telephone: (312) 413-1520; (312) 413-0453 (TTY)
Fax: (312) 996-6942
E-mail: rrtcadd@uic.edu
Web site: http://www.rrtcadd.org
The RRTCADD works to improve the support that individuals with disabilities receive through all stages of their lives. As life expectancies have increased, new issues and areas of needed support have arisen. The RRTCADD works to understand these new needs through research, and promotes solutions through evidence-based practice and the dissemination of results. The RRTCADD ultimate seeks a society where individuals with disabilities are fully integrated into the community and lead independent and fulfilling lives.

Self Advocates Becoming Empowered (SABE)
P.O. Box 30142
Kansas City, MO 64112
E-mail: SABEnation@gmail.com
Web site: http://www.sabeusa.org
Self Advocates Becoming Empowered is a U.S.-based self-advocacy organization. SABE's goals include replacing institutions with affordable, accessible housing and other personalized services; obtaining national health care for all; and ensuring equal employment opportunities and pay for all.

Sibling Support Project
A Kindering Center Program
6512 23rd Avenue, NW, #213
Seattle, WA 98117
Telephone: (206) 297-6368
Fax: (509) 752-6789
E-mail: donmeyer@siblingsupport.org
Web site: http://www.siblingsupport.org
The Sibling Support Project is dedicated to providing life-long support to the siblings of individuals with disabilities, special health needs, or mental health concerns. Because these conditions affect all members of a family, the project works with parents and service providers to understand the needs and issues faced by siblings. The program works through training, creating local support groups, seminars, and providing information.

Society for Disability Studies (SDS)
The City University of New York
101 W. 31st Street, 12th Floor
New York, NY 10001
Telephone: (212) 652-2005
Fax: (646) 344-7249
E-mail: pratikp1@gmail.com
Web site: http://www.disstudies.org
The Society for Disability Studies promotes the study of disabilities as an academic discipline. It uses research, artistic production, teaching, and activism to "augment understanding of disability in all cultures and historical periods, to promote greater awareness of the experiences of disabled people, and to advocate for social change." The SDS also publishes the Disability Studies Quarterly, *an academic journal.*

Special Olympics International
1133 19th Street, NW
Washington, DC 20036-3604

Telephone: (202) 628-3630; (800) 700-8585
Fax: (202) 824-0200
E-mail: info@specialolympics.org
Web site: http://www.specialolympics.org
The Special Olympics tells the world that "people with intellectual disabilities can and will succeed if given the opportunity." The Special Olympics promotes dignity, acceptance, and achieving one's potential by providing sporting opportunities to people with intellectual disabilities. Beyond sports, the Special Olympic promotes quality health care and research to improve the lives of those with disabilities.

TASH

1025 Vermont Avenue, NW, Suite 300
Washington, DC 20005
Telephone: (202) 540-9020
Fax: (202) 540-9019
E-mail: Operations@TASH.org
Web site: http://tash.org
TASH stands against the segregation and isolation of those with disabilities or other conditions that traditionally separate individuals from the rest of society. TASH works internationally, advocating for civil rights and full integration of its member population. TASH works through legislation, litigation, scientific investigation, and dissemination of positive information about people with disabilities.

Through the Looking Glass (TLG)

2198 Sixth Street, Suite 100
Berkeley, CA 94710-2204
Telephone: (800) 644-2666; (510) 848-1112; (510) 848-1005 (TTY)
Fax: (510) 848-4445
E-mail: TLG@lookingglass.org
Web site: http://lookingglass.org/index.php
Through the Looking Glass (TLG) is a nationally recognized nonprofit agency devoted to providing direct services, training, assistive resources, and research for parents with disabilities. While TLG serves parents with a wide range of disabilities, intellectual disabilities have been a major focus of their efforts over the years. The organization has concentrated on improving practices in many mainstream systems, including child protection services and early intervention systems like Head Start.

United Cerebral Palsy (UCP)

1660 L Street, NW, Suite 700
Washington, DC 20036
Telephone: (800) 872-5827; (202) 776-0406

Fax: (202) 776-0414
E-mail: info@ucp.org
Web site: http://www.ucp.org
United Cerebral Palsy provides services through its affiliates to more than 176,000 adults and children with disabilities every day. These services include housing, therapy, training, assistive technology, and family support. Beyond these services, UCP has a national office in Washington, D.C., that raises funds for affiliates, advances best practices, disseminates information, and advocates for legislation.

United States International Council on Disabilities (USICD)

1710 Rhode Island Avenue, NW, 5th Floor
Washington, DC 20036
Telephone: (202) 207-0338
Fax: (202) 207-0341
E-mail: info@usicd.org
Web site: http://www.usicd.org
The United States International Council on Disabilities is a coalition of individual advocates, organizations for people with disabilities, nongovernmental organizations (NGOs), and government members. This broad base of membership allows for a large international voice supporting the global disability rights agenda. The main goal of this agenda is to improve the lives and circumstances of those living with disabilities.

World Institute on Disability (WID)

510 16th Street, Suite 100
Oakland, CA 94612
Telephone: (510) 763-4100; (510) 208-9493 (TTY)
Fax: (510) 763-4109
E-mail: wid@wid.org
Web site: http://www.wid.org
The World Institute on Disability advocates for the removal of barriers that inhibit social integration, employment, and economic security for people with disabilities. Primarily run and staffed by individuals with disabilities, WID focuses on programs, education, training, research, tools, and public advocacy that advance the ability of those with disabilities to live independent lives.

Seven

Selected Print and Electronic Resources

Tamar Heller, Sarah Parker Harris,
and Jeannie Zwick

This chapter provides a list of suggested resources to assist readers in further inquiry of topics relating to disability through the life course. Resources are annotated and presented in two sections: (1) print resources and (2) electronic resources.

Print Resources

Books

Birren, J. E., & Schaie, K. W. (Eds.). (2006). *Handbook of the psychology of aging* (6th ed.). Burlington, MA: Elsevier Academic Press.
The Handbook of the Psychology of Aging *(6th edition) is a central reference for information on the psychology of development and aging. In its 22 chapters, this handbook offers a comprehensive exploration of several areas, including concepts in the psychology of aging, biological and social influences on aging, as well*

as complex behavioral concepts and processes in aging. The handbook is useful for researchers and professional practitioners working with the aging populations and for students exploring the psychology of aging.

Cuskelly, M., Jobling, A., & Buckley, S. (Eds.). (2002). *Down syndrome across the life span.* London: Whurr.

Down Syndrome Across the Life Span *offers information on the latest research efforts for persons with Down syndrome across the lifespan. Cuskelly, Jobling, and Buckley encourage readers to consider a social model perspective when viewing the challenges of living with Down syndrome. According to the authors, quality of life is determined more by environmental factors and less by the developmental difficulties that are associated with Down syndrome.*

Davidson, P. W., Prasher, V. P., & Janicki, M. P. (Eds.). (2003). *Mental health, intellectual disabilities, and the aging process.* Oxford, UK: Blackwell.

Mental Health, Intellectual Disabilities, and the Aging Process *is the third book in a series designed to address issues of health, adult development, and aging for persons with intellectual disabilities. The book is divided into three parts: prevalence and characteristics, diagnosis and treatment, and service system issues. Readers will gain practical advice for supporting and treating those with intellectual disabilities through the aging process.*

Drew, C. J., & Hardman, M. L. (2006). *Intellectual disabilities across the lifespan* (9th ed.). Englewood Cliffs, NJ: Prentice Hall.

Drew and Hardman's research-based book addresses the impact of intellectual disabilities across the lifespan. Through personal stories, the authors highlight educational, psychological, and social issues individuals with intellectual disabilities face from conception through old age.

Grigal, M., & Hart, D. (2010). *Think college! Postsecondary education options for students with intellectual disabilities.* Baltimore: Paul H. Brookes.

Meg Grigal and Debra Hart, two of the leading experts in the field of post-secondary education for persons with intellectual disabilities, address how to support students with disabilities at all stages in the college transition process. Handbook contents include three current models for post-secondary education, common barriers in post-secondary education for students with disabilities, transition services and support, employment, legislation, and the future of post-secondary education options. This book is person-centered, offering first-person narratives from students and families as well as profiles of real post-secondary education programs.

Hammel, J., & Nochajski, S. M. (Eds.). (2000). *Aging and developmental disability: Current research, programming, and practice implications.* New York: Haworth Press.

Aging and Developmental Disability *explores research findings on aging experiences and issues for people with disabilities. Readers will learn about specific interventions targeted toward aging adults with developmental disabilities and benefit from understanding the direction of future research in this area.*

Kemp, B. J., & Mosqueda, L. (2004). *Aging with a disability: What the clinician needs to know.* Baltimore: Johns Hopkins University Press.
Kemp and Mosqueda's handbook offers thoughtful, patient-centered guidelines for treating persons aging with a disability. Through the perspectives of persons with disabilities and their families, the authors offer a survey of the physiological and functional changes as people age, a discussion of treatment options and specific conditions, as well as possible directions for future research.

Lakin, K. C., & Turnbull, A. (Eds.). (2005). *National goals and research for people with intellectual and developmental disabilities.* Washington, DC: American Association on Mental Retardation.
Lakin and Turnbull's work introduces the collective knowledge of several leaders and scholars in the disability field on the topic of goal fulfillment in 12 critical areas for people with intellectual disabilities and developmental disabilities. These areas include, but are not limited to, education, positive behavior support, health support, biomedical research, employment, and self-advocacy. The chapters are divided into a developmental framework, each one addressing a distinct phase across the lifespan from young child to older adult. This book hopes to "increase independence, inclusion, opportunity, and self-determination of Americans with intellectual and developmental disabilities."

Lefley, H. P. (1996). *Family caregiving in mental illness: Vol. 7. Family caregiver applications series.* Thousand Oaks, CA: Sage.
Lefley's book examines the role of families in caring for adults with mental illness. This volume offers a historical overview of family caregiving as well as a glimpse into the experiences of parents, adult children, and siblings caring for family members with a mental illness across the lifespan. Readers will learn about family coping strategies, service supports for families, and the effects of advocacy movements on caregivers.

Marshak, L., Seligman, M., & Prezant, F. (1999). *Disability and the family life cycle: Recognizing and treating developmental challenges.* New York: Basic Books.
Marshak, Seligman, and Prezant offer an in-depth overview of the common challenges people with disabilities encounter across the lifespan. This book is divided into eight chapters that reflect a lifespan timeline, with each section designated to a life period from infancy to old age. Readers will gain an understanding of the disability experience from a "developmental perspective."

Noonan-Walsh, P., & Heller, T. (Eds.). (2002). *Health of women with intellectual disabilities*. Oxford, UK: Blackwell.
Health of Women With Intellectual Disabilities *is the first book in a series with the International Association for the Scientific Study of Intellectual Disabilities (IASSID). This publication addresses issues of healthy aging for women with intellectual disabilities. Noonan-Walsh and Heller's book includes 14 chapters of international authorship, case studies, and an evidence-based approach to addressing the context of health, health status, and issues of health promotion across the lifespan for women with intellectual disabilities.*

Odom, S. L., Horner, R. H., Snell, M. E., & Blacher, J. B. (Eds.). (2007). *Handbook on developmental disabilities*. New York: Guilford Press.
Handbook on Developmental Disabilities *offers an overview of current information about developmental disabilities in the areas of health and genetics, early intervention for young children, school-age education and intervention, post-school and adult issues, behavior supports, and family issues. Readers gain further insight on intervention strategies to assist children with developmental disabilities and their families across the lifespan.*

Parens, E., & Asch, A. (Eds.). (2000). *Prenatal testing and disability rights*. Washington, DC: Georgetown University Press.
Parens and Asch present a collection of essays that debate the implications of prenatal testing for people with disabilities. Key topics in the book include a disability rights perspective on prenatal diagnosis, familial perspectives on prenatal testing and selective abortion, the repercussions associated with prenatal testing argued from both sides, and strategies for policy-making in the future.

Prasher, V. P., & Janicki, M. P. (Eds.). (2002). *Physical health of adults with intellectual disabilities*. Oxford, UK: Blackwell.
Physical Health of Adults With Intellectual Disabilities *is the second book in a series produced with the International Association for the Scientific Study of Intellectual Disabilities. Prasher and Janicki employ a global perspective to the exploration of health issues particularly prevalent in the intellectual disability community. Chapters address issues of epidemiology, sensory functions, and pathologies, and present a framework for understanding research on physical health and health promotion.*

Priestley, M. (2003). *Disability: A life course approach*. Cambridge, UK: Polity Press.
Priestley's book explores important disability issues and debates. The chapters cover issues relevant to people with disabilities across the lifespan, such as birthrights, youth transitions, old age, and dying. Three concepts are central to the author's message: disability, generation, and the life course. The book has an international scope and will appeal to a diverse readership.

Putnam, M. (Ed.). (2007). *Aging and disability: Crossing network lines.* New York: Springer.

Michelle Putnam's book explores the intersection of aging and disability, with a particular focus on the crossing of care-boundaries between the aging community and those with disabilities. In this volume, Putnam addresses why aging and disability networks have historically been separated and how to bridge the divide so that populations with disability and those aging into disability obtain necessary services. Putnam presents current research and resources that highlight this collaboration.

Quinn, P. (1998). *Understanding disability: A lifespan approach.* Thousand Oaks, CA: Sage.

Understanding Disability: A Lifespan Approach *is written largely for the social worker or family member of a person with disabilities who needs guidance on what to expect across pivotal developmental stages for those with disabilities. Readers will gain a social model perspective to understanding various types of disabilities—such as Down syndrome, visual impairments, cerebral palsy, and spina bifida—across the lifespan. Additionally, a wide range of resources, both electronic and print, are located in the book's appendix.*

Sands, D. J., & Wehmeyer, M. L. (Eds.). (1996). *Self-determination across the life span: Independence and choice for people with disabilities.* Baltimore: Paul H. Brookes.

Sands and Wehmeyer's book considers issues of self-determination within an educational, ecological, and familial context. While anyone interested in the field of disability could benefit from reading this book, it is particularly relevant for parents of adolescents with a disability.

Wehman, P. (2006). *Life beyond the classroom: Transition strategies for young people with disabilities* (4th ed). Baltimore: Paul H. Brookes.

Wehman's book compiles the latest information on effectively transitioning individuals with mild to severe disabilities through different stages of life. Transitions include schooling, post-secondary education, moving into the community, and employment. Other areas covered are assistive technology, Social Security benefits, and testing.

Journal Articles

Ailey, S., Marks, B., Crisp, C., & Hahn, J. (2003). Promoting sexuality across the life span for individuals with intellectual and developmental disabilities. *Nursing Clinics of North America, 38*(2), 229–252.

This article promotes sexuality as a human right for people with intellectual and developmental disabilities. Societal barriers that have historically thwarted the sexual development of this population are juxtaposed against an emerging paradigm shift that supports the sexual development of people with cognitive impairments. Readers gain an in-depth perspective into the sexual lives of individuals with intellectual disabilities through detailed case studies and an exploration of sample sexual education program activities for individuals with intellectual disabilities across the lifespan. According to the authors, learning to enjoy sexuality requires people with cognitive impairments to develop "a positive self-esteem, make choices, give consent, receive information, experience mutuality, experience pleasure, and have legal recourse if they are abused."

Aronson, K. J., & McColl, M. A. (Eds.). (1999). Ageing and disabilities [Special issue]. *Disability and Rehabilitation, 21*(5/6), 193–310.

This special issue on aging and disabilities consists of 11 articles written by researchers in Australia, Canada, and the United States. The articles address issues such as the growing population of older-aged people in western society and issues they face in terms of disability and activity limitation, the elimination of chronic conditions in older people, the advent of new technology to help aging populations, and the effects of aging in specific populations, such as people with spinal cord injuries, strokes, and developmental disabilities. This series adds to the growing discussion on disablement and aging, offering an optimistic view on services and policy emerging in the field.

Bailey, D. B., Jr., (Ed.). (2007). Family adaptation to intellectual and developmental disabilities [Special issue]. *Mental Retardation and Developmental Disabilities Research Reviews, 13*(4), 291–378.

This special issue of Mental Retardation and Developmental Disabilities Research Reviews *features nine articles that represent future directions in research on how families adapt to intellectual and developmental disabilities. The following key areas are addressed: the role of parents in developmental outcomes, siblings of individuals with autism, and stress management interventions.*

Biegel, D. E., & Schulz, R. (Eds.). (1999). Interventions for family caregivers [Special issue]. *Family Relations, 48*(4), 341–436.

This special edition of Family Relations *offers an overview of the family caregiving experience. Authors present a comparative analysis of illness conditions and other contextual factors that affect caretaking abilities and experiences. Educators, researchers, and family practitioners will benefit from an overview of caregiver interventions and outcome studies.*

Blanck, P., & Schartz, H. (Eds.). (2005). Corporate culture and disability [Special issue]. *Behavioral Sciences and the Law, 23*(1).

This special issue of Behavioral Sciences and the Law *contributes to the understanding of corporate culture and disability. Authors in this series highlight the importance of including persons with disabilities in employment. The impact of civil rights legislation is also discussed along with the implications of the Americans with Disabilities Act of 1990.*

Block, P. (Ed.). (2002). Parents with disabilities [Special issue]. *Sexuality and Disability, 20*(1), 1–104.

Block introduces a series of essays in this special edition of Sexuality and Disability *that offer a positive view of parenting with a disability. Through these essays, readers will gain an understanding of how people with disabilities view sexuality, parenthood, and resources. Authors present new research approaches and practical parenting strategies for parents with a disability.*

Conyers, L. M., Koch, L. C., & Szymanski, E. M. (1998). Life-span perspectives on disability and work: A qualitative study. *Rehabilitation Counseling Bulletin, 42*(1), 51–76.

Conyers, Koch, and Szymanski's article explores the lives of nine employed college graduates from diverse ethnic backgrounds in their employment settings. From this qualitative study, people with disabilities, parents, and advocates can gain a better understanding of the meaning of work for people with disabilities, accessibility of careers, and the influence of disability on career development and advancement. Results from this study can be used to assist people with disabilities and career counselors in the job search process.

Ducharme, S. H. (Ed.). (1993). Sexuality [Special issue]. *Sexuality and Disability, 11*(3), 185–249.

This special collection of articles focuses on the sexuality of people with various types and degrees of disability. Articles address issues of genetic counseling, male fertility, parenting, adoption, and sexuality across the lifespan. Particular attention is given to spinal cord injuries and effects on pregnancy and delivery.

Heller, T. (Ed.). (2004). Family and service system supports [Special issue on aging, Part 2]. *American Journal on Mental Retardation, 109*(5), 349–442.

This special edition of American Journal on Mental Retardation *is the second in a two-part series focused on aging and developmental disabilities. Seven articles, written from a variety of perspectives and employing multiple methodologies, address the implications of the aging process on the family and on health and social service system supports. The studies span several countries and employ a variety of research methods, such as cross-sectional studies and life history narratives. Readers will learn about current research in the following areas: support for families, grandparent caregivers, service utilization by adults with disabilities, end-of-life care services, and lives of older women with intellectual disabilities. Authors emphasize a need for better support for families.*

Kennedy, J. (Ed.). (2002). Disability and aging—beyond the crisis rhetoric [Special issue]. *Journal of Disability Policy Studies, 12*(4), 226–284.

This special edition of Journal of Disability Policy Studies *encourages readers to abandon negative views about the aging U.S. population. While thinking about the aging population as a crisis may spur people to respond, it may not yield the best solutions to the problem. This special issue encourages policymakers and others to address the needs of all people with disabilities, with particular attention to how needs are currently being met or not met. Articles included in this issue address Medicaid policies, rehabilitative services, housing, personal assistance, onset and duration of disability, and social and political implications of an aging population.*

Marks, N. F. (1996). Caregiving across the lifespan: National prevalence and predictors. *Family Relations, 45*(1), 27–36.

Marks's article highlights a national survey used to generate population estimates for in- and out-of-household caregiving for persons of all ages. This research examines whether social demographic factors like gender, age, education, and employment can predict the likelihood of caregiving among adults. Marks's work encourages researchers and practitioners to adopt a lifespan perspective in future research for making policy decisions regarding caregiving and offers insight into types of caregivers who may need more service considerations.

McDermott, S., & Turk, M. A. (Eds.). (2010). A disability perspective on the issue of physician-assisted suicide. *Disability and Health Journal, 3*(1), 1–70.

This special edition of Disability and Health Journal *examines issues related to assisted suicide and disability. Legal considerations for assisted suicide are addressed across personal, disability rights, and population perspectives. Readers will gain an understanding of the complicated debate surrounding disability and aid in dying.*

Mona, L. R., & Shuttleworth, R. P. (Eds.). (2000). Disability, sexuality, and culture [Special issue, Part 1]. *Sexuality and Disability, 18*(3), 153–225.

This is the first of two special issues of Sexuality and Disability *that feature articles from the conference titled Disability, Sexuality, and Culture: Societal and Experiential Perspectives on Multiple Identities. Articles from this conference present disability and sexuality-related issues from a social rather than a medical perspective.*

Murphy, G., & Feldman, M. A. (Eds.). (2002). Parents with intellectual disabilities [Special issue]. *Journal of Applied Research in Intellectual Disabilities, 15*(4), 281–419.

Murphy and Feldman present a series of articles focusing on a historically neglected area of research: parenting with intellectual disability. Issues such as sexuality, parenting, stress, support networks, and home-based programs are brought together to illustrate the diversity and breadth of research emerging on this topic.

These articles illustrate a shift from the absence of people with disabilities in the decision-making process to the inclusion of input from parents with disabilities in the intervention strategies.

Nosek, M. A. (Ed.). (2001). Center for Research on Women with Disabilities [Special issue, Part 1]. *Sexuality and Disability, 19*(1), 1–87.
This special issue of Sexuality and Disability *is the first of a two-part series that provides an overview of the research conducted at the Center for Research on Women With Disabilities. Margaret Nosek, guest editor, introduces a series of articles that address the following issues: reproductive health care, dating, physical and sexual abuse, and access to health care. Nosek also presents a short review of findings from the National Study for Women with Disabilities. Readers will learn about current research in the areas of sexuality, self-esteem, and reproductive health and access for women with disabilities.*

Nosek, M. A. (Ed.). (2001). Center for Research on Women with Disabilities [Special issue, Part 2]. *Sexuality and Disability, 19*(3), 163–235.
Nosek introduces the second of two special issues of Sexuality and Disability *that highlight the work at the Center for Research on Women with Disabilities. This issue offers an overview of some of the emerging areas of research in abuse and access to reproductive health care for women with disabilities. Additionally, parents with disabilities, family members, and advocates will learn how the Americans with Disabilities Act can be used to access health care.*

Rumrill, P. D., Jr. (Ed.). (2001). Postsecondary education and disability [Special issue]. *Journal of Vocational Rehabilitation, 16*(3/4), 141–245.
This special issue of the Journal of Vocational Rehabilitation *provides a central resource for teachers, counselors, and family members of persons with intellectual disabilities who need assistance in the college decision-making process. Guest editor Phillip Rumrill introduces a series of articles that discuss issues related to post-secondary education for people with disabilities in the United States. The articles address the key role of the vocational rehabilitation personnel, the disability service providers, and the students in the college transition process. Rumrill also includes current research on post-secondary education programs and studies that have assessed career outcomes following post-secondary education experiences.*

Seltzer, M. M., Greenberg, J. S., Floyd, F. J., Pettee, Y., & Hong, J. (2001). Life course impacts of parenting a child with a disability. *American Journal on Mental Retardation, 106*(3), 265–286.
This study examines the extent to which having a child with either a developmental disability or a serious mental health problem may alter the parents' life course options, health, and well-being at two stages in the parents' adult life: mid-30s and

early 50s. Readers will gain an understanding of how parents cope at various life stages with their child's disability and how coping levels can vary depending on type and degree of disability.

Seltzer, M. M., Greenberg, J. S., Orsmond, G. I., & Lounds, J. (2005). Life course studies of siblings of individuals with developmental disabilities. *Mental Retardation, 43*(5), 354–359.

Sibling relationships tend to outlast even parent–child relationships and tend to be cemented through both genetic and experiential similarity. Typically these relationships are egalitarian, reciprocal, and mutual. This article studies how the sibling relationship differs when one member of the sibling pair has a disability. Moreover, this article seeks to understand the source of variation in these relationships. It raises the question: Is variation due to differences in genetics or background experiences faced by the sibling with the disability versus the sibling without the disability?

Seltzer, M. M., & Heller, T. (Eds.). (1997). Family caregiving for persons with disabilities [Special issue]. *Family Relations, 46*(4), 317–468.

This special issue of Family Relations *features work, compiled by guest editors Marsha Seltzer and Tamar Heller, on families who provide care to a son or daughter with a disability. These articles consider the factors that influence the caregiving context for parents of children with disabilities. Such factors include cultural context, type of disability of child receiving the care, sociodemographic characteristics of the family, age, and formal services that parents receive. Each article includes discussions of service provision and intervention.*

Seltzer, M. M., Heller, T., & Krauss, M. W. (Eds.). (2004). Aging [Special issue, Part 1]. *American Journal on Mental Retardation, 109*(2), 81–194.

This special edition is the first in a two-part series focused on aging in individuals with intellectual and developmental disabilities. It features nine articles, focused primarily but not exclusively on individuals with Down syndrome and their increased risk for early onset of dementia. Readers are introduced to a 12-week fitness intervention and health education program and its physical and psychosocial outcomes. Readers also gain an understanding of how to enhance health and quality of life for people with Down syndrome and other developmental disabilities. This collection of articles has the potential to contribute to the disability field as well as to the study of aging in the broader, general population.

Shuttleworth, R. P., & Mona, L. R. (Eds.). (2000). Disability, sexuality, and culture [Special issue, Part 2]. *Sexuality and Disability, 18*(4), 227–308.

This is the second of two special issues of Sexuality and Disability *that feature articles from the conference Disability, Sexuality, and Culture: Societal and Experiential*

Perspectives on Multiple Identities. These articles highlight recent research, issues of cultural representation, and an assessment of past and current approaches to disability and sexuality research.

Szymanski, E. M. (1994). Transition: Life-span and life-space considerations for empowerment. *Exceptional Children, 60*(5), 402–411.
Szymanski's article stresses the importance of lifespan and life-space considerations in transition planning for persons with disabilities. Transition planning must focus on students in the context of their everyday life. Parents, advocates, and transition specialists will learn insights on how to best promote empowerment with transition planning and how to relinquish power to individuals with disabilities so those individuals can best self-advocate and set their own goals.

Wishart, J. G., & Fraser, W. I. (Eds.). (1993). Learning disabilities in childhood [Special issue]. *Journal of Intellectual Disability Research, 37*(4), 341–435.
This special edition addresses current and future research directions for children with learning disabilities. People with autism and Down syndrome are among the populations surveyed in the articles.

Electronic Resources

Access Living. (2008). Retrieved from www.accessliving.org
Access Living is a nonprofit, cross-disability organization run largely by and for people with disabilities. Its mission, based on the philosophy of the Independent Living Movement, is to "empower people with disabilities so they may lead dignified, independent lives and to foster an inclusive society for all people—with and without disabilities." Access Living is a resource hub for people with disabilities, offering support for housing, personal assistance, and transportation options. Access Living offers a vital link to youth and peer-based programs that provide independent living skills training. Access Living's Web site offers links to articles, brochures, a referral directory, and legal documents.

Center for Independent Living. (2005). Retrieved from http://www.cilberkeley.org
The Center for Independent Living (CIL), the world's first organization "run by and for people with disabilities," helps individuals with disabilities live independently by offering resources in the following areas: housing or work issues, installing assistive technology, and improving independent living skills. CIL provides free services and referrals to individuals with disabilities and advocates for policy changes to improve access to public places and transportation. CIL also runs fee-based consultation services for private employers on how to improve accommodations for individuals with disabilities.

Center on Disability Studies, University of Hawai'i at Manoa. (2008). Retrieved from http://www.cds.hawaii.edu

The Center on Disability Studies develops and conducts interdisciplinary education, research, and evaluation of programs to benefit those living with disabilities. The center has four component programs: Hawaii University Center for Excellence in Developmental Disabilities Education, Research, and Service; Pacific Basin University Centers for Excellence in Education, Research, and Service for Individuals with Developmental Disabilities; National Center for the Study of Postsecondary Educational Supports; and the National Center on Secondary Education and Transition. The Center on Disability Studies Web site offers links to key publications, current events, and other national organizations that are working toward the shared purpose of training and research to benefit the lives of people with disabilities.

Center on Human Development and Disability, University of Washington (2010). Retrieved from http://www.depts.washington.edu/chdd

The University of Washington's Center on Human Development and Disability (CHDD) encompasses two major programs: the Eunice Kennedy Shriver Intellectual and Developmental Disabilities Research Center and its University Center for Excellence in Developmental Disabilities. The CHDD offers professional training programs and clinical services for families as well as additional research and resources in the following areas: infant and youth mental health, autism, adults and elders, disability studies, clinical training, community disability policy, education, and genetics.

Center on Human Policy, Law, and Disability Studies, Syracuse University. (n.d.). Retrieved from http://thechp.syr.edu

The Center on Human Policy (CHP) is a research and advocacy organization based at Syracuse University. The center promotes and studies the inclusive community opportunities for people with disabilities. The center works to advance its goals at all levels of government. CHP's Web site includes a wide host of publications, Web links, education and training materials, and information on academic programs in disabilities. The center distributes bulletins, research reports, articles, and information packets related to the inclusion of people with disabilities. Research topics include disability policy, educational programs, institutional life, and building inclusive community.

Disabilities, Opportunities, Internetworking, and Technology. (2010). Retrieved from http://www.washington.edu/doit

Disabilities, Opportunities, Internetworking, and Technology (DO-IT), an information network at the University of Washington, focuses on using information technology to increase the participation of people with disabilities in academic programs and careers. DO-IT believes the use of computers and their associated technology can increase both the independence and productivity of individuals with disabilities.

DO-IT's Web site includes links to research programs for distance learning, post-secondary education, and career training, as well a searchable publication database.

Disability Law Lowdown. (2010). Show 47—Especially for teens [Podcast]. Retrieved from http://english.disabilitylawlowdown.com
Show 47 of the Disability Law Lowdown Podcast is aimed at teenagers who are in the process of transitioning out of high school. Jacquie Brennan, host of the podcast, discusses a new information sheet published by Pacer Center that presents information on how high schoolers can advocate for themselves and plan their future by taking an active role in developing their Individualized Education Program (IEP). The podcast, which is also available on iTunes, also discusses an array of electronic and print resources that can help students with disabilities learn how to take a more active role in the development of their IEPs.

Disability Resources, Inc. (2010). Retrieved from http://www.disabilityresources.org
Disability Resources, Inc. offers information about print and electronic resources, government agencies, nonprofit organizations, telephone hotlines, and online services that help people with disabilities live independently. This Web site offers access to a Disability Resources Monthly newsletter that reviews and reports on new resources.

Disability Scoop. (2010). Retrieved from http://www.disabilityscoop.com
Disability Scoop is considered the premier source for developmental disability news. This news organization serves the developmental disability community by offering educational, legal, and counseling services, and an active discussion forum.

Equip for Equality. (2009). Retrieved from http://www.equipforequality.org
Equip for Equality, an independent, private, nonprofit organization, works toward its mission to "advance the human and civil rights of children and adults with physical and mental disabilities in Illinois." This state-based organization offers advocacy services by topic area that empower individuals, including legal services, training seminars, a special education helpline, electronic links to news and events, abuse investigation handbooks, and resource guides.

Eunice Kennedy Shriver Center, University of Massachusetts Medical School. (n.d). Retrieved from http://www.umassmed.edu/shriver
The Eunice Kennedy Shriver Center at the University of Massachusetts Medical School works to expand research, education, and services for individuals with developmental disabilities and their families. The center works to advance understanding of the neurological, cognitive, and behavioral development associated with developmental disabilities, specifically focusing on mental retardation. The center studies both the biological and environmental causes of mental retardation and abnormal development in the hope of providing better services. The Eunice Kennedy Shriver Center offers a wide range of

electronic resources, including access to leadership training, distance learning opportunities, publications and newsletters, biomedical research, bio-behavioral research, and behavioral science research. Additional services available include clinical evaluation, treatment, consultation, and resources through its ADHD and autism clinics.

Family Support Center on Disabilities: Knowledge and Involvement Network. (n.d.). Retrieved from www.familysupportclearinghouse.org

The Family Support Center on Disabilities: Knowledge and Involvement Network (KIN) offers an extensive range of options to individuals with disabilities and their families. This site offers information on early intervention and education, employment, legislation and policy, housing, transportation, and recreation. KIN offers families access to a valuable network of peers and experts in the field of disability services and family support. Families can participate in online discussion forums, seminars, and disability conferences.

Family Village: A Global Community of Disability-Related Resources. (2009). Retrieved from http://www.familyvillage.wisc.edu

The Family Village, sponsored by the Waisman Center at the University of Wisconsin–Madison, is a Web site for children and adults with disabilities and their families. Family Village is a global community that brings together information, resources, and networking opportunities on the Internet in a creative, organized, accessible directory. Central to the Family Village resources is the library, where families and persons with disabilities can access information and resources about various disabilities. The Web site also contains information about assistive technology, legal rights, special education, and support groups.

Independent Living Institute. (n.d.). Retrieved from http://www.independent living.org

The Independent Living Institute (ILI), located in Stockholm-Johanneshov, Sweden, works to develop consumer-driven policies that will increase freedom of choice for persons with disabilities. The institute provides information and training about its policies throughout Sweden and internationally. ILI's area of expertise is in designing systems of direct payment for personal assistance services and assistive technology. ILI's Web site offers an extensive, full-text virtual library on independent living and related subjects, interactive services, a global networking database, and various links to disability and independent living resources.

Independent Living Research Utilization Program (ILRU). (2008). Retrieved from http://www.ilru.org

The Independent Living Research Utilization Program works to increase knowledge about independent living by collecting and disseminating information about

the latest research in the area. Since 1977, it has become a national center for information, training, and research about independent living. ILRU is a program of the Institute for Rehabilitation and Research.

Institute on Community Integration, University of Minnesota (2010). Retrieved from http://ici.umn.edu

The Institute on Community Integration (ICI) at the University of Minnesota is a University Center for Excellence in Developmental Disabilities (UCEDD) dedicated to improvement of policies and practices for people with disabilities across the lifespan. University of Minnesota's UCEDD offers collaborative research, training, and information sharing through newsletters and briefs, research guides, curricula, reports, brochures, and multimedia.

Interwork Institute, San Diego State University. (2008). Retrieved from http://interwork.sdsu.edu

The Interwork Institute at San Diego State University focuses on "promoting universal design in all aspects of the community." The goal of this design is to completely integrate individuals with disabilities into the community and all aspects of life. The institute promotes this goal through research, training, and education. The institute Web site offers links to other disability Web sites, university resources, rehabilitation counseling services, and job assistance.

Kennedy Center, Inc. (2010). Retrieved from http://www.thekennedycenterinc.org

The Kennedy Center, Inc. operates out of Connecticut on a not-for-profit basis to rehabilitate both children and adults with disabilities. The Kennedy Center is community based and works to treat all people with the respect and dignity they deserve while providing cost-effective services that will ultimately allow those with disabilities to live independent lives and be included in their communities. The Kennedy Center's Web site includes links to local and national organizations and information regarding the organization's early intervention program for youth with disabilities, school-to-career trainings, and community inclusion efforts.

Lifespan Family Research Program, University of Wisconsin–Madison. (2009). Retrieved from http://www.waisman.wisc.edu/family/index.html

The Lifespan Family Research Program at the University of Wisconsin–Madison is dedicated to the advancement of knowledge about changes over a lifetime in families with a member who has a disability. The program focuses on two areas. The first is how families manage daily life, their unique challenges and their coping mechanisms, and resources used to overcome their difficulties. The second is how an individual's disability changes over a lifetime and how individuals with disabilities face major life changes, such as adulthood and moving out of the parental home to a non-family living environment. The Lifespan Family Research Program's current research includes family caregiving in families that include a family member with autism and fragile X syndrome.

Minnesota Governor's Council on Developmental Disabilities. (n.d.). *Parallels in time I and II: A history of developmental disabilities.* Retrieved from http://www .mnddc.org/parallels/index.html
Parallels in Time I and II: A History of Developmental Disabilities, an interactive resource produced in collaboration with the Minnesota Governor's Council on Developmental Disabilities, offers an exploration of developmental disabilities through history, from the ancient era to present day.

NADD: An Association for Persons with Developmental Disabilities and Mental Health Needs. (n.d.). Retrieved from http://www.thenadd.org
NADD advocates for the mental health of people with developmental disabilities, primarily by promoting improved mental health care. NADD works along several dimensions: disseminating information, providing education and training about mental health, promoting relevant research, and advocating for government policies benefiting mental health. NADD's Web site offers information on upcoming conferences, training and educational products, and an extensive array of links to related organizations and resources.

National Center on Physical Activity and Disability (NCPAD). (2010). Retrieved from http://www.ncpad.org
The National Center on Physical Activity and Disability (NCPAD) is an information center at the Department of Disability and Human Development at University of Illinois Chicago that works to bring an active lifestyle to all people. Central to NCPAD's philosophy is the belief that "exercise is for everybody" and an active lifestyle promotes general health and well-being. NCPAD provides the information necessary for individuals to pursue whatever type of activity that would make them happy and healthy. This information can range from how to start an exercise program, to how to play or participate in popular activities, and even where to pursue different sports.

National Dissemination Center for Children with Disabilities (NICHCY). (n.d.). Retrieved from www.nichcy.org
The National Dissemination Center for Children with Disabilities (NICHCY) is a central hub of information on children and youth with disabilities (birth to age 22). Families, educators, administrators, and students will find an abundance of information on the following topics: disabilities in infants, toddlers, children, and youth; legislation like the Individuals with Disabilities Education Act (IDEA) and No Child Left Behind (as it relates to children with disabilities); early intervention services; special education; disability organizations; and transition to adult life.

National Rehabilitation Information Center (NARIC). (n.d.). Retrieved from www.naric.com

National Rehabilitation Information Center (NARIC) is a central resource for disability- and rehabilitation-oriented information throughout the United States. NARIC provides interactive information to the disability and rehabilitation community through online publications, searchable databases, and timely reference and referral data.

Quality Mall. (2008). Retrieved from www.qualitymall.org

Quality Mall is a hub of free information on person-centered supports for people with intellectual and developmental disabilities. The Quality Mall is divided into 21 stores, each featuring a person-centered support category—such as family, future planning, and self-advocacy resources—with internal links that include books, electronic media, organizations, and programs, as well as key people in the field.

Research and Training Center on Independent Living: Lifespan Institute, University of Kansas. (2010). Retrieved from http://www.rtcil.org

The Research and Training Center on Independent Living (RTC/IL) at the University of Kansas is dedicated to research that will allow individuals with disabilities to live more independent and fulfilling lives. The center has consumer involvement, realizing that consumers and service providers can provide insights into the needed services and how best to provide them. This RTC/IL features information on projects committed to the enhancement of independent living for people with disabilities, a searchable database for information on independent living resources, training opportunities, and products to enhance the lives of people with disabilities in the following areas: advocacy, employment opportunities, full participation in the community, and disaster preparedness.

Think College! (2010). *College options for people with intellectual disabilities.* Retrieved from http://www.thinkcollege.net

The Think College! Web site is a project of the Institute for Community Inclusion at the University of Massachusetts-Boston. The Web site offers a searchable database of post-secondary education options for people with intellectual disabilities, a list of training sessions and events, advice about college, and a newsletter for students, families, and professionals interested in post-secondary education for students with intellectual disabilities.

Vanderbilt Kennedy Center, University Center for Excellence in Developmental Disabilities. (2010). Retrieved from http://kc.vanderbilt.edu/kennedy/ucedd

The Vanderbilt Kennedy Center's University Center for Excellence in Developmental Disabilities (UCEDD) offers training, education, research, and services to people with

developmental disabilities and their families at the statewide and national level. Vanderbilt Kennedy Center's mission is to "improve the quality of life for persons with developmental disabilities by supporting and applying scientific research to bring better services and training to the community." Its resources include a family outreach center, services for educators, clinical and community training, as well as printable resources and materials by topic.

YAI Resource Center. (2010). Retrieved from http://www.yai-rc.org

The YAI Resource Center supports those working in the field of intellectual and developmental disability by offering educational and training materials, activities, and resources covering a broad range of topics, including supported employment, relationships and sexuality, and aging. The YAI online community also offers access to a professional community that allows interested members to communicate with and learn from others around the world.

Glossary of Key Terms

ACIP   *See* Advisory Committee on Immunization Practices

Activities of Daily Living (ADL)   A term used in health care to describe daily self-care tasks such as feeding, bathing, dressing, or communicating. The ability to perform ADLs provides a measurement of an individual's levels of disability and functioning.

ADA   *See* Americans with Disabilities Act of 1990

ADAAA   *See* Americans with Disabilities Act Amendments Act of 2008

ADL   *See* Activities of Daily Living

Advisory Committee on Immunization Practices (ACIP)   A group of experts selected by the Secretary of the U.S. Department of Health and Human Services that develops recommendations—based on scientific data, safety and efficacy, and cost-effectiveness—regarding which vaccines children and adolescents should receive, and their dosing intervals.

Aging and Disability Resource Centers   Funded by the Administration on Aging, these centers provide a coordinated system of long-term supports and services for disabled and elderly individuals in the United States and promote health and long-term care initiatives that benefit both groups.

Aging Well   An adaptation of the successful aging model that views aging as a lifelong process, dependent on events occurring at younger ages. It defines positive outcomes as (1) maintaining health and function (physical and mental health and independence); and (2) active engagement with life (friendships, contributions to society, and community participation).

Aging With Disability   A term used to describe people with early-onset disabilities as they grow older, as opposed to people who have mid- or late-life onset of disability (who are said to have "disability with aging").

Americans with Disabilities Act Amendments Act of 2008 (ADAAA) Passed in response to judicial interpretations that narrowed the scope of the ADA, this law reestablished the broad range of impairments that qualify as a disability and confirmed that mitigating measures should not be considered in determining whether a person's impairment qualifies as a disability.

Americans with Disabilities Act of 1990 (ADA)   This sweeping civil rights law prohibits discrimination against people with disabilities in employment, public transportation, public accommodations, and telecommunications. Under Title 1 of this law, individuals are considered to have a disability if they have a "physical or mental impairment that substantially limits one or more major life activities" or are "regarded as having such an impairment."

Assistive Technology (AT)   This term describes a variety of devices and strategies that serve to increase the independence and community participation of people with disabilities by aiding them with seating and mobility, communication, access, environmental control, or activities of daily living.

AT   *See* Assistive Technology

Caregiver Burden   A concept that applies to stress, financial hardship, perceived inequity in the division of labor, and other factors experienced by people who care for family members with disabilities.

Cash and Counseling   A consumer-directed Medicaid policy that disburses funds to people with disabilities through monthly cash subsidies in conjunction with counseling services, with the goal of fostering greater autonomy and choice.

CFC   *See* Community First Choice Option

Chronic Sorrow   Coined in the 1960s, this term describes the reaction of parents to the diagnosis of disability in a child as a form of long-lasting grief.

CLASS   *See* Community Living Assistance Services and Supports

Cognitive Development   A theory advanced by educator Jean Piaget that says children progress through four stages of increasingly sophisticated cognitive ability—sensorimotor, preoperational, concrete, and formal operational—which are finalized by the end of adolescence.

Community First Choice (CFC) Option   A Medicaid program, available to states as a waiver option, that provides home- and community-based attendant services and supports for activities of daily living to individuals with disabilities who meet income requirements and who would otherwise require an institutional level of care.

Community Living Assistance Services and Supports (CLASS)   Established under the Patient Protection and Affordable Care Act (PPACA), this voluntary national long-term care insurance program provides individuals with a cash benefit if they have functional limitations or disability.

DALY   *See* Disability-Adjusted Life Years

Developmental Stages   An influential concept in developmental psychology and pediatrics that says children progress through a universal sequence of cognitive, social, and personality development.

Disability   An evolving concept that results from the interaction between persons with impairments and attitudinal and environmental barriers that hinder their full and effective participation in society on an equal basis with others.

Disability Rights Movement   An advocacy movement that began in the 1970s, drawing upon earlier successes of the civil rights and women's liberation movements. It was instrumental in pressuring Congress to adopt various disability policies and laws.

Disability Studies   A diverse, interdisciplinary academic field that examines the social, cultural, and political implications of disability.

Disability With Aging   A term used to describe people who develop disabilities as they reach mid- or late life, as opposed to people with early onset disabilities who grow older (who are said to be "aging with disability").

Disability-Adjusted Life Years (DALY)   A summary measure created by the World Health Organization (WHO) to represent the burden of disease in terms of years of life lost due to either disability or premature death.

Dismodernism   A concept of identity development that acknowledges the interdependent nature of humanity and the universal experiences of bodily limitation.

Early Intervention   Educational programs that target children from birth to three years old and are designed to improve the children's developmental, social, and learning outcomes; such programs often include speech and language therapy, physical therapy, occupational therapy, and social work.

Elementary and Secondary Education Act of 1965 (ESEA)   This legislation funded educational programs for economically disadvantaged children and children with disabilities in both elementary and secondary schools, as well as Head Start and Title I programs; in 2001 it was reauthorized as No Child Left Behind (NCLB).

Emerging Adulthood   A phase distinct from both adolescence and young adulthood that occurs predominantly in industrialized societies and is marked by exploration of social and economic roles without definite commitment, as made evident by factors such as occupational instability and residential mobility.

ESEA   *See* Elementary and Secondary Education Act of 1965

Eugenics Movement   A form of social Darwinism that sought to promote "genetic purity" by preventing "inferior" people, including individuals with disabilities, from having children.

Fair Housing Act Amendments of 1988   Legislation that provided individuals with disabilities with protection against discrimination in housing, the right to make reasonable modifications to rented housing, and the right to accommodations in housing rules, policies, and practices.

Family Demography   The study of the ties that bind people and households together in family units, conducted with the goal of better understanding the behavior of both individuals and society.

Family Systems Health Model   A normative, preventative model for the assessment and intervention of families who face the caregiving demands of chronic disorders over time. The model outlines three dimensions: psychosocial types, major phases in their natural history, and family systems variables.

Function   The normal physiological action or activity of a body part, organ, or system.

Genetic Engineering   Direct human manipulation and alteration of an organism's genetic material in a manner that does not occur naturally.

Gerontology   The scientific study of aging, which takes into account biological and cultural perspectives, lifespan changes in allocation of resources, systematic theory of adaptive psychological aging, and theories of psychological aging in specific domains.

Herd Immunity   The fact that unvaccinated individuals indirectly benefit from vaccinated individuals, because those who are vaccinated prevent the transmission of disease within the entire population.

Home and Community-Based Services Program   A consumer-directed Medicaid program that offers people with disabilities and their families such services as home modification, case coordination, respite, pre-vocational and educational habilitation, and supported employment.

ICF   *See* International Classification of Functioning, Disability and Health

I/DD   *See* Intellectual and Developmental Disabilities

IDEA   *See* Individuals with Disabilities Education Act of 1990

Identity   A term that may refer to an individual's core characteristics (personal identity) or definition of self in relation to others (social identity).

Idiographic Development   A psychological approach that involves gathering information that is unique to an individual's development instead of measuring that individual's adherence to or deviance from a common construct or norm.

IEP   *See* Individualized Education Program

IFSP   *See* Individualized Family Service Plan

Impaired Role   A modification of the sick role that applies to individuals whose condition is unlikely to change, as in the case of a permanent disability. Individuals within this group are expected to live up to normal societal expectations, within the limitations of their impairment, and to make the most of their situation.

Impairment   Any loss, abnormality, or disturbance of psychological, physiological, or anatomical structure or function that interferes with normal activities and may be temporary or permanent.

Individualized Education Program (IEP)   Mandated by the Individuals with Disabilities Education Act (IDEA), the IEP documents and guides the process of identifying and referring eligible school-age children for special education services, assessing their needs, planning and implementing individualized programs to meet their needs, and monitoring and evaluating the programs' effectiveness.

Individualized Family Service Plan (IFSP)   Mandated by the Individuals with Disabilities Education Act (IDEA), the IFSP documents and guides the early intervention process for young children with disabilities and their families, with the goal of improving the children's physical, cognitive, social, and emotional growth.

Individuals with Disabilities Education Act of 1990 (IDEA)   This legislation amended and updated the Education for All Handicapped Children Act (EHA or EAHCA) and established the legal definition of disability used in special education law.

Intellectual and Developmental Disabilities (I/DD)   Severe, chronic disabilities that can be attributed to mental or physical impairments, are manifested in childhood and continue throughout life, create substantial functional limitations in activities of daily living, and result in a need for individualized services and supports.

International Classification of Functioning, Disability and Health (ICF)   Released in 2001 by the World Health Organization (WHO), this conceptual model of disability integrates the medical and social models; it views disability and functioning as outcomes of the interactions between health conditions and contextual factors. The relevant domains within this model are impairment, activity limitation, and participation restriction.

Katie Beckett Waiver   Established as a provision of the Tax Equity and Fiscal Responsibility Act of 1982, this program allows states to provide Medicaid benefits to children with disabilities who would not ordinarily qualify because of parents' income or resources. These waivers offer families the means to provide care for children with medically complex needs at home, as opposed to placing them in institutions.

Least Restrictive Environment (LRE)   A mandate of the Individuals with Disabilities Education Act (IDEA) that requires children with disabilities to receive their education in settings that provide greatest participation in the regular classroom while ensuring maximum educational benefit.

Life Course Approach   A conceptual model that addresses disability issues across generations and through various life stage transitions. It views individuals' life trajectories as the result of a complex interplay between four dynamic factors: historical and geographic location, social ties, human agency, and variations in timing of events and social roles.

Life Stage Categories   Generational stages—including birth, childhood, youth, adulthood, aging, and death/dying—that are shaped by cultural and social influences.

LRE   *See* Least Restrictive Environment

Medical Model of Disability   A conceptual model that focuses on diseases, injuries, and conditions that impair the physiological or cognitive functioning of an individual; it defines disability as a condition or deficit that resides within the individual and can be cured or ameliorated, or its progression stopped, through a particular treatment or intervention.

Medicalization of Disability   A perspective that views physical and cognitive diversity as pathology, or medical issues that require study, measurement, treatment, and cures.

NCLB   *See* No Child Left Behind Act of 2001

No Child Left Behind Act of 2001 (NCLB)   Sweeping education legislation that established accountability measures, academic standards, and high-stakes testing designed to ensure that all students gain the skills needed to succeed in college and the workforce. Under NCLB schools are required to report to the state educational authority (SEA) and demonstrate adequate yearly progress (AYP) toward a goal of 100% proficiency of all tested students by 2014.

Normative Approach   A theory of human development that compares individuals and groups along commonly defined psychological constructs, or norms.

Patient Protection and Affordable Care Act of 2010 (PPACA)   Sweeping health care reform legislation that requires that all Americans have health insurance; bars health insurance companies from discriminating based on pre-existing medical conditions, health status, or gender; prohibits lifetime limits on coverage; prohibits rescission (dropping) of customers by insurers; creates insurance exchanges; requires employers with 50 workers or more to offer health insurance benefits or pay a fee; expands Medicaid and provides premium assistance; and creates temporary insurance pools for consumers with pre-existing conditions until insurance exchanges open in 2014.

Personal Care Program   A consumer-directed Medicaid program that offers people with disabilities such services as home health care and assistance with personal care, activities of daily living, and housekeeping chores.

Persons With Disabilities   Individuals who have long-term physical, mental, intellectual, or sensory impairments that, in interaction with various barriers, may hinder their full and effective participation in society on an equal basis with others.

PPACA   *See* Patient Protection and Affordable Care Act

Psychosexual Stages   A concept originated by Sigmund Freud that views human development in a series of four psychosexual stages, each of which presents a conflict in a child's life. Freud contended that when the conflict is resolved, the child moves on to the next stage; but if the conflict remains unresolved, the individual remains "fixated" at that stage, which dominates his or her adult personality.

Psychosocial Stages   Developed by Erik Erikson as an alternative to Freud's psychosexual stages, this concept views human development in a series of eight psychosocial stages that extend from infancy through adulthood, each of which involves a basic conflict that either positively or negatively influences an individual's personality development.

Section 504   A provision of the Rehabilitation Act of 1973 that states that no qualified individuals with disabilities can be excluded from, denied the benefits of, or subjected to discrimination under any programs receiving federal financial assistance. Section 504 requires that school districts provide a free and appropriate public education to qualified students in their jurisdictions who have a physical or mental impairment that substantially limits one or more major life activities.

Self-Determination   Actions that enable a person to serve as the primary causal agent in maintaining or improving his or her own quality of life. Self-determination is a central construct in the independent living and consumer movements across disabilities, in which advocates strive for greater autonomy, choice, and personal control of their lives.

Sick Role   A prominent sociological approach to disability that relieves unhealthy individuals from complying with social behavioral norms, but also obligates them to be both compliant to and appreciative of medical intervention.

Social Model of Disability   A conceptual model that focuses on the barriers an individual with disabilities faces when interacting with the environment; it defines disability as a problem that lies primarily outside the individual, in the lack of accommodations in the surrounding environment, and in the negative attitudes of people without disabilities.

Social Security Disability Insurance (SSDI)   A federal government program that provides wage replacement income for individuals who have worked and paid Social Security taxes and become disabled according to Social Security criteria; its benefits are paid to disabled workers, their widows, widowers, and children, and eligible adults disabled since childhood.

SSDI   *See* Social Security Disability Insurance

SSI   *See* Supplemental Security Income

Successful Aging   A predominant paradigm within gerontology that contends that aging well is marked by high cognitive and physical functioning, low incidence of disease and disability, and active engagement with life.

Supplemental Security Income (SSI)   A federal government income supplement program that is designed to help low-income people who are elderly, blind, or disabled meet their basic needs for food, clothing, and shelter.

Supports Outcome Model of Aging Well   A modification of the concept of aging well that is specifically geared to persons with disabilities by emphasizing the primacy of the environment and individualized supports in influencing outcomes for individuals across the life course.

Ticket to Work and Work Incentives Improvement Act of 1999 (TWWIIA)
A federal government program intended to help pave avenues to employment for people with disabilities; it also allows people with disabilities to maintain Medicare eligibility for four additional years.

Title V   A provision of the Social Security Act of 1934 that gives federal grants to individual states to support maternal and child health services; many Title V programs are vitally important to children with disabilities and their families, including programs providing rehabilitative services, case management, care coordination, and other critical services for children with special health care needs.

Transition   A disruption in an individual's day-to-day life, including both proximal (daily hassles and stressors) and distal (major events) changes, that results in progression to a new life stage (e.g., from school to work, from single to married, from living with parents, to living alone).

TWWIIA   *See* Ticket to Work and Work Incentives Improvement Act of 1999

Index

Note: Page numbers in italics refer to tables and figures.